The Teacher and the World

Teachers the world over are seeking creative ways to respond to the problems and possibilities generated by globalization. Many of them work with children and youth from increasingly varied backgrounds, with diverse needs and capabilities. Others work with homogeneous populations and yet are aware that their students will encounter many cultural changes in their lifetimes. All struggle with the contemporary conditions of teaching: endless top-down measures to manipulate what they do, rapid economic turns and inequality in supportive resources that affect their lives and those of their students, a torrent of media stimuli that distract educational focus, and growth as well as shifts in population.

In *The Teacher and the World*, David Hansen provides teachers with a way to reconstruct their philosophies of education in light of these conditions. He describes an orientation toward education that can help them to address both the challenges and opportunities thrown their way by a globalized world. Hansen builds his approach around cosmopolitanism, an ancient idea with an ever-present and ever-beautiful meaning for educators. The idea pivots around educating for what the author calls reflective openness to new people and new ideas, and reflective loyalty toward local values, interests, and commitments.

The book shows how this orientation applies to teachers at all levels of the system, from primary through to university. Hansen deploys many examples to illustrate how its core value, a balance of reflective openness to the new and reflective loyalty to the known, can be cultivated while teaching different subjects in different kinds of settings. The author draws widely on the work of educators, scholars in the humanities and social sciences, novelists, artists, travelers and others from both the present and past, as well as from around the world. These diverse figures illuminate the promise in a cosmopolitan outlook on education in our time.

In this pioneering book, Hansen has provided teachers, heads of school, teacher educators, researchers, and policy-makers a generative way to respond creatively to the pressure and the promise of a globalizing world.

David T. Hansen is Professor and Director of the Program in Philosophy and Education at the Teachers College, Columbia University.

Teacher Quality and School Development Series
Series Editors: Christopher Day and Ann Lieberman

The Teacher and the World

A Study of Cosmopolitanism as Education

David T. Hansen

Routledge
Taylor & Francis Group

LONDON AND NEW YORK

First published 2011
by Routledge
2 Park Square, Milton Park, Abingdon, Oxon OX14 4RN

Simultaneously published in the USA and Canada
by Routledge
711 Third Avenue, New York, NY 10017

Routledge is an imprint of the Taylor & Francis Group, an informa business

British Library Cataloguing in Publication Data
A catalogue record for this book is available from the British Library

Library of Congress Cataloging in Publication Data
Hansen, David.
The teacher and the world : a study of cosmopolitanism and education /
David Hansen. – 1st ed.
p. cm.
1. Education and globalization. 2. Cosmopolitanism. 3. Critical pedagogy.
4. Education–Sociological aspects. I. Title.
LC191.H2595 2011
306.43–dc22
2011012234

ISBN: 978-0-415-78331-6 (hbk)
ISBN: 978-0-415-78332-3 (pbk)
ISBN: 978-0-203-80332-5 (ebk)

Typeset in Galliard
by Keystroke, Station Road, Codsall, Wolverhampton

For my students

"The earth knows longing for the rain, the sky knows longing . . ." And the world longs to create what will come to be. I tell it "I share your longing."

Marcus Aurelius

Contents

Series Editors' Introduction

The Teacher and the World is a rare publication, overtly and explicitly concerned with offering an antidote for teachers to counter the intensifying and, for many, debilitating turbulence of the stream of government-imposed policy reforms which promise, but do not always deliver, improvements in schools and classrooms. It does so, not by providing sets of bullet-pointed solutions, rational planning models or prescriptions for action but, on the contrary, five closely written chapters and an epilogue which offer what David Hansen calls a "cosmopolitan orientation."

Hansen argues that this philosophy provides teachers with resources to strengthen, broaden, deepen and sustain their ability to interact well with "students, colleagues, parents and community members" on the one hand, and, on the other, with "friends, family and significant others." Cosmopolitanism in this sense, then, is offered as a way of professional living in the world for teachers, however confusing the world is. In terms of their professional lives, Hansen claims that it will strengthen their sense of agency, broadening their aesthetic, ethical, moral and intellectual horizons. It will fuel their sense of moral purpose within an ethic of social responsibility in their quest to make it possible for the children and young people whom they teach to grow as responsible, knowledgeable learners.

This cosmopolitan perspective does not provide solutions to problems but directly addresses the education of teachers' sense of being, the quality of their discernment and judgement. Thus, regardless of the positive and negative effects of the speed of globalization which, Hansen suggests, has "washed away many traditional modes of life around the world," they will remain able to fulfil their "irreplaceable role in cultivating reflective openness to the new and reflective loyalty to the known." Through this, they may engage their students in participatory inquiry, treating their lives in ethical, artful and creative ways in order that they may develop the capacities to grow in these ways as well as those associated with the traditional educational purposes of socialization, knowledge acquisition and preparation for an economic life.

It is tempting to associate this stance of education being about standing back as well as standing in with those who promote reflective teaching, acknowledge the "hidden" or "enacted" curriculum in classrooms and research teachers' emotions and identities; and indeed there are associations. Yet Hansen goes much further. He associates cosmopolitanism with "a democratic political commitment with its fundamental value of universal justice." Cosmopolitanism as democracy, he suggests, does not depend first upon the establishment of democratic institutions. Rather, it is based upon educated individuals who are characterized by their habit of "keeping habit itself responsive, dynamic and expansive . . . through the continued reconstruction of experience." It is more than engaging in reflective processes, although it is associated with them. Hansen argues that education should never become a tool for the promotion of particular interests, but a means by which learning, reflective openness and loyalty propels us forward as individuals and social beings. Education can, from this cosmopolitan perspective, teach students how to, "focus their minds, expand their spirits and discover best how to deploy their individual bent." To achieve this takes a teacher with particular values, qualities, knowledge and competencies.

As in his earlier books, *The Call to Teach* (1995) and *Exploring the Moral Heart of Teaching: Towards a Teacher's Creed* (2001), Hansen continues to emphasize the dynamic roles that teachers play in "making it possible for people for learn." Yet his own vision in this book is wider than in the other two. For him, the term "cosmopolitanism" deepens the importance of education by "clarifying the value of what is irreducible and unique about human beings" and "widens the significance of education by shedding light on the value of the common and shared features of human life."

This is not an easy-read book. Though it is well written and cogently organized, it demands the reader's full attention in a way that those books which purport to offer "practical" guidance for teachers do not. The chapters are long, their titles and content spanning broad concepts, their subjects the work of such distinguished philosophers as Plato, Confucius, Socrates, Michel de Montaigne, Marie de Gournay, and Alain Locke, all of whom in their own ways sought, as does Hansen, to challenge forces which seek to diminish educators' autonomy and authority. This is not a book for the faint hearted for it unashamedly plays to teachers as thinkers, as reflective practitioners, as professionals who wish to revisit and re-examine their fundamental values and, through this, clarify and strengthen the moral and ethical basis for their practices. Nor is it a book which can be skim read. Its contents will challenge. Like good teaching and learning, it demands sustained engagement. When readers, as teacher educators, school principals or teachers, do engage, they will notice the relative absence of references to research on schools and classrooms. Yet, alongside this, they will be rewarded with profound and deeply humane insights into new possibilities for ways of being and conducting themselves in schools and classrooms which will reinforce and extend the quality of their thinking and practices as professional educators.

Christopher Day, University of Nottingham
Ann Lieberman, Stanford University
2011

Acknowledgements

Writing this book has been an odyssey marked by numerous points of departure, all in quest of arriving at an inhabitable philosophy of education. Along the way many individuals have taken the time to comment on the work, and I remain grateful to them.

David Granger, Brian Keith, M. Mei-lin Ng, and Shilpi Sinha read an earlier draft of the book and provided trenchant, wide-ranging criticism. Nimrod Aloni, René Vicente Arcilla, John Baldacchino, Nicholas Burbules, William Gaudelli, Deborah Kerdeman, Luise Prior McCarty, Shirley Pendlebury, Jin Shenghong, Lalitha Vasudevan, and Leonard Waks have all provided helpful criticism of particular portions of the account. My colleague at Teachers College, Megan Laverty, has read numerous earlier writings leading up to the book and has shared her questions, her views, and her support. Stephanie Burdick-Shepherd, Jeff Frank, Cara Furman, Kyung Hwa Jung, Avi Mintz, and Terri Wilson have provided essential bibliographic assistance, not to mention enlightening conversation.

I have had the benefit of testing the ideas in the book in lectures and seminars at the following institutions: University of Humanistics (Utrecht), University of Manitoba, University of Kyoto, University of São Paulo at Ribeirao, State University of Londrina, Teachers College (Columbia University), Institute of Education (University of London), University of Stirling, Sibelius Academy (Helsinki), University of Oslo, Leuven University, University of Hong Kong, Indiana University, Université Laval, Xiamen University, Orebro University, Oulu University, University of Helsinki, Al-Quds University, University of Porto, Universidad Complutense Madrid, and Nanjing Normal University. My thanks to faculty and students in these settings for their hospitality and for their questions and suggestions, many of which still feel ahead of me and which I hope one day to address. Thanks also to colleagues and students for their criticism at presentations I gave on the topic at annual meetings of the American Educational Research Association (New York City, San Diego), the Association for Moral Education (New York City), the Graduate Student Conference on Philosophy and Education (New York City), the Philosophy of Education Society of China (Ji Nan), the Philosophy of Education Society of Great Britain (Edinburgh), the Philosophy of Education Society (North America: Boston,

Montreal), the Progressive Education Conference (Tel Aviv), and La Société Francophone de Philosophie de l'Éducation (Paris).

For generously making available some splendid summer work spaces – and adding, as a bonus to me, their criticism of the project – my thanks to Randall Allsup, Eileen Ball, and Caroline Heller. My wife, Elaine, has been a great listener and conversational friend.

Earlier versions of some of the ideas in this book appeared in the following journals, whose publishers I thank for permitting me to draw upon them: "Chasing butterflies without a net: Interpreting cosmopolitanism," in *Studies in Philosophy of Education*, 29 (2010), 151–166; "Cosmopolitanism and education: A view from the ground," in *Teachers College Record*, 112 (2010), 1–30, published online 2008, http://www.tcrecord.org ID Number: 15411; with Stephanie Burdick-Shepherd, Cristina Cammarano, and Gonzalo Obelleiro, "Education, values, and valuing in cosmopolitan perspective," in *Curriculum Inquiry*, 39 (2009), 587–612; and "Curriculum and the idea of a cosmopolitan inheritance," in *Journal of Curriculum Studies*, 40 (2008), 289–312.

I have had the pleasure of teaching students from many parts of the world, each bringing to bear on education a distinctive perspective and sensibility. I cannot imagine this book taking the form it has without their endlessly productive questions. Whatever deficiencies in the book that remain are my responsibility; whatever strengths that might endure mirror these students' intellectual passion and generosity. I dedicate this effort to them.

Preface

What does it mean to speak of "the teacher and the world"? The teacher and the classroom, the teacher and the school or university, the teacher and the community: these are the typical ways of describing the teacher's realm of experience. They sound right because teachers dwell in highly particular settings. They work with specific groups of students, colleagues, administrators, parents, and others. Their focus is necessarily inward, upon the human beings they are charged with educating. Wherever they work, and at whatever level of the system, teachers rightly need to give themselves over to their localized, face-to-face tasks.

In an interconnected world like our own, however, there are better and worse ways of enacting this down-to-earth vocation. I do not mean keeping one foot in the global arena of human affairs while keeping the other in the classroom. Teachers need both feet planted firmly on the ground they share, and come to share, with their students. I mean becoming mindful about how the larger world is always already a part of the teacher's experience.

Especially today it is impossible for a teacher to be unaware of global influences via the media and human movement. Teachers can try to ignore these factors. But such ignorance does not mean their influence disappears. Rather it means this influence will work its way in their classrooms and schools with no reflective response. Teachers are well positioned to help students, and themselves, to learn to respond to the world: to draw upon the knowledge and skills they cultivate to shape their lives creatively, rather than merely being shaped by forces over which they have no control.

In the chapters that follow I will portray the teacher's relation with the world through a cosmopolitan lens. Cosmopolitanism is an ancient concept with ever-present and ever-beautiful meaning. The term evokes images of moral solidarity with people the world over. However, cosmopolitanism is not a synonym with universalism. Rather it signifies the human capacity to be open reflectively to the larger world, while remaining loyal reflectively to local concerns, commitments, and values. The idea arose millennia ago in tandem with globalization, itself a long-standing process which in recent centuries has accelerated and become unstoppable through mechanisms of trade, artistic and scientific exchange, migration, and communications technology. Cosmopolitanism is an orientation through which people can respond, rather than merely react, to the complex and sometimes intense pressures of globalization. A cosmopolitan outlook positions people to sustain their integrity and continuity through the vicissitudes of unpredictable change.

This orientation is being enacted by educators the world over, in spirit if not in name. There are teachers, teacher educators, heads of schools, and educational researchers everywhere who deeply value learning from other persons and cultures. They value the distinctiveness and singularity of local community and of individual character. They are women and men who grow. Their education is continuous; it did not come to an end when they earned their teaching, administrative, or scholarly credentials. However, like countless families and communities around the globe, educators wonder how to balance the values of openness and loyalty. They are mindful of the wider world with its endless possibilities for learning and transformation. They feel an equally compelling attachment to that which lies close to heart and mind. At the same time, educators struggle with the conditions of teaching today: endless top-down measures to manipulate what they do, rapid economic turns and inequality in supportive resources that affect their lives and those of their students, a torrent of media stimuli that distract educational focus, and growth as well as shifts in population.

Cosmopolitanism provides no solutions to these contemporary predicaments. But it does offer a way of looking, thinking, and acting that makes possible better rather than worse responses to them. Its virtues are threefold:

- **Suppleness**. Cosmopolitanism is not a partisan ideology but an attentive outlook on life. Its expressions in cultures the world over are incalculably diverse and marvelously unscripted. I will document this claim by drawing on historical examples as well as contemporary field-based research that has been examining cosmopolitanism "on the ground" in various quarters of the globe. These examples will illuminate what it means to be open reflectively to the new and loyal reflectively to the known, which I take to be a core value in educational work in our time.

- **Longevity**. Cosmopolitanism is not a fashionable idea. It is not another instance of "the latest thing." Rather it has stood the test of time for millennia, albeit in a rough and ready manner, as a generative outlook on the human prospect. As mentioned, it has constituted a thoughtful *response* to change rather than a blind *reaction* to it. The chapters ahead range widely over the history and philosophy of cosmopolitan responsiveness and imagination. Their aim, in part, is to provide educators confidence in the reality and efficacy of this orientation.

- **Hopefulness**. Educational work the world over is under great pressure today to serve purely short-term, strategic interests. Many people worry that education is becoming just another commodity to buy – a ticket to the next predetermined stop – rather than an *experience* that invites human beings to a life of aesthetic, ethical, intellectual, and social meaningfulness. A cosmopolitan orientation can help educators respond to the contemporary ethos while staying true to their own creative vocation. This challenging task calls for a maturing, hopeful sense of constraint and possibility that contrasts with both blind optimism and fatalistic pessimism.

A cosmopolitan outlook can help teachers, within the terms of their work, to ripen their experience. All teachers have an influence of one sort or another on students, colleagues, administrators, and others. I hope to illuminate how this influence can become richer, perhaps even wiser, as teachers more and more envision themselves as persons *in* and *for* the world in which we all live. This perspective, in turn, helps educators cultivate a sense of past, present, and future, and thus to realize much more the time-honored significance of what they do.

Educational work has always been one of humanity's most imaginative undertakings. It has always been a deeply formative way to be with people, whether they be students, colleagues, parents, or others. These truths have become more vivid, and more priceless, in light of an increasingly fast-changing, crowded human condition.

David T. Hansen
January 2011

1 A Perspective on Teaching and Education for Our Time

Introduction

The Cosmopolitan Prism

A prism is a piece of translucent material that alters the angle of light. It transforms the tone, the texture, and the substance of color. We are surrounded by such prisms. There is an arresting moment in Krzysztof Kieslowski's film, "The Double Life of Veronique," in which the main character, played by the fine actress Irene Jacob, is riding a train to visit an ailing aunt. She looks out the window, at the world rushing by, through a small round prism that she holds delicately in the fingers of her right hand. As she gazes through the prism, light concentrates, colors intensify, and shapes distend or extend. Moreover, it is not only for her that the prism transforms the curve and light of the world. The viewer's world is also changed. The viewer is no longer a spectator but becomes a participant in the woman's seeing. Kieslowski captures in her gesture, and in the viewer's response, the possibility of leading a different life because the world would be seen differently.

Cosmopolitanism holds out the prospect of a different life, even as people subscribe to values to which they have long adhered. Cosmopolitanism constitutes an orientation in which people learn to balance reflective openness to the new with reflective loyalty to the known. The orientation positions people to learn from rather than merely tolerate others, even while retaining the integrity and continuity of their distinctive ways of being. In this respect, when viewed through a cosmopolitan prism education deepens and widens in significance. Cosmopolitanism deepens its importance by clarifying the value of what is irreducible and unique about human beings. Despite the massive size of nation-based systems today, education continues to happen (if it happens at all) one person at a time. The process necessarily draws out the individual person's agency because nobody can give him or her an education, as if they were passing along a bag of goods.

Teachers know this. They are not warehouse managers dispensing parcels of information on order. Instead they play a dynamic role in making it possible for people to learn. Still, every person has to reach out for education. Every person's education becomes as irreproducible as their character and spirit as a human being.

Cosmopolitanism widens the significance of education by shedding light on the value of the common and shared features of human life. Although people differ in the values they cherish, they share the capacity to value in the first place. Although they find meaning in quite varied forms of art, family life, friendship, and work, they share an underlying quest for meaning in life rather than desiring a mere stone-like existence. A cosmopolitan-minded education can help people recognize these common features as a renewed basis for mutual understanding and cooperation.

The cosmopolitan prism renders visible the symbiotic relation between points of view that may, at first glance, seem incommensurable. In theoretical terms, a claim about what is universal may sound universalistic, that is, homogenizing, reductive, and oppressive. A defense of the local may sound narrow, that is, separatist, closed-minded, and walled-in. However, in this book the relevant contrast will be between, on the one hand, cosmopolitanism as *embodying* affiliations with the local and, on the other hand, forces that are homogenizing and parochial. Cosmopolitanism is not synonymous with universalism. The local is not synonymous with parochialism. As mentioned above, cosmopolitanism means learning to hold in productive tension the values in reflective openness to the new and reflective loyalty to the known.

Cosmopolitanism has sometimes been associated with the well-to-do and privileged who treat the world as a smorgasbord of fresh delights. The term can conjure the image of today's elite urban dweller – in Bangkok, Buenos Aires, Hong Kong, London, Mumbai, Nairobi, New York, St. Petersburg, Sydney, or Tokyo – enjoying cuisines and music from around the world, following international news, dressing cross-culturally, and traveling far and wide. There is nothing inherently wrong with any of these doings. Aside from the pleasures they provide, they can promote or even incarnate a cosmopolitan orientation. But they may not. They may plunge persons into the consumerist and exploitative dimension of globalization in which everything becomes a commodity to be used up – a phenomenon quite different from the participatory and responsive ethos that cosmopolitanism represents.

Traveling, reveling in art from the world over, and the like, are not in themselves markers of a cosmopolitan disposition, and nor are they necessary for it. As research, journalism, films, novels, poetry, and everyday experience make clear, a local baker, janitor, or cab driver, or a small-town schoolteacher, fisherman, or market seller, may have a livelier cosmopolitan sensibility than the most globe-trotting, well-connected executive, who in any case is all too often camped out in airport lounges and chain hotels. Put another way, the most widely traveled person can be the most parochial of all in outlook and sense of judgment. A cosmopolitan-minded education does entail traveling, but with an accent not on physical movement per se but on intellectual, ethical, and aesthetic journeying.

Closer and Closer Apart, Further and Further Together

A central thesis in what follows is that a cosmopolitan-minded education assists people in moving closer and closer *apart* and further and further *together*. This trope springs from my long-term study of life in classrooms. In that life, as a teacher and group of students interact over the school year they often come to learn a great deal about one another's interests, personalities, dispositions, habits, strengths, weaknesses, hopes, and yearnings. In this respect they become closer to one another as the weeks and months roll by. However, they are in fact moving closer and closer *apart* precisely through a deepening recognition of what renders each of them a distinctive person. Here, closeness derives not from collapsing differences but from their sharpened emergence. This closeness is real, vital, and dynamic. It renders classroom life fascinating and rewarding, at least for serious-minded teachers and students. It also accounts for some of that life's frustrations and mysteries (for example, regarding the unpredictable ways in which people change).

At the same time, the teacher and students are moving further and further *together* through a course of study and the myriad experiences that accompany it. Whether in art, history, mathematics, physical education, or science, and whether at the primary, secondary, or university level, they come to share over the course of a term or year an uncountable array of questions, inquiries, assignments, problems, challenges, difficulties, understandings, and more. These experiences do not render them a peaceable kingdom. Disagreements, resentments, and confusion typically crop up again and again. But teacher and students return to their work. Their shared experiences substantiate their movement together through time and activity. As with their closeness, their participatory togetherness through the sometimes bumpy adventure of education is real, vital, and dynamic. The more engaged that teachers and students are, the more formative as well as compelling will be their fellow traveling.

I addressed this image of closeness and distance in a previous book, *Exploring the Moral Heart of Teaching* (2001, p. 156, *passim*). That book, as well as an earlier study, *The Call to Teach* (1995), has led to the present inquiry into cosmopolitanism and education. What does it mean to be a teacher in a globalized world? Are teachers the hand-servants of the particular state or nation in which they reside? Are they paid functionaries carrying out the dictates of inward-looking authorities? Are they representatives of what might be called "the republic of education" that reaches across political borders and that regards the endeavor as something more than the maintenance of particularistic or nationalistic values? Are teachers charged by the very meaning of education to help young people develop broad, deep, and rich understandings of self, community, and world? What would it mean to be a teacher who grasps and can convey the value of being open reflectively to new ideas, purposes, and people, while also being loyal reflectively to particular beliefs, traditions, and practices? Such a teacher would be on the road to balancing, if uneasily, the values embedded in the local institution that has hired her or him with those of a wider human horizon.

These questions reach back to the very beginning of education itself, which surfaced historically in tension with socialization though not necessarily in conflict with it. If socialization means coming into a form of life – learning a language and a set of cultural customs – education means learning to reflect about that form of life while acquiring knowledge of subjects and of the larger world.

The idea of teaching as a calling or vocation, and the idea that teaching is a moral practice, both have roots in the emergence of education millennia ago. To conceive teaching as a calling, rather than as solely a job or occupation, elevates teaching to its proper place as one of humanity's most dignified and important social undertakings. Teaching's values reside in what it crystallizes, namely knowledge, and in what it cultivates, namely the aesthetic, ethical, and intellectual capacity of the individual human being. There is nothing portentous or solemn about this portrait. Teaching has always required a lightness of touch – not to be confused with lightheartedness – if it is to support education rather than, say, dogmatism, indoctrination, or other one-sided outcomes. Lightness is the other side of seriousness (cf. Calvino, 1993, pp. 3–29). It connotes being responsive, nimble, and patient in the act of teaching, while also retaining a sense of educational purpose.

To conceive teaching as a moral activity recognizes the fact that morals such as thoughtfulness and generosity, and principles of conduct such as fair-mindedness and respect for truth, are always at play in teaching. Whether in primary school, after-school settings for adolescents, or seminars for medical students, people are constantly learning these morals and principles – or their opposites – even if indirectly more than overtly. Thus much more is at issue in educating than the transfer of knowledge, important as that is. The *ways* in which teaching and learning happen (or fail to) embody moral dimensions, for better or for worse. It appears there is never a moral vacuum in education: at every moment its meaning, values, and consequences for human beings hang in the balance, however microscopic the scale. Happily these facts do not mean the teacher must walk on eggshells, though it does make sense to be mindful of how one is treading.

Teaching across human history has always been a moral undertaking, and it has also been a calling, at least for a good number of its practitioners. Today, as the world becomes smaller, and as human beings find it increasingly difficult to wall out external influences, teachers can advance an education that equips people not just to deal with these circumstances but to reconstruct their approach toward them. Instead of merely reacting to being thrown together in more crowded conditions, people can respond – as many do today – by engaging others in creative communication and exchange. As they do so, they can transform their proximity from one of accident and force of events into an educational relationship, in which they can learn with one another how to dwell more efficaciously, purposefully, and humanely in their settings. They can learn to move closer and closer apart. They need not abandon their individual and cultural uniqueness. On the contrary, they can come to perceive and comprehend differences in a clearer light, however partial, incomplete, and provisional their insight will often be. At the same time, thanks to their ongoing education they can learn to move further and further together in the very process of shaping humane and fulfilling ways of interaction. This self-created social tether does not diminish their distinctiveness but gives it a more robust, sustainable integrity.

Closer and closer apart, further and further together: the image frames teaching and education when viewed through a cosmopolitan prism. Here and in the chapters that follow I will elucidate this perspective. I will try to vindicate it in the face of claims that human creativity, as embodied in a cosmopolitan outlook, is hopelessly constrained by biological, psychological, economic, and socio-cultural forces. Such constraints are real. But it is a different matter to claim that they predict or determine human conduct. Such claims pale in comparison with the inexhaustible accomplishments observable across space and time in the field of human endeavor (including the accomplishment of conceiving the idea of determinism!). Thus, in what follows I will illustrate a cosmopolitan orientation through examples drawn from history, philosophical inquiry, the arts, ethno-graphic research, and everyday life. The analysis will show why cosmopolitanism dwells vibrantly today on the ground rather than constituting an ivory tower or merely theoretical posture.

A Respectful Distance from Utopian Idealism

The discussion will also temper the longstanding utopian impulse behind cosmo-politanism. This impulse finds expression in questions such as: What would a truly cosmopolitan world look like? Would it be a world in which human beings could move in peace through diverse communities, sharing, communicating, participating, learning, taking interest and even delight in one another's differ-ences as well as similarities? A world with no harsh dogmas and ideologies, in which people had the confidence in their values to live them in calm gratitude rather than loudly assert that others must abide by them? A world in which poetry in its broadest sense had made a fabled return, triumphing over today's debilitating, distracting commercialism? Would a truly cosmopolitan world be one where economic and political resources had been redistributed such that everyone, rather than a privileged few, could realize their full human capacities?

Is this the world seen through a cosmopolitan prism? Or is it rather *our* world that becomes more fully illuminated, *our* world with its dismaying imperfections and terrible injustices that persist alongside its piercing beauty, its inspiring goodness, its iridescent joy and unbounded love? Utopian visions can constitute valuable alternative standpoints for criticizing present arrangements (Leung, 2009, p. 372). But they can just as easily unmoor the human spirit from the here and now. Anne-Marie Drouin-Hans (2004, pp. 23–24) reminds us of the double gesture in utopia: it can connote a "good place" (from the Greek *eu-topos*) but also "no place" (Gr. *ou-topos*). The world viewed through a cosmopolitan prism is neither Edenic nor hellish, neither a comedy nor a tragedy, neither good nor bad. It is neither a scene of inevitable progress nor, as Immanuel Kant once sadly put it, a place of bitter atonement for what seem like long-forgotten sins. The world has aspects of all these attributes.

From a cosmopolitan perspective, however, the world is what human beings make of it, subject to conditions of their mortality, vulnerability, and fallibility. For millennia, people have justifiably turned to education as a source of "making," of generating humane, inhabitable ways of life. Education in a cosmopolitan perspective merits a hearing because of its roots in everyday life, especially at the ever-appearing crossroads of the new and the known to which all people are subject in varying degrees and ways. That crossroads can be a scene of learning, and cosmopolitanism itself, as stressed in the subtitle of this book, can be understood as an educational orientation in the world.

The sections that follow provide historical background for the inquiry and a sense of the contemporary research landscape on cosmopolitanism (several extended footnotes offer references and theoretical clarification). The sections also illuminate the method of working adopted in this book and they anticipate themes in the chapters to come.

Background Notes on the History of Cosmopolitanism

Philosophical traditions which originate in the Mediterranean world have rendered the cosmopolitan idea in its most extended forms. Accordingly I will focus upon them in this book. However, these forms have never been self-contained (or "purely" Western, whatever that could mean), nor are they at all points the most influential in the world today. For one thing, the Mediterranean has always been a cultural crossroads,[1] ranging historically from the Moorish, Christian and Jewish milieu of medieval Spain in the west to the multilingual, multicultural ethos of the Levant in the east, not to mention the Phoenician, Carthaginian and Magrebian cultures of North Africa and the Greek and Roman cultures of southern Europe. For another thing, cosmopolitan motifs appear in numerous philosophical lineages deriving, for example, from the Hindu *Upanishads* (first millennium BCE) and Confucius' *Analects* (sixth century BCE). Contemporary scholars have articulated cosmopolitan themes in these and other long-standing traditions (Giri, 2006; Kwok-bun, 2005; Levenson, 1971). They have made plain that the movement in cosmopolitan ideas has often been, in global terms, east to west (Bhattacharya, 1997; Bose and Manjapra, 2010; Sen, 2006; Shayegan, 1992; Tuan, 1996; Weiming, 1998) and south to north (Fojas, 2005; Loss, 2005; Salomon, 1979). They call into question stereotypical (or "essentialized") notions of West and East.[2]

The term cosmopolitanism derives from the Greek *kosmopolites*, typically translated as "citizen of the world." As Pauline Kleingeld and Eric Brown show in their concise review of the history of the cosmopolitan idea (Kleingeld and Brown, 2006; also see Kleingeld, 1999), there are indices of it in Socrates' (470–399 BCE) eagerness to talk with persons from anywhere. One can also discern a cosmopolitan attitude in the practices of the traveling Sophists, Socrates' contemporaries who were itinerant educators and among the very first persons in Western culture who were paid for their educational services. As far as scholars have been able to determine, the idea finds its first formal expression in the voice of Diogenes (*c*.390–323 BCE), a so-called Cynic philosopher who famously declared that he came from the world rather than from a particular culture or polity. One of his teachers, Antisthenes (455–360 BCE), helped originate Cynic philosophy, including its cosmopolitan aspect. The Cynics were persons who treated local governance and custom as in many respects narrow-minded and out of tune with nature. They construed what is called moral obligation as a form of allegiance to humanity itself, a significant portion of which they knew given the poly-vocal cultural ethos of the Mediterranean world at the time (Branham and Goulet-Cazé, 1996; Schofield, 1991).

The Cynics' influence percolated through subsequent renderings of cosmopolitanism, although with marked differences from their deliberate distancing from public life. The idea reached an apogee in the ancient world among the Hellenistic and Roman Stoics, who in various forms suggested it was possible to devote oneself both to local and larger human community. They sought to frame ways of life in which one could be attuned both to particularized obligations and to the needs and hopes of humanity writ large – a view that informs what I have called reflective openness to the new fused with reflective loyalty to the known. Writers as varied as Cicero, Seneca, Epictetus, and Marcus Aurelius ventured cosmopolitan ideas throughout their texts. Recent research on these and other figures dissolves the stereotype of the Stoic as an aloof, isolated, long-suffering ('stoic') individual. Scholars have demonstrated that the Stoics, through a diverse array of practices, were often public-minded and politically active, even as they focused on cultivating their ethical, aesthetic, and intellectual ways of being (Brown, 2006; Foucault, 2005; Hadot, 1995; Long, 1996; Nussbaum, 1994; Reydams-Schils, 2005; Sellars, 2003). In Chapter 2, I return to Socrates and the Stoics as well as their cosmopolitan-minded descendants, showing how rich their legacy is for the teacher in today's globalized world.

In the wake of the Renaissance, with its rediscovery of Plato and other ancient sources, writers such as Desiderius Erasmus (1466–1536) and Michel de Montaigne (1533–1592) put forward portraits mirroring those of the Stoics about the importance of tolerance and mutual exchange. They sought an ecumenical approach that could reduce the religious strife prevalent at the time, even as they respected human differences in culture, in the arts, and more (Kraye, 1996; Toulmin, 1990). During the eighteenth century, many writers, jurists, business people, artists, and others from across Europe sought to break out of what they viewed as narrow, royalty-centered absolutism. For some it was risky to do so, and they generated a remarkable armoire of rhetorical devices that masked their identities while also letting them advocate cosmopolitan ideals of human solidarity that reach across the borders of national and tribal custom (Jacobs, 2006; Rosenfeld, 2002; Schlereth, 1977).

Commentators rooted their cosmopolitan claims, in part, in the view that because human beings are capable of reason and moral agency, they must be treated with respect. They are not things with a merely economic or cultural value, but are beings with dignity. They are creative rather than merely created creatures. They are ends in themselves rather than mere means to others' ends (Kant, 1990, pp. 51–52 (434–435 KW)). This outlook led cosmopolitan thinkers, in contrast with some of their Enlightenment confreres, to condemn war, slavery, and imperialism (Kant, 1963b; Carter, 2001; Muthu, 2003). Immanuel Kant (1724–1804) eclipsed his own cultural biases in showing that moral respect – deriving from the German *achtung*, which can also be rendered as "reverence" – translates into the duty to make possible for all people an education that positions them to shape the course of their lives. Kant gave the cosmopolitan idea an enduring boost through his moral philosophy and through his oft-cited argument for how to generate peace among states and communities.[3]

The Current Research Landscape

In recent years scholars from many disciplines and many parts of the world have reanimated the cosmopolitan idea. They have demonstrated cosmopolitanism's remarkably diverse manifestations in human life as well as the permeability of the idea to influence from anywhere. This community includes philosophers and political theorists who undertake conceptual work, historians who study past instances of cosmopolitan-minded practice, literary critics examining aspects of world literature, field-based researchers who seek to illuminate "actually existing cosmopolitanism" (Malcolmson, 1998) or what can be called cosmopolitanism on the ground (Hansen, 2010a), and scholars in education focusing on the ramifications of cosmopolitanism for educational thought and practice.[4] This wide-ranging interest mirrors the fact that the idea has historically been a source of creative thinking about political and moral concerns.

Some of today's scholars combine cosmopolitan ideas with familiar notions of humanism, liberalism, and multiculturalism. Others address a different unit of analysis than what is suggested by those concepts. In heuristic terms, their point of departure is neither humanity nor the individual as such, as in humanism and liberalism, nor the community as such, as in multiculturalism. Rather, as I interpret it, the focus is on what a person and community are in the present moment, juxtaposed with what they might become through a reflective response to new influence fused with a reflective appreciation of their roots and values. Put another way, liberal and multicultural exchange spotlights the adjudication of existing values – values taken as given and self-contained. Cosmopolitan-minded exchange highlights the emergence, however modest in their terms and scope, of transformed values (Earle and Cvetkovich, 1995, p. 102, *passim*) – values for which descriptive language may not yet exist. This movement does not mean abandoning prior values. The term transformation, in cosmopolitan perspective, accents not radical change but incremental reconfiguration. As we will see, it emphasizes continuity in values and beliefs, but not their fixity. The orientation implies learning from rather than merely tolerating value differences. From a cosmopolitan point of view, to learn is to absorb, to metabolize the new into the known such that the latter itself takes on new qualities (more on these points below).[5]

The current interest in cosmopolitanism also embodies a desire to move beyond perceived dead-ends in what has been called identity politics, with its background presumptions of cultural and individual purity that, in some articulations, makes mutual understanding across difference inconceivable. From a cosmopolitan perspective, purity and fixity of identity are impossible, given the unpreventable porosity of cultures and individuals to influence from the larger world. All the fingers in the cosmos cannot plug the dike and keep such influence out. The barriers individuals and groups may erect attest in their very construction to the permanent presence of external influence. These barriers cannot wall the world out, at least not for long, though they can wall people in.

To presume as cosmopolitanism does that permeability and porosity are the rule rather than the exception in human affairs is not to adopt a liberal individualist or aesthete's view that this condition is "good" and that people ought to revel in it. It is not to celebrate the privileged, consumerist nomad sampling the world's smorgasbord of arts, cuisines, and other customs. Moreover, it is not to ignore the homogenizing pressure that globalized forces exert on local community and individuality. The threat of cultural dissolution can lead naturally to turning inward in a manner that may evoke identity politics, on the one hand, and rootless individualism, on the other hand. These impulses may represent an attempt to survive rather than necessarily to separate oneself off from others. An inhabitable cosmopolitan outlook requires compassion and respect for this deeply human response (Hollinger, 2002, p. 230). The cosmopolitan premise that individual and cultural purity is impossible suggests that influence from without is unceasing and that, given an increasingly crowded world, people would be well served to respond to it thoughtfully – as contrasted with reacting to it passively or violently – if they wish to retain individual and cultural integrity.

Kwame Anthony Appiah captures the spirit of much of the current research on cosmopolitanism. "We can learn from each other's stories," he writes, "only if we share both human capacities and a single world: relativism about either is a reason not to converse but to fall silent" (2005, p. 257). Appiah refers to capacities rather than to values. He knows as do persons everywhere that economic, artistic, religious, family, and other values differ markedly the world over. Their diversity is incalculable. Moreover, persons who subscribe to the same values often hold or express them differently. Two painters who cherish the color red may express their valuing in contrasting ways in their work. Two teachers who revere science may conduct experiments and other classroom activities in distinctive fashion. The examples here seem infinite. Thus Appiah takes care to refer not to values but to capacities. I take him to mean shared human capacities to think, to speak, to listen, to tell and follow stories, to learn, and to be able to begin again when things go awry.

People can cultivate these shared capacities while holding different values. Indeed, the flowering of these capacities can help people appreciate differences and negotiate conflicts in values without having to resort to radical either/or decisions. Such communication and mutual understanding will rarely be ideal or complete. As the world continues to transform there will always be a need for reopening dialogue and crafting new arrangements. However, to borrow a mathematical image from Eva T. H. Brann (1979, p. 5), a partial understanding of another person or culture has to none a ratio of infinity. One can (re)build a whole world on the basis of this truth.

Today's proliferating scholarly literature frames cosmopolitanism in varied ways. For heuristic purposes, Pauline Kleingeld and Eric Brown (2006) summarize much of cosmopolitan thought under the headings of political, economic, moral, and cultural cosmopolitanism. I will touch on each category as a way to further illuminate the approach toward education and teaching taken in this book.

Political cosmopolitanism focuses on institutions, policies, and laws that transcend national jurisdictions and that are intended to protect human rights and ways of life. While some figures advocate a single world government, others respect the value of nations but urge a reconstructed political order in which nations could thrive without nationalism (Calhoun, 2007; Kristeva, 1993). Scholars and activists in this line of thinking focus on human rights and peace organizations, international agencies ranging from the United Nations to the International Criminal Court, and the ever-expanding array of non-governmental organizations that work across political and geographic boundaries (while also, in some cases, generating new forms of boundary).

Economic cosmopolitanism constitutes a critique of neoliberalism, which is an ideology that conjoins a full-blown endorsement of "free market" principles with privileging individual self-interest over the interests of mutual well-being. In a neoliberal outlook, critics argue, instrumentalist mentalities – wherein everything becomes, in effect, a means to profit-making ends – have been rapidly colonizing business, educational, health, and artistic endeavors the world over to the detriment of fundamental human needs and hopes. Critics chastise neoliberalism for fueling what many people regard as the dark side of globalization, in which consolidated economic interests (e.g., multinational companies) often run roughshod over political, moral, environmental, and cultural concerns (Habermas, 1998; Papastephanou, 2005). These critics conceive forms of economic cosmopolitanism that are deeply shaped by concerns for social justice (Barnett et al., 2005; Tan, 2004). For example, the capabilities approach to social and economic development, as conceived by Amartya Sen (1999) and others (DeMartino, 2000; Nussbaum, 2000), rejects a focus on wealth creation because such a one-sided aim has led historically to a harsh assault on the environment and to the impoverishment of moral values. Instead, the approach highlights educational and training programs designed to position people everywhere, especially the downtrodden, to develop the skills and political agency to participate more fully in shaping their circumstances and possibilities.[6] The capabilities approach, in this sense, can be understood as a mode of economic cosmopolitanism reconstructed through values derived from political and moral cosmopolitanism.

Moral cosmopolitanism addresses questions such as whether and how human obligations extend to people outside one's immediate circle (Beck, 2004). For universalists such as Martha Nussbaum (1997a, 1997b, 2002), people need to treat their moral obligations as global in nature and significance. In her outlook, the fact that every person is born into a particular culture constitutes an accident.

What is not accidental, in her view, is being born a human being in a world of human beings. For "rooted" cosmopolitans such as Appiah (2005, 2006), people can respect universal rights but at the same time legitimately regard their moral obligations as intimately tied to, and as springing from, local community. From this perspective, to characterize a person's cultural origins as accidental or incidental, especially from a moral point of view, unnecessarily diminishes a longstanding and dynamic source of guidance.

Cultural cosmopolitanism highlights new social configurations emblematic of the increased intermingling of people, customs, and practices in many parts of the world. Cultural cosmopolitans argue that people can be rooted meaningfully (that is, morally, aesthetically, intellectually) in more than one culture or community (Hollinger, 2002; Waldron, 2000, 2003). Just as strong (e.g., Nussbaum) and moderate (e.g., Appiah) versions of moral cosmopolitanism mark the literature, so there are vibrant internal debates concerning cultural cosmopolitanism. On the one hand, some observers celebrate hybridity and the possibility of what they see as endless cultural borrowing and exchange made possible by contemporary media, internet technology, increased mobility, urban change, and the like. Others caution that there are deep differences between what can be called an additive versus a transformative model of cultural cosmopolitanism. In the former, individuals in effect approach cultural diversity as shoppers: pick some from here and some from there. Critics claim this movement hardly constitutes genuine hybridity. In their view, hybridity necessitates transformation of some kind in one's values, beliefs, and commitments. Such a process can be difficult, confusing, unpredictable, and time-consuming.

According to Pratap Bhanu Mehta (2000, pp. 620, 627–629), Harri Englund (2004, pp. 296, 297, 312), and other critics, the promise in cultural cosmo-politanism resides not in new forms of so-called hybridity as such. Rather it positions people to appreciate how difficult it can be to discern how other persons *see* the world. It is one thing to "hear" another's words and arguments; it is another thing to picture the way of seeing the world that is the source of those words and arguments. A cosmopolitan orientation makes possible picturing cultural and individual differences more clearly, while also grasping just how challenging it can be to take on new perspectives and habits. The latter does happen time and again (Bailin, 2006), but the process can be slow, uneven, and marked as much by discomfort as by pleasure in the new. To move closer and closer apart, and further and further together – whether in the classroom or elsewhere – is rarely a simple or straightforward affair.

The distinctions between the modes of cosmopolitanism Kleingeld and Brown (2006) identify are not hard and fast.[7] Each can be viewed as emphasizing rather than as isolating a particular body of questions and concerns. The notion of *educational cosmopolitanism* featured in this book resonates most closely with concerns associated with moral and cultural cosmopolitanism. Their perspectives, to which I will return in the pages ahead, shed light on the experience of being open reflectively to the new and loyal reflectively to the known. I will suggest that such experience is transformative, however minute the scale may be, rather than merely additive. These experiences touch self and community. They modify people's perceptions and conduct in the world.

On Patience, Truth, and Justice in Teaching

As with all education, a cosmopolitan approach cannot be forced or rushed. The urge to educate quickly, so characteristic of our times, in order to compete with others inevitably leads to ephemeral outcomes – or problematic ones, if we consider by analogy the environmentally destructive consequences the world over of what could be dubbed hasty agriculture.

Nor can education be meaningful if it is rendered into a mere means to an end, however compelling that end may be (cf. Aloni, 2002). To put the intellectual and emotional integrity of the present moment in thrall to a future outcome is to dissolve the meaningfulness and integrity of that moment. As Hannah Arendt (1961) argued, a paradox of education is that teachers must often turn their back to the future for the very sake of the future, precisely by concentrating fully on the here and now while drawing in as best as possible the cultural legacy bequeathed by the past. This emphasis on the educational value of the present moment contrasts with presentism, which is the dogmatic assumption that contemporary outlooks, values, and interests are self-justified and superior simply by virtue of being current.[8]

A related challenge is that teachers naturally wish to shape *in their own image* the persons in their charge, for it is hard to keep in view any other (especially when emotion and hope are at play). Our prisms can be difficult, at times, to turn. However, at numerous points along the way education disconfirms expectations rather than validates them, and this is so for teachers, students, parents, and communities. Education entails a real encounter with the new rather than merely a rehearsal of the known. It means regarding subject matter as an occasion for new thinking rather than for merely projecting into it prior understandings and assumptions.

Education involves surprise and discovery, as well as frustration and discomfort (Mintz, 2008). To develop a new understanding of self, other, and world is often to lose a previous one. This experience can be as painful, figuratively speaking, as for the snake that sheds its skin in order to grow. In his famous essay "Circles," Ralph Waldo Emerson (1803–1882) writes: "The way of life is wonderful; it is by abandonment" (1983, p. 414). He evokes how wondrous it is that a human being can transform *at all* in aesthetic, moral, and intellectual terms, given the weight of social custom as well as of built-in psychological and biological constraints. At the same time, he shows that this transformation, by which he means education, involves real loss ("abandonment") as well as real gain. He does not mean forgetting one's history or that of one's community. On the contrary, memory itself affirms the realities of loss and gain through education.

The accent on the qualifier "real" in the paragraph above sheds light on education's relation to truth and justice – two of humanity's most longstanding, oft-cited, and sometimes elusive ideals. In public comments on the writer's task in a conflicted world, Susan Sontag (2001) asked "Should we serve justice or truth?" To the surprise of some in the audience, she replied: "It has to be truth, in order to serve a justice which is not yet." She meant that in the absence of the discipline of truth-seeking, the passion for justice can produce unjust methods of striving for it. The passion for truth, however, is poignantly disinterested, in her view, because it is guided by the spirit of "a justice which is not yet" – which is to say, a justice that we cannot fully describe because we have yet to experience or witness it. It is a justice that we can aspire to, that we can move closer to, just as we can picture and draw nearer to ways of love and friendship we have yet to see in the world. However, to conceive this justice, much less to realize it, necessitates rigorous, thoughtful, and dispassionate inquiry (in her remarks, Sontag praised W. G. Sebald as exemplary[9]). In Sontag's view of the writer, to serve truth constitutes the most just way to serve justice. Perhaps she would say the same of the judge, the politician, and the journalist. Truth-seeking can be public and can guide the building of just laws, institutions, and policies.

As an instance of Sontag's outlook, consider Chinua Achebe's well-known novel, *Things Fall Apart*. The author's style fuses his intimate knowledge and feeling for Igbo cultural life in Nigeria with literary motifs drawn from other parts of the world (such as the title of the novel, taken from W. B. Yeats' poem, "The Second Coming"). As such, Achebe's writing enacts an element of cosmopolitanism that we will meet again and again in the chapters ahead: namely, a human capacity to create meaning that is not reducible to any single cultural source. Achebe's novel tells a tale of the breakdown of Igbo culture and tradition under the impress of British colonialism. At the same time, it constitutes a tenacious search for truth. In unsparing terms, Achebe sketches the flawed character of Okonkwo, the leading protagonist in the story, while also illuminating the man's gifts. He portrays in equally frank terms what can be judged flawed aspects of Igbo culture, such as its passion for war, its gender inequality, and its infanticide of twins, while also coloring-in its many-sided sensitivity. In a powerful way, these accounts humanize the Igbo such that the colonial undertaking stands out all the more for its monstrousness – since that endeavor was all too often predicated on the assumption that the colonized were *not* fully human. They were considered "primitive" and "simple" – rather than, as Achebe amply documents, complicated, contradictory, inconstant, ambivalent about some of their values and practices, creative and destructive, and so much more. Achebe crystallizes the inhumanity of the colonial project not by romanticizing the Igbo or by eliding their cultural discontinuities, but precisely by painting a true picture. This truth helps us see the meanings of justice and injustice.

"It has to be truth," claims Susan Sontag, "in order to serve a justice which is not yet." To be sure, teachers are not dramatists or public informants. Their tasks differ from those of the novelist, journalist, and general writer. Teachers work directly *with* the children, youth, or adults in their charge, and they work directly *with* the subject matter of education, ranging from art, to engineering, to zoology. Nonetheless, in a broad sense they share a concern for human well-being. When it comes to truth and justice, the educator needs passionate dispassion: a commitment to truth, rather than to self-interest or to ideology, fused with a love of justice.[10] This paradoxical way of casting passion mirrors the paradox of education touched on above. All the ends of education that can be conceived, ranging from higher scores on standardized tests to a stronger devotion to democracy, can too easily sunder the endeavor by overlooking the fullness of the present as well as by either eliminating or harnessing too tightly various methods that have elsewhere proven their merit. The pursuit of high scores may elbow aside opportunities for open-ended, interpretive discussion of ideas, texts, and events, including what it means to practice a democratic way of life. The striving for democratic dispositions may pass right over the development of the thinking and knowledge of the world requisite for playing a truthful and just role in its trajectory.

Teachers can draw students and themselves into the ever-generative space where reality and imagination meet. With patience and steadfastness (Hansen and Laverty, 2010), they can come to grips with the problematic consequences of what is colloquially called "spin," in which mask-making triumphs over reality such that anything goes and truth flies out the window. It is an ethos of fantasy and often of will to power, rather than of imagination. It has been exacerbated by the astounding explosion of communications technology in our time, which has in other ways led to much human good. The counterpart of a universe of spin would be an ethos of brute fact that ejects imagination from the scene. In his novel *Hard Times*, Charles Dickens immortalized such an atmosphere in his depiction of Mr. Gradgrind's dolorous classroom.

All of this contrasts with the disciplined work of articulating ideas, inter-pretations, and arguments – with seriousness and lightness – as well as of trying to see the world truly through art and other makings. To serve truth, as Sontag puts it, does not mean having or possessing truth. For the teacher, as for the scholar, truth constitutes a regulative ideal. It may not be attainable in some final sense, and yet serves as a beacon that lights a more just way. Its pursuit calls upon imagination, that is, conceiving and picturing possibilities – "that which is not yet" – that are richly rooted in the actual world of people, things, events, and meanings. A cosmopolitan orientation in education pivots around respect for reality and truth, patiently yet earnestly cultivated.

Remarks on Method

I have written this book for teachers, teacher educators, heads of school, researchers interested in teaching in a globalizing context, and colleagues involved in policy-making. I also have in view readers interested specifically in cosmo-politanism. To write for this diverse audience is no straightforward matter. For this reason, both here and in what follows I take pains to clarify terms, a practice I found necessary in the aforementioned research on the moral dimensions of teaching. In presenting that work publicly and in writing about it, I have sometimes had to devote as much time to explaining what I do *not* mean by the concept moral as what I do perceive in it. In my view, for example, the moral differs from concepts such as value, custom, ideology, and convention. Teachers and students can cultivate a shared morality in the classroom – understood as an emergent, generative mode of regarding and treating one another, subject matter, and world – without subscribing to the same values or ideologies (Gallas, 2003, pp. 133–134; Hansen, 1992).

Debate continues in education about the meaning of the moral, just as it does in the scholarly field known as moral philosophy. Like the moral, cosmopolitanism is also an "essentially contested concept" (Gallie, 1956). The scholarly community has not settled on a single definition of the term and is unlikely to do so. While some scholars bemoan this condition, since in their view it makes things unnecessarily messy, others are content to try to characterize or describe the concept rather than define it. For them any definition becomes an instant straitjacket, corralling a concept whose value resides in its very movement as it aspires to respond to the movement of the human world itself.

Scholars addressing cosmopolitanism today are attuned to the fact that there are better and worse ways of characterizing the concept. For example, Catherine Lu (2000), in her sketch of "the one and many faces" of cosmopolitanism, shows how writers less familiar with the history of the idea and the contemporary research literature continue to assert, mistakenly, that cosmopolitanism connotes political aloofness, moral rootlessness, disguised ethnocentrism, and/or elitist aestheticism (touched on previously with regards to today's wealthy nomadic tourist). As another example, Sharon Todd (2009), in her "rethinking" of cosmopolitanism, shows why conflating cosmopolitanism with uncritical universalism undercuts the potential in the concept to illuminate humane modes of social interaction across differences. If cosmopolitanism is reduced to a synonym for a universalistic, flattening outlook, then the very point in deploying the term falls away.[11]

Contemporary scholarship has not dissolved the charges levied against the idea. But it has engaged them seriously and, in so doing, has made it possible to give cosmopolitanism a fresh and fair hearing. It has shown, for example, that like any human orientation cosmopolitanism can morph into an outlook that excludes some people, but that such a possibility is not inherent either in the idea or in its manifold historical and contemporary enactments. A comparable point can be made about the concept moral: it can morph into moralism, a one-sided if not oppressive approach toward justice and other people. But this outcome is in no sense immanent in the idea or across its historical expressions.

Thus, to clarify terms constitutes more than an exercise in logic. It can become a social act of vindicating terms, which includes grasping their limits, so that they can help people think and make decisions. Teachers are perpetual vindicators and clarifiers. In primary and in university settings, and at all points in between, they are in the business of enacting and defending careful thinking about terms. It can be valuable to see the clear edges of things, at least to the extent possible, rather than to leave them in a blur.

A related methodological point is that, as seen in this chapter, I will circle back again and again to core aspects of cosmopolitanism and educating in the world today. One reason for this practice is the impossibility of addressing every pertinent question readers may have about a given claim when it first arises. To stop to do so would likely mean never getting started. I regret taxing readers' patience, if it comes to that, but hope that by the end of the book the parts have formed a whole (if not something larger than that).

The method of working in this book also embodies the conviction that the past continues to "speak" in the present. More strongly, the past often speaks to us as if it came from the future rather than from what has come before. To be sure, every writer – past and present – embodies some of the prejudices of his or her era. But this commonplace does not capture what is interesting in writers, which from a cosmopolitan point of view has to do with the ways in which they push the boundaries of both the familiar and the strange. I will draw upon a range of philosophical and other writers from the past, some of whose perspectives not only reside outside their time (even while reflecting their temporal conditions) but reach beyond our own. I will deploy a style of writing that aspires to be responsive to the varied register of these sources. For example, it will be appropriate to write statements such as "Plato says" rather than "Plato said," not because the man himself still lives (which is obviously not the case) but because his ideas and questions do. They are as alive as any persons living today, or even more so as a poet chagrined with the present age might put it. Jean-Luc Nancy writes:

> A contemporary is not always someone who lives at the same time, nor someone who speaks of overtly "current" questions. But it is someone in whom we recognize a voice or gesture which reaches us from a hitherto unknown but immediately familiar place, something which we discover we have been waiting for, or rather which has been waiting for us, something which was there, imminent.
>
> (Nancy, 1996, pp. 107–108)

Another way to make this point is to revise the familiar adage that all who live and work today stand on the shoulders of those who came before. That adage remains powerful: to forget the past is fundamentally to forget ourselves, which is to say to forget the very question of what it means to be a human being. But this truth can be wedded with the idea that those in the past stand, in turn, on our shoulders. Through our remembrance – our willingness to take up their voices in dialogue – and through our own words and deeds in the here and now, we continue to diffuse their creativity into human consciousness and practice. We allow their future to continue to be ahead of them, in a manner that Maurice Merleau-Ponty conjures when he writes of paintings:

> If no painting comes to be *the* painting, if no work is ever absolutely completed and done with, still each creation changes, alters, enlightens, deepens, confirms, exalts, re-creates, or creates in advance all the others. If

creations are not a possession, it is not only that, like all things, they pass away; it is also that they have almost all their life still before them.

(Merleau-Ponty, 1964, p. 190)

Merleau-Ponty evokes how the past can be as vitally present, today and tomorrow, as what people normally take the present to mean.

Finally, this book will feature metaphor. A metaphor is a term of art. It fuses a concept or image drawn from one field of activity with an activity in another field, in order to illuminate the truth of experience. "The stormy sea of politics today," "this dinner is heavenly," "my classroom feels like an oasis," "their arrangement was a house of cards": metaphor is the stuff of life. "A cosmopolitan prism," "a cosmopolitan crossroads": these and other terms will continue to be the bricks and mortar in what is to come. Their use assumes that metaphor is more than metaphorical, so to speak. Metaphor is not a second-best way to talk, or a poor cousin of sharp logic. Metaphor is often the very essence of meaningful communication, and human life would be a dry and shriveled affair without it. Research and anecdote alike have demonstrated how heavily teachers rely upon metaphor to accomplish their work and to characterize their philosophies of education.[12]

Overview of the Book

Chapters 2 and 3 focus upon philosophy as "the art of living." This longstanding tradition of thought and action, initiated by influential figures such as Confucius and Socrates, offers still-timely cosmopolitan and educational values. The tradition emphasizes arts of human flourishing. It recognizes that a dimension of human nature is to keep in question that very nature. It heeds conditions of human constraint and possibility in the world: the reality of porosity and permeability to influence, the uncontainable range of human diversity, the ubiquity of human vulnerability and fallibility, and the instability of the natural and social world. In the face of such aleatory conditions philosophy as the art of living has historically put forward "exercises" or "practices" humans can engage in to craft lives of meaning and purpose. Such activities include reflective ways of writing, speaking, listening, observing, and contemplating. The tradition illuminates a cosmopolitan-minded orientation toward life. It constitutes a beautiful resource for teachers in a globalizing world, regardless of where they work or what they teach.

Chapter 4 focuses upon cultural creativity, with culture comprehended at three levels: sociolinguistic communities (the French, the Japanese, etc.), communities of art or artfulness (the cultures of teaching, medicine, sport, law, dance, architecture, etc.), and the individual person seeking to cultivate (or "culturate") his or her capacities as richly as circumstances permit. Cultural creativity at all three levels is bound up with values, or, more precisely, with how people hold and express their values in interaction with others. It is impossible to be a human actor without valuing something. Even a thoroughgoing relativist has to value relativism. But it is possible, as touched on previously, to express values in quite different ways. People can be hardened and defensive about them, or supple and generous; willful and violent, or deliberative and peaceful; reckless and heedless, or cautious and mindful (Hansen et al., 2009, p. 592). From a cosmopolitan perspective, every act of rethinking how one holds values mirrors what it means to be open reflectively to the world *and* loyal reflectively to the local (including to one's values). Every such act constitutes a form of cultural creativity at one or more of the three levels touched on above. Put another way, every such act transforms the world, in however modest or microscopic a way, by generating an additional instance of thoughtfulness.

The chapter illustrates these claims by drawing upon recent field-based research on cosmopolitan-minded ways of life among immigrants, working-class people, artists, religious persons, and many others – the children of whom take their seats in the world's classrooms today and whom teachers are charged with educating. By knowing something about the dynamics of cosmopolitanism on the ground, teachers in our globalizing era can cultivate their educational work that much more wisely. I will also draw on historical precursors of the current scholarly literature, in order to underscore that cosmopolitan-mindedness has been around for a long time. Taken together, these sources yield a dynamic tableau of cosmopolitan dispositions and practices which align in fruitful ways with what can be learned from philosophy as the art of living.

One way they come together is by highlighting the differences between traditionalism, understood as a backward-looking, reactionary attitude toward change, and tradition or "a sense of tradition", understood as a reflective response to new influence while retaining reflective loyalty to time-honored ideals and values. A feeling for tradition, as contrasted with traditionalism, helps people grasp what it means to leave home in the walled-in sense of the term while also remaining at home – and esteeming it – in a windows-open sense. As Mohandas Gandhi wrote: "I do not want my house to be walled in on all sides and my windows to be stuffed. I want the cultures of all lands to be blown about my land as freely as possible. But I refuse to be blown off my feet by any" (in Bhattacharya, 1997, p. 64).

In these chapters I approach education as something larger in scope and often more persistent in impact than schooling. Education can take place in countless settings, from the home, to the community center, through the internet, and to the street itself. Thus the subtitle of the book refers to cosmopolitanism *as education* rather than *as schooling*. Teachers at all levels of the system can benefit from being mindful of the manifold influences their students may be experiencing. They can benefit equally from imagining the life influences informing their own orientations. All such influences variously complement and complicate educational work. A good teacher preparation program can help teachers bring this issue to the surface, in the spirit of cultivating their own reflective openness to the new and reflective loyalty to the known.

Most teachers do work in formal institutions, from kindergarten through to university. Thus Chapter 5 culminates the book with a focus on curriculum and pedagogy in cosmopolitan perspective. I sketch the idea of curriculum understood as a cosmopolitan inheritance. Because the subjects which typically constitute curriculum embody longstanding human responses to the quest for meaning and a fulfilling life, all curriculum can be regarded as a shared human patrimony. This posture does not mean approaching the course of study unreflectively and unaware of its particularistic dimensions. Quite the contrary. Curriculum as cosmopolitan inheritance generates valuable resources for thinking through difficult human predicaments and concerns, as well as for conceiving new possibilities.

The chapter also attends systematically to teaching, a practice which like curriculum has ancient roots that continue to give it life, however obscure the nourishment may have become in the standards-driven, bureaucratic school systems found around the globe. The discussion centers upon how teachers can play significant roles in helping students, and themselves as a professional community, to move closer and closer apart as well as further and further together. This cosmopolitan-minded educational approach encompasses several dimensions: the aesthetic, having to do with developing perceptivity, sensibility, and responsiveness; the moral, pointing to how persons regard and treat people as well as the other things of this world; the reflective, denoting the ability to stand back though not apart from situations in order to think and imagine; and the ethical, spotlighting what it means to cultivate the self to deepen these aesthetic, moral and reflective capacities. Chapter 2 will address this notion of ethics. The qualifier reflective that accompanies openness and loyalty connotes more than the cognitive, logical, or analytical, although as we will see it contains aspects of all these terms. The reflective hangs together with the aesthetic and the moral. In their absence, it can become desiccated and unmoored from actual human affairs.

Many teachers already enact cosmopolitan solidarity even if not in so many words. This book aspires to provide such words, on the premise that how teachers think about their work, and how they describe it both to others and to themselves, has powerful consequences for what they actually do. This claim casts another light on the question of what it means to be a teacher in a globalized world. Among other things, teachers at all levels of the system are as much as ever guardians of conceptual awareness and lucidity. It matters how people describe the world, whatever their age and circumstance. It matters what concepts they use to do so and how they characterize or imagine those concepts (Laverty, 2010). Through their own ongoing education, teachers can enhance their ability to work with students in developing mindful communication.

In the Epilogue I emphasize that education viewed through a cosmopolitanism prism accompanies a democratic political commitment. Authoritarian and totalitarian regimes have historically persecuted cosmopolitan-minded people, whereas democratic societies have proven to be far more tolerant of contrasting values, beliefs, and practices. However, democratic ideas and structures have historically been more an outcome than a precondition for cosmopolitan-minded ways of life. For millennia, cosmopolitan orientations and habits have emerged through the course of everyday interaction, just as they do today. These ways of life do not await top-down initiatives, which can in fact just as easily undermine as support them. However, the right kind of institution-building can sustain the cosmopolitan impulse and extend it. While that process grows, as it seems likely to do in the future despite any number of obstacles, educational work on the ground can deepen people's reflective openness to the new and reflective loyalty to the known.

2 Becoming a Teacher in and of the World

The tradition of philosophy known as "the art of living" includes persistent inquiry into what it means to be human, juxtaposed with reflection on what many have called the human condition. The tradition features a practical focus on methods of self-improvement. The latter term may conjure today's racks of self-help books available online and at the local bookstore – and there are indeed family resemblances between the best of these works and the ancient line of philosophizing I take up here. However, this longstanding tradition has a deeply educational and public aspect. It connotes intellectual, moral and aesthetic self-transformation fused in the most cosmopolitan-minded of its iterations with a maturing sense of social responsibility.

A central purpose of this and the following chapter is to show how intimately the tradition supports the teacher in a globalized world. Philosophy as the art of living, itself emergent through reflection on human diversity and change, provides teachers with resources to strengthen, broaden, and deepen their ability to interact well with others: students, colleagues, parents, community members, as well as friends, family, and significant others. It does not provide direct solutions to problems, much less blueprints for action. Rather it addresses the teacher's sense of judgment and calls upon her or him to cultivate it through a variety of activities, which the tradition calls exercises. In so doing, the teacher finds herself or himself more and more capable of making decisions and taking a stand on matters of importance, while also sustaining open-ended communication with others. This process means, in turn, that the teacher comes further *into* the world – as a listening, responsive figure – while becoming a representative and spokesperson *of* the world – as a knowledgeable figure for whom the world and its future matters.

The first part of the chapter sketches the outlook of an array of well-known practitioners of philosophy as the art of living, among them Confucius and Socrates. Each figure emerges as a role model for teachers, not in a spirit of mimicry but in the sense of illustrating what it can look like to cultivate artfulness in all the affairs of one's work and life. The second section outlines practical steps these figures undertook. They are steps that any teacher today can practice in order to ready herself or himself for the challenges, difficulties, and opportunities of teaching in globalizing circumstances. The ensuing chapter contextualizes practicing the steps in a context of incessant social change and of unfathomable individual and community diversity.

A Cosmopolitan Lineage

Confucius' Opening Act

Among other beginnings, philosophy as the art of living can be traced to Confucius' (*c*.551–479 BCE) passionate concern for the values in self-improvement juxtaposed with practicing justice toward others. Confucius led a remarkable life that included notable public service, extensive teaching and mentoring, and periods of contemplative withdrawal. I will not pretend to offer here an adequate overview of his thought, any more than I will for the other figures sketched in this chapter. My purpose is to illustrate the contribution they make to cosmopolitanism and education through their reflections on the art of living.

Confucius' aphoristic style in *The Analects* is compulsively quotable, not unlike the style of other figures associated with the tradition such as Michel de Montaigne and Friedrich Nietzsche. At the center of Confucius' view of life as an art is the idea of humaneness. That term translates the Chinese *ren*, a concept that points to a fusion of "person" and "two," thus connoting the idea of relationality (Dawson, 1993, pp. xx–xxi; Jaspers, 1990, p. 49; Weiming, 1998, p. 304; for discussion, see Weiming, 1985). Humaneness is neither a purely psychological nor sociological quality. Rather it is at once an orientation toward other people and a mode of conduct. It has sometimes been translated as "virtue." However, this term works only if it is characterized in the manner of Kant. Kant, who was himself heavily influenced by this tradition of philosophy through the auspices of Stoic writers (whom I discuss below), claimed that virtue denotes "the moral disposition in conflict" (1993, p. 88). In other words, virtue is not a state of mind, a purely psychological attribute, or a final accomplishment. Rather it dwells *in* life itself, in moments of challenge, confusion, doubt, or confrontation that call upon whatever capacities of responsiveness the person embodies.

Confucius argues that a person who aspires toward humaneness does not withdraw from life to cultivate a private garden, although this move can be taken. Such a person does not duck the predicaments and problems that social life constantly generates. "The humane man puts difficulties first," Confucius says, "and success in overcoming them second" (*The Analects*, 1993, p. 22, Book 6.22). Put another way, humaneness privileges *learning from others* over resolving tensions to one's personal satisfaction. The impulse to flee from problems can lead people to resist engaging other persons with their differing experiences and points of view. However, for Confucius humaneness foregrounds broad rather than partisan sympathies (p. 7, Bk. 2.14). He freely admits he is describing an ideal that can guide conduct but that can never be fully realized. Referring at one point to how others probably regard him, he says "That is the one who works away at it although he knows it's no good, isn't it?" (p. 58, Bk. 14.38). For Confucius, it is the "working away at it" that counts rather than the outcomes per se. As the Stoic thinker Marcus Aurelius puts it, in describing one of his teachers: "The sense he gave of *staying* on the path rather than being *kept* on it" (2003, p. 9, Bk. I.15). In Confucius' view, a person can have a measure of genuine control over how she interacts with others, whereas it is hard to predict or exercise control over the actual results of interaction. "The failure to cultivate virtue, the failure to put into practice what I have learnt, hearing what is right and being unable to move towards it, being unable to change what is not good – these are my worries" (p. 24, Bk. 7.3).

Because humaneness is a mode of work rather than a final achievement, it requires focus and cultivation. Confucius addresses a wide array of practices, or arts, that he argues can help bring a person closer to humaneness – and thereby closer and closer apart, and further and further together, with other people. He speaks of ways of walking (modestly and uprightly), of listening (patiently and tenaciously), of speaking (straightforwardly and in moderation), and of greeting other people (respectfully and courteously). He refers to artful ways of expressing one's views, of deferring to others in conversation, and if necessary postponing reactions until another time when all participants will be more likely to benefit. Chan Kwok-bun (2005) characterizes these practices as a cosmopolitan etiquette "that requires a willingness to wait and see, the capacity to listen and a desire to understand the other, which is crucial to conciliation" (p. 7).

Confucius attends continuously to formal education as central to humaneness. Such learning does not mean acquiring information as such, but rather absorbing as best as one can insights from tradition – from philosophical texts, documents, songs, manuals on manners and ritual, and the like. Confucius does not endorse blind obedience to past values and customs. But intellectual and value continuity (not to be confused with mere replicability) remains vital to him. Tradition bequeaths people resources to fuel humaneness itself. At all times, in his view, the aim of education is not cultivating knowledge in itself but rather knowledge allied with moral perspective. Humaneness triggers images of a working harmony between one's unique bent as a person and a strong sense of social connection with others.

Like his Stoic confreres on the other side of the globe, Confucius understands the lure of withdrawal, of getting away from the tensions and strife of public affairs. But in his view to be human is not to isolate oneself from others. Rather, as Karl Jaspers (1990) puts it in his reading of Confucius, "to be human means to be in communication" (p. 49). Authoritarian regimes that prohibit communication – whether they are governments or institutions – are undertaking more than strategic political moves. They are preventing human beings from realizing their potential and capacities.

In summary, Confucius articulates methods of self-discipline and self-control that spring to life in human interaction. He believes these methods can assist people to dwell morally with one another in a tumultuous, often bewildering world. His aim is not to eliminate human difference and disagreement. Rather it is to enable people to learn from these features of experience. Interaction with other people, which will include conflict and misunderstanding, provides the spark that can "release" (Kwok-bun, 2005, p. 7) or unleash aspects of the person or of his or her community that would otherwise remain dormant. Put another way, it is the *engagement* with life that draws out the capacities in people. Confucius seeks not "unity" between people per se but a kind of unity in flux – a unity without uniformity (cf. Tresch, 2007, p. 93). Such unity becomes another term for sustaining communication as best as possible through the unpredictable vicissitudes of life. For Confucius, life becomes artful to the degree that it is responsive to other people, to one's own potential to grow, and to the goods he identifies in nature and the cosmos (he refers again and again to notions of a dynamic though not homogenizing harmony).

These remarks are introductory but I hope suggestive enough for my returning throughout this chapter and book to the idea of humaneness. Confucius' thinking does not have a point-by-point correspondence with his Stoic counterparts in Europe who also articulate philosophy as the art of living. Among other things, their notions of nature, of ritual (*li*), and of government differ. However, I believe Pierre Hadot (1995, p. 212) is right to argue that the practices associated with philosophy as the art of living do not depend upon a single, preordained background picture of the cosmos. They do need a background, or grounding, which in this book I provide through a cosmopolitan framework. However, it is precisely the practical aspect of the arts that gives them their staying power across the generations and that render them invaluable to teachers in our era.

Socrates and his Successors

In almost the same era as Confucius, Socrates (469–399 BCE) enacts a persistent, public interest in talking with people from anywhere, fellow Athenians and foreigners alike. Time and again, Socrates considers what it might mean to lead his life according to other people's values. His practice points to why cosmopolitanism implies more than tolerance of difference. It suggests, instead, a willingness to learn from or with other traditions and human inheritances. This orientation does not entail endorsing other people's tastes and customs. But it does mean regarding them as indices rather than as departures from the human. Socrates was often relentless in trying to come to grips with his own and other people's underlying commitments. He never hesitated to take inquiry to the most universal plane. Moreover, as Eric Brown (2000) underscores, Socrates did not conduct himself as if his fellow Athenians merited greater attention than other people. As mentioned, Socrates examined issues as intensively with foreigners as with his compatriots. At the same time, he did appreciate the fact that Athens allowed greater freedom of speech than many other polities he and his peers knew about. In addition he remained profoundly loyal to his local culture, so much so that even when threatened with execution he refused to go into safe exile.

While Socrates' moral and intellectual courage are exemplary, his down-to-earth openness to new ideas combined with loyalty to local values has been practiced, albeit in more modest form, by countless teachers and students who have taken discussion seriously. In the best of such discussions, it is never a question of abandoning outright one's prior views or self-conceptions, nor is it a question of defending a standpoint at all costs. Rather the process is transactive: heeding others, participating, and keeping thought open to influence. The experience often broadens and deepens a person's understanding and outlook. From this perspective, discussion practices centered on interpretive inquiry – whether in art, history, literature, or science – mirror philosophy as the art of living. Discussion is not a mere means to an end but constitutes an enactment of significant values of listening, articulating, respecting others, and sustaining human community.

Socrates' arts have a cosmopolitan aspect. In a critical spirit, they welcome rather than merely tolerate new views and new people. On his part, Plato generates cosmopolitan images through a number of staging decisions he makes in *The Republic*. For one thing, he has Socrates and his interlocutors conceive the *kallipolis* or just city while meeting in the cosmopolitan port of Piraeus rather than in Athens (cf. Sallis, 2006, p. 18). Allan Bloom (1968, p. 441) characterizes the Piraeus, located some six miles from Athens, as "a center for innovations in everything" in part because of its cultural diversity. For another thing, Plato has the dialogue take place in the home of Cephalus, a "metic" or resident foreigner (he was originally from Syracuse in Sicily). According to Athenian custom metics had to pay taxes and contribute in other ways to communal upkeep, but they lacked the full rights of citizenship. Still another move Plato makes is to have Socrates complement at the very start of the dialogue the creativity of a community other than Athens.

I take Plato to be suggesting that resources from any society are welcome if they fuel inquiry into the most just forms of association. I also hear him implying that people everywhere can deliberate about justice and the good, and that it is therefore important to keep the door, or port, open to their perspectives. This idea of an open door or port, a quintessential cosmopolitan trope, would apply as much to the individual mind as to the mind of a given community. To be sure, humans have exhibited a formidable capacity to build walls around and between themselves. But Plato puts forward in dramatic fashion the image that humans can also be, to echo an aphorism from Ralph Waldo Emerson, both makers and openers of doors to one another.

This cosmopolitan dimension of thinking reached an apogee in the ancient world among the Hellenistic and Roman Stoics. These diverse figures included at one end of the socioeconomic scale royalty and high-ranking counselors, and at another end humble teachers and leaders of materially modest communities. In their writing and teaching, they dwelled on how to lead a humane life in a world where individual and cultural differences abound and remain unfathomable in their range, variability, and intensity. They sought to frame ways of life in which they could be loyal to particularized obligations and to what they conceived as a universal humanity. Writers as different as Chrysippus, Epictetus, and Marcus Aurelius expressed cosmopolitan ideas throughout their texts. As mentioned in

Chapter 1, recent research on these figures undermines the stereotype of the Stoic as a solitary, aloof, disengaged individual. Many participated in public affairs or were otherwise involved in their respective communities. I return below to examples of their approaches toward enacting philosophy as a way of life.[1]

These writers returned time and again to the figure of Socrates (cf. Hadot, 1995, pp. 147–178). They were fascinated with what they saw as his determination to cultivate himself as fully as possible as a humane person. They were taken with his pedagogical efforts to lead others to do the same. They lauded his ability to reason, to inquire, to argue and to weigh issues with considered judgment.

At the same time they took seriously the place of emotion in human lives. Their reflections are saturated with both worry and appreciation for the power of feeling. They sought to tame unconstrained passion – for example, the "passionate intensity" of dogmatic ways of thinking which W. B. Yeats evokes in his powerful poem, "The Second Coming." They endeavored to channel passion and fuse it with ends articulated through reason. This posture meant easing the hold of passion while liberating feeling itself: "To be free of passion," writes Marcus Aurelius, "and yet full of love" (2003, p. 7, Bk. 1.9).

Moreover, the Stoic accounts of passion and desire themselves often ring with undisguised passion and desire. Some yearn in affective terms to render life as meaningful as possible. In this respect they were not Platonists in the traditional sense of trying to separate the soul or spirit from the body.[2] They were not proto-Cartesians conceiving mind as independent from the material. For some figures in the tradition, among them Michel de Montaigne (1533–1592), philosophy as the art of living meant learning to regard the human being as a unity: as a being of feeling, spirit, body, and mind. This unity does not imply an easy or stable harmony. Like other Stoic-minded writers, Montaigne dwells at length on the frustrations, mysteries, and joys of being a creature that is difficult to know.

Stoic and many subsequent cosmopolitan-minded thinkers fuse deep respect for reasoning with a sense of vigilant modesty in addressing human differences. Writers continually contrast cosmopolitan meanings with what they regard as chauvinistic, anti-rational, and often explosive aspects of political and inter-communal life. In this respect the imprint of Plato as well as of his student Aristotle on their thought seems evident, even if indirect. In *The Republic*, Plato conjures the incessant demagoguery and belligerency of a great deal of Athenian politics when he declaims that "hardly anyone acts sanely in public affairs" (Plato, 1992, s. 496c6). He advocates not a withdrawal from politics but a wiser, more balanced approach. In that approach education plays on ongoing, dynamic, and perennially controversial role. Plato is acutely, almost preternaturally conscious of the despair that the course of public affairs can induce – a sensibility shared by many writers on philosophy as the art of living and a testament to their concern for rather than retreat from life. Plato observes that time and again, "What the most decent people experience in relation to their city is so hard to bear that there's no other single experience like it" (s. 488a1-3). In the face of persistent injustice, the very love of justice brings heartbreak after heartbreak. But cosmopolitanism originates, in part, in the attempt to extract and apply humane lessons drawn from pondering different forms of political life.

Writing in the midst of the religious wars in France during the sixteenth century, Montaigne (a close reader of Plato) conceives an educational approach that he believes can help people "judge sanely" (*juger sainement*) their own and other people's ways of life (1991, p. 177). He regards sanity neither as an individualistic, psychological state, nor as an oppressive societal marker of what is taken to be normal (cf. Foucault, 1988). Rather Montaigne posits the term as a moral orientation characterized by a deepening awareness of human limitations and differences, and by an interest (indeed pleasure) in learning from others rather than merely putting forward one's own values. For Montaigne, to judge sanely is to dwell interactively with others in ways that contrast with judgmentalism, which is the dogmatic (and lazy) habit of *passing* judgment rather than putting in the time and effort to *reach* a considered judgment.

In a comparable vein, the often caustic critic of American public life, John Dewey – himself indebted, like Montaigne, to Stoic lines of thought (for example, through the influence of Emerson) – writes that the notion that a person can barge through life without thinking through shared human concerns constitutes "an unnamed form of insanity which is responsible for a large part of the remediable suffering of the world" (1985, p. 49). Here Dewey echoes his argument that what English speakers call "mind" (as contrasted with "brain") exists transactionally with other people and the world rather than being cooped up inside the skull. Thus people use phrases like "mind your manners," "mind out for that car coming," and "she's always mindful of others." All of these uses reveal mind's place *in* the ongoing affairs of life. In Dewey's view, to reject the reality that mind is in the world (rather than constituting a private, inner entity) means in an organic sense to be out of one's mind, i.e. out of the world or cosmos.

Consider, finally, the philosopher Alain Locke's cosmopolitan-minded analysis of cultural relativism. Locke illuminates differences between relativism and being relativistic: the former can denote a serious regard for cultural distinctiveness, while the latter simply undermines any meaningful form of judgment including of one's own roots. Locke argues, on the one hand, against an "all-inclusive orthodoxy of human values" which would dissolve both the local and the cosmopolitan. On the other hand, he argues against holding cherished values and cultural symbols irrationally, as if the application of reason and criticism is *ipso facto* acidic rather than substantiating. To think matters through – including one's bedrock values – can help lead, in Locke's view, to "a safer and saner approach to the objectives of practical unity" amongst people (1989, p. 71).

A recurrent theme of cosmopolitan philosophizing is the value of reasoned judgment juxtaposed with a thoughtful regard for differences and similarities in belief and form of life. Locke captures this theme in emphasizing the difference between "practical" unity – once more, a unity without uniformity – and "theoretical" unity. Philosophy as the art of living comprehends the lure and the appeal of attaining universal agreement about the meaning of truth, knowledge, beauty, and justice. However, its dispensation is not to wait for such agreement to be achieved, presuming it can be, but to work out methods for dwelling humanely in the here and now. Put another way, truth-seeking becomes a regulative ideal, guiding practice, rather than something to be possessed, owned, or controlled (cf. Chapter 1, p. 14). Education plays a central role in this project, particularly with regards to how each person, in concert with others, can work to improve herself or himself from an intellectual, moral, and aesthetic perspective.

The tradition of philosophy as the art of living takes on further cosmopolitan expressions in Renaissance and early modern writers, among them Erasmus (1466–1536) and the aforementioned Montaigne, who are deeply influenced by ancient commentators. They aspire to strike a note of critical tolerance and of enduring interest in all matters human (rather than in just their own concerns), and all of this in the midst of an era of accelerating political, economic, religious and cultural change. Erasmus instantiates in a quite literal sense the stereotype of the peripatetic cosmopolitan. Throughout much of his life he moved from one center of learning to another across Europe, while also publishing knowledgeable texts on religious, philosophical, and other questions. In his writing he returns again and again to questions of humaneness, to deploy Confucius' term: that is, to how people can render themselves just toward others, and toward themselves, through education, reflection, and modesty. Erasmus was among the most widely-read figures of his time, in part because of his shrewd talent for taking advantage of the newly emergent printing press. Readers from all ends of the ideological spectrum acknowledged his extraordinary fair-mindedness, his sense of judgment and balance, his elegance as a writer, and his sense of humor. Stefan Zweig (1956) dubs him "the first conscious European and cosmopolitan" (p. 8).[3]

At the same time, many religious, political, and other well-known figures criticized Erasmus for refusing to locate himself on the ideological spectrum of the day – a refusal characteristic of numerous writers in the tradition with regard to their own eras. Zweig criticizes Erasmus for, in his view, failing to be more executive in adjudicating the intensifying clash between the Church and the Protestant reformers. Johan Huizinga (1952), in his rich study of Erasmus' life and influence, echoes the criticism. He cites a famous call to action from the artist Albrecht Dürer, who knew Erasmus well and rendered his portrait several times:

> O Erasmus of Rotterdam, where will you be? Hear, you knight of Christ, ride forth beside the Lord Christ, protect the truth, obtain the martyr's crown . . . [work] in behalf of the Gospel and the true Christian faith [Dürer sympathized with Luther]. . . . O Erasmus, be on this side, that God may be proud of you.
>
> (cited in Huizinga, 1952, pp. 148–149)

In my view Zweig and Huizinga overlook the fact, as did Erasmus' contemporary critics, that to resist taking a stand along the popular spectrum does not mean retreating from public life. Erasmus was as much an activist in his own way as the most partisan Catholic or Protestant of his era. He was relentlessly active on behalf of sanity as that term has been characterized here. He felt called to write, and to keep writing, as a means of teaching, advising, counseling, and inspiring mindfulness. To borrow a term of art from the philosopher Susan Haack, he was a passionate moderate in all things human.

Unlike Erasmus, Montaigne resided for much of his life in one place, namely the modest estate near Bordeaux he had inherited. Moreover he remained deeply rooted in his local French traditions and never broke from them. In his pioneering essays (he gave this mode of writing a unique and highly influential stamp), he makes plain that he could not communicate at all without them. At the same time, he submits his culture's mores, habits, and ideals – and himself – to withering criticism, relying directly upon perspectives from other cultures, societies, and historical eras. In one and the same life, and often in one and the same moment, he learns from his neighbor and he learns from the stranger. He learns from what he calls "this great world of ours" with its extraordinary variability. In an echo of the cosmopolitan prism, he describes the world as a "looking-glass" into which any person can gaze to render life more comprehensible and meaningful, although not necessarily more comfortable as he also underscores (1991, p. 177). What Montaigne learns, in short, is not merely new information but ways of being in which he simultaneously retains reflective loyalty to the known and reflective openness to the new.

Women's Participation

With the early modern period in Europe women begin to come into their own as public writers and thinkers, and join in both prose and example the stream of philosophizing on the art of living. Before then they had little official access to the universe of publishing and teaching, though they did participate in social arrangements informed by the ethos of philosophy. Gretchen Reydams-Schils (2005) illuminates, for example, the agentive and egalitarian role women played in a variety of communal relations in the Roman period that were modeled around motifs of the art of living. She shows how various Stoic and other thinkers and teachers, among them the influential Musonius Rufus (first century CE), not only advocated but in some cases helped establish formal educational provision for women. Musonius Rufus also argued that because both women and men reason about life matters, women should be allowed to practice philosophy publicly (Reydams-Schils, 2005, pp. 153–159; also see Dillon, 2004).

However, it is with the era of Erasmus, Montaigne, and afterward that women gain access to publishing as well as modes of leadership in philosophizing. In her numerous writings, for example, Marie le Jars de Gournay (1565–1645) emphasizes values in the arts of inquiring, reading, writing, conversing, and more, all of which she regards as both self-formative and as influencing society for the good. One of the tragedies as well as outrages of her time, she argues, is that social convention conspires to shut down the public voice of half its population. Addressing her male readers, she writes:

Blessed indeed are you, who can be wise without committing a crime, since your sex accords you the privilege of every proper action and speech, as well as the favor to have what you say believed, or at least listened to. As for me, if I wish to put my auditors to the sort of examination that involves, it is said, strings that female fingers cannot touch, even had I the arguments of Carneades [a second-century BCE Skeptic], there is no one so much a weakling that he will not rebuke me, to the grave approbation of the company present, with a smile, a nod, or some jest, which will have the effect of saying, "It's a woman speaking" [*C'est une femme qui parle*].

(Gournay, 1998, pp. 35, 34)

In these instructive remarks Gournay attacks one-sided convention and the cruelty it can embody. The critique of cruelty surfaces across the tradition of philosophy as the art of living (cf. Montaigne, "On Cruelty," 1991, pp. 472–488). It is a suffering, as Dewey would put it, that is remediable (see his remarks above, p. 27).

Like the other figures touched on here, Gournay's work reveals the influence of her precursors in the tradition. For example, she returns repeatedly to the ancient writers mentioned previously and she treats them as mentors on how to conduct her life. Richard Hillman and Colette Quesnel (in Gournay, 2002) highlight the importance of Plato to her evolving sensibility. She also translated Diogenes Laertius' (third-century CE) widely read life of Socrates. Gournay refers continuously to Montaigne's *Essays*, an unsurprising gesture given that she served as editor of their final version which was published in 1595. She also wrote a lengthy, elaborate preface (Gournay, 1998) that accompanied the various printings of the *Essays* for several decades. The reader can discern in its pages the ways in which she self-consciously orients herself as a student of these writings. In so doing she enacts a longstanding practice in philosophy as the art of living in which a particular author's oeuvre, or a single text like Confucius' *Analects*, becomes an important, lifelong source of guidance and perspective (cf. Gournay, 1998, p. 85). I return to the important role of educative and edifying handbooks later in the chapter, and will describe their pertinence for teachers today.

In her preface, Gournay defends Montaigne's essays from charges that they are licentious as well as subversive in their flouting of convention, precious in their use of language and coining of terms, obscure in their structure and flow, and obnoxious in their focusing on the self (Montaigne makes himself the central object of inquiry in his writing). All of these criticisms were in one way or another lodged against Gournay's own work. She had already published a novel, *Le Proumenoir de Monsieur de Montaigne* (*The Paths/promenade of Monsieur de Montaigne*, 1594), which among other things engaged questions of women's psychology and sexuality. To those who criticize Montaigne's detailed accounts of his everyday tastes and judgments, Gournay replies that they ought to be praising him for showing that "the great things depend on the small ones . . . Life itself is merely a composite of little details . . . There is nothing important that is slight: it has its weight, if it touches us" (1998, p. 77). As she defends what she sees as Montaigne's philosophical maturity, creativity, and integrity, she argues that her rapport with him illuminates why genuine friendship, loyalty, and mutual support can traverse gender boundaries. She demonstrates that the art of living is at once a personal, social, and lifelong way of being (cf. pp. 67, 75, 89). Such an art leads, ideally, to the cultivation of a wise sense of judgment (pp. 31, 83).

Gournay enacts this outlook in her subsequent and long publishing career. For example, she returns to motifs of the art of living – as well as to a remarkable array of other themes in the arts, sciences, and social ethos of her day – in texts such as *Égalité des Hommes et des Femmes* (*The Equality of Men and* Women, 1622) and *Grief des Dames* (*The Ladies' Complaint*, 1626) as well as in her widely published poetry. She translates texts from ancient writers including Cicero, Ovid, Virgil, and the aforementioned Diogenes Laertius. In the face of continued gender prejudice as well as ever-present financial constraints, Gournay achieved a noteworthy degree of public recognition and prominence. Not only was her work read and cited but it led to her active involvement in the founding of the French Academy (1635), an institutional expression in the country of its love for and commitment to the French language.

Along with other contemporaries, Gournay's writing as well as her example widened the doorway for women to enter public intellectual life. This impact can be seen, for example, in the emergence in Paris and other locales of the famed salons which among other foci partook vibrantly in philosophizing on the art of living. Initiated in the seventeenth century and taking off in the eighteenth (Gournay participated in several herself), these social gatherings were organized and sustained by women. They featured environments marked by tolerance, expanded sympathies and understandings, and open-minded and self-critical inquiry. They surfaced elsewhere in Europe, for example in Berlin where, as Amos Elon (2002) shows, many were led by Jewish women. The salons featured sustained dialogue on issues in culture, politics, social affairs, the emerging sciences, and more. Participants read work both by women and men, and by contemporary as well as ancient authors. In brief, they engaged in two historic modes of philosophizing: the one as theory (What is knowledge?), the other as the art of how to live (How can I become more just?).

The salons served both as agora and as informal schools for developing arts of expressivity, judgment, and mutual regard (more on these arts below). According to Kenneth Clark (1969), the salons constituted one of the finest enactments in their era of that ever-fragile human achievement known as civilization. For Clark, civilization means, among other things, the establishment of conditions that allow people to flourish intellectually, morally, and aesthetically. He also argues that civilization emerges in its most robust forms during moments of open trans-cultural and international exchange. Such was the ethos in the salons. Although they began at court and in the abodes of the aristocracy, many morphed over time into more egalitarian settings in which searing critiques of convention became commonplace. They were open to women and men, to locals and foreigners, and to freethinkers and religious devotees. Participants became each other's teachers. They were places where what Gandhi might call "free air" circulated (cf. Chapter 1, p. 18).

These voices in the cosmopolitan lineage of philosophy as the art of living – Confucius, Socrates, Montaigne, Gournay, and many others – give rise in the modern and current era to a cosmopolitan-minded array of thinkers. Like the writers mentioned thus far, these figures remain fundamentally· unclassifiable in part because they are so non-traditionalistic in their reception of the past and in their outlook toward the present and future. One might say these writers who address in depth the art of living (and, to be sure, many other topics) take tradition with the utmost seriousness precisely through their conversational and critical rather than idolatrous approach to it. Thinkers as different as Goethe, Emerson, Dewey, Locke, George Eliot (née Maryann Evans), José Enrique Rodó, W. E. B. Du Bois, Virginia Woolf, Rabindranath Tagore, and George Orwell merge universal motifs about justice and goodness with fine-grained concern for questions of self-improvement.

In Chapter 4, we will meet considerably less well-known people from everyday walks of life who enact in their distinctive fashion a comparable orientation. Their doings document, on the one hand, why a cosmopolitan orientation is not the preserve of the well-to-do, who can be parochial and self-serving despite the best educations (or, at any rate, university degrees) that money can buy. People in everyday walks of life also demonstrate that cosmopolitanism is not a disposition found only among universally esteemed artists, scientists, political and religious leaders, and others. These highly creative individuals do have much to teach people everywhere. No doubt readers could identify figures other than those named above whose example seems endlessly edifying and enlightening. These persons are, in Nietzschean terms, a kind of spiritual vanguard (as contrasted with being an upper-class elite), illuminating the creative potential persons and communities alike might strive to cultivate. And yet, cosmopolitanism also finds expression in the ordinary ways in which people combine reflective openness to the new with reflective loyalty to the known. There is much to learn from these people as well: lessons, once more, of value the world over.

The Art of Living as an Educational Outlook

From a cosmopolitan point of view, philosophy as the art of living can be understood first and last as an educational outlook, and in between as an often sharp critique of unexamined custom. This critique does not emerge from a single or unified lens, but through an ever-changing armoire of perspectives. As emphasized, the writers in this tradition are highly distinctive and noninter-changeable in outlook. Nonetheless, a shared concern in much of their writing and practice (i.e. why they can be considered participants in a tradition in the first place) has been on how a person can learn to draw as fully as possible upon prior human achievements, and one's own life encounters, to craft a humane, meaningful life, even or especially when extant conventions seem to reject, thwart, or cheapen this project.

There are at present a range of forces that threaten to diminish if not belittle teachers' educational autonomy and authority: top-down testing regimes in schools, mechanistic standards for teacher preparation, incessant pressure to reduce education to a mere economic means, and more. The writers in the tradition of philosophy as the art of living address this condition, if not in so many words – for it is a condition which in one form or another has always confronted teachers. (Confucius often had to move in the face of authoritarian threats; Socrates was executed for challenging the state's monopoly on what is taken to be true.) The tradition calls on teachers "to work on themselves." Rather than becoming dogmatic or close-minded in response to pressure, or abandoning educational work outright, teachers can ready themselves, through a variety of exercises, for the challenges, difficulties, and possibilities of education in a globalizing environment.

How does this perspective play out in the teacher's classroom and institutional setting? A cardinal purpose of this chapter and the next two is to bring together the elements that address the question. Put another way, my row-by-row tilling of ideas in these pages is necessary in light of the complexity of the teacher's relation with the world in our time.

Evoking the Fusion of Ethics and Morality

For many writers in the tradition, a cosmopolitan-minded life would seek to be responsive to the demands of justice toward others and of the desire for self-improvement. The former refers to what today is called *morality*: the ongoing task of regarding and treating other people fairly and responsively. Self-improvement refers to what the tradition sometimes calls *ethics*: the ongoing project of cultivating as richly as possible one's intellectual, moral, and aesthetic being.

The question of ethics can be traced at least as far back as Confucius' remarks in *The Analects* and Socrates' inquiries in Plato's *Gorgias*. How shall I live my life? What is the best way to live? What is the way that will draw out my fullest humanity? This concern runs through Epictetus, Marcus Aurelius, and other ancient writers, on through Montaigne and Emerson, and up through the present. The question of morality is equally old: How shall I regard and treat other people? What is the best or the right way to respond to them? How far-reaching and substantive are my obligations to others? A time-honored Stoic response to the questions is the metaphor of life as a process of moving across concentric circles, the nearest encompassing family and friends, the farthest humanity writ large. A mainstay of Stoic philosophy, in some of its forms, has been the idea of compressing the circles, of bringing humanity as a whole as close to feeling as possible (Nussbaum, 1997b, 32–33).

As appealing as the image of concentric circles may be, however, it is too categorical. For one thing, even the most intimate inner circles of family and friends often feature in their values, customs, and interactions a mélange of strands from diverse cultures and individuals (Fischer, 2007, p. 156). For another, consider the complicated issue of proximity to others in determining moral obligation. On the one hand, it can be hard to conceive – much less enact – moral duty toward unknown people. On the other hand, it can be more efficacious to discharge such duty, for instance through systematic charitable giving, than it is to dwell with one's immediate family or community – the circles presumed to be "closest." "Proximity, spiritual or otherwise," Appiah (2005) reminds us, "is as conducive to antagonism as it is to amity. Giacomo Leopardi, in his *Pensieri*, says that 'a certain wise man, when someone said to him, 'I love you', replied, 'Why not, if you are not of my religion, or a relative of mine, or a neighbor, or someone who looks after me?'" (p. 256; also see Forman-Barzilai, 2005). Leopardi captures the universal experience of alienation and estrangement persons can feel toward the local. This condition can motivate them not to abandon their moral impulse but to extend it to other horizons of people. The reverse happens time and again as well: a person who meets disappointment in trying to establish broadened moral arrangements may withdraw, figuratively speaking, to her or his own garden.

The metaphor of concentric circles can conjure reified boundaries between local, regional, and global spaces, thereby eliding modes of permeability that Stoic thinkers were themselves adept at identifying. Moreover, it can suggest a simplistic picture of how to prioritize moral obligations, as if, as Veit Bader (1999) puts it, "there is just one throw of one pebble, and the obligations are strongest the closest by, getting weaker and weaker the farther away from the center" (p. 391). The idea of concentric circles is equally misleading if applied to the individual's ethos, since it may connote an image of a pristine "core" in the inner circle untouched by influences from the other rings. Finally, the notion of preset circles crystallizes the unsettling picture of a person or community circumscribing within their epistemic circle other people and the world – rather than appreciating the necessity, for humaneness and peace, of a two-way cultural transaction.

A better metaphor is Emerson's idea of "drawing a new circle" from moment to moment, and from contact to contact (1983, p. 414). To learn from another person, event, or idea implies transforming one's circle of experience and understanding. This change is something other than an expansion of the circle. It is not merely quantitative; it will lead to more than the acquisition of new information or facts. It will be qualitative, however modest in comparison with the totality of the person's outlook. Consider the poet who decides after a long meditation to delete a stanza, or the sculptor who prunes away what had hitherto seemed essential, or the composer who finally eliminates a passage before signing off on the work. These are not cases of merely subtracting material in a brute manner. They involve genuine transformation in both the person – whose sense of craft and of judgment has been touched by the experience – and the object at hand as it enters culture.

Put another way, the ethical and moral consequences of contacts in the world include "losings" rather than solely gains or measurable increases. To develop a new understanding can mean losing a previous one. To broaden an horizon of concern implies losing a previously narrower one. To conceive new perspectives destabilizes and may dissolve prior views. What the poet and classicist Anne Carson calls "decreation" constitutes the other side of creativity. As mentioned in the previous paragraph, the need to dismantle is as vital, at moments, as building. The idea holds for the teacher's urging to students to be clear about their concepts. Deconceptualization, or removing a particular content or understanding that has encrusted a concept, can be an important part of thinking – as can be seen with the idea of cosmopolitanism itself.

These changes do not imply that people must reject the old out of hand. A cosmopolitan orientation involves remembering the roads abandoned or not taken, and reconfiguring them through time. In terms that echo philosophers on the art of living, the poet Robert Frost writes:

> All reasoning is a circle I say. At any rate all learning is a circle. We learn A the better to learn B the better to learn C the better to learn D the better to learn A. All we get of A is enough to start us on the way to take it up later again. We should circulate among the facts not progress through them leaving some forever behind.
>
> (Frost, 2007, p. 662)[4]

Frost's insight pertains as much to moral learning as it does to any other form of tuition. Moral learning is neither linear nor cumulative in a direct manner. It involves circulating back and forth between previous experience and point of view, and that which seems called for by current circumstance. To remember how one saw people as a child, for example, or at any earlier stage of life, can suddenly shed valuable light on what is at stake in the present moment.

This artful process coheres with picturing ethics and morality as modes of drawing a new circle. The ancient idea of ethics as the cultivation of the self invites persons everywhere toward receptivity: to attend to and learn from the ways, mores, and arts of others, not in a celebrant's or aesthete's spirit but as a possible inheritor of these ways, mores, and arts. Such learning is not merely other-directed. It is equally directed toward the individual's particular bent and aspirations toward living as full and humane a life as possible. This participatory attitude can, in turn, move persons further toward a willingness to engage questions of morality precisely because it can trigger a substantive acknowledgment of the humanity in others. This attitude guides persons to regard others and themselves as ends rather than as mere means. It orients human beings from whatever background or origin to come closer and closer apart – as they discern and understand, however partially, their distinctiveness – and to move further and further together – as they confront new problems and act upon possibilities that emerge in the rapidly shifting scenes of public life.

Writers on the art of living illuminate how in actual life morality and ethics are mutually implicated, such that the distinction is useful for purposes of inquiry and understanding rather than as marking out two separate spheres of experience. The influential thinker and teacher Epictetus (*c*.50–130 CE) urges: "Set up right now a certain character and pattern for yourself which you will preserve when you are by yourself and when you are with people" (1983, p. 22, paragraph 33). He articulates a fusion of ethics and the moral redolent of the classical ideal of fusing *logos* and *ergon*, or word and deed (I return to this ideal later in the chapter). He seeks to draw upon notions of justice as well as his conviction in the vitality of personhood.

Epictetus charts a path that heeds both local and universal values while recognizing the ever-challenging nature of the journey. In this outlook, persons put trust not solely in established custom and habit but also in their capacities to perceive, discern, criticize, and appreciate – capacities triggered, in part, by their encounters with differences from local norms. This always unfinished process generates what the tradition describes as exercises or practices of the self. Such practices include deliberative ways of speaking, listening, interacting, reading, writing, and more, which are at all times arts in development since their aim is not serving the self but rather improving it. Thus what Michel Foucault (1994, 2005) and other scholars of the tradition dub "the care of the self" contrasts markedly with a narcissistic or self-absorbed posture (see, for example, Ambrosio, 2008; De Marzio, 2007a, 2007b; Domanski, 1996; Hadot, 1995; Nehamas, 1998; and Shusterman, 1997). In this viewpoint it is precisely by shifting attention from oneself to listening, to speaking thoughtfully, and to thinking as best as one can about the meanings of experience that the human being can most fully come into her or his own. The focus on such practices constitutes another reason for perceiving philosophy as the art of living as an ongoing educational encounter in and with the world. We discern again its living pertinence for the teacher in our tumultuous globalizing situation, which calls out to every educator to be open reflectively to new influences and possibilities, and loyal reflectively to local values and customs.

Staying Clear of a "Total Attitude"

Foucault, Hadot, Nussbaum, Reydams-Schils, and other scholars cited previously have shown that these arts took on diverse forms across Stoic and other like-minded groupings that sprang up around the Mediterranean world in the Hellenistic and Roman eras (see also P. Brown, 1971, p. 60, *passim*). They helped people in the moral task of mutual recognition and support, and in the ethical task of self-transformation. To judge from remarks by Epictetus and others, their progress in both trajectories was typically modest and uneven, a fact that does not reflect poorly on them but rather attests to the inevitable confusion and ambiguity that accompanies engaging new ideas and customs. Their experience points to the symmetry between the diverse arts of listening, speaking, and interacting they sought to cultivate and the image of cosmopolitanism on the ground. Such arts are deeply rooted in local interaction, exchange, and participation. At the same time, they can assist people in keeping attuned to how differently human beings approach questions of purpose, of value, and of meaning in their affairs.

These practices can also help persons in the complicated task of discerning how and when to be open reflectively to the new and loyal reflectively to the known.

I raise this issue, in part, because the juxtaposition of the strange and the familiar is not necessarily tension-laden, much less threatening. Children and adults alike often respond spontaneously to cultural and individual difference with fascination, pleasure, even excitement. This response is not "reflective" in the sense of taking a step back from events. On the contrary, it is more like jumping into a pool on a fresh summer day, becoming absorbed in the new in a wondrously naïve, unselfconscious manner. In a fundamental sense, cosmopolitanism begins in open-hearted responsiveness to "this great world of ours," to recall Montaigne's trope. The person is rare who has not had this experience in childhood, however constrained or pinched it may have been. Without it, the reflective aspect of dealing with tension-laden encounters between old and new can be a dry and formal task.

However, a cosmopolitan outlook is not all-encompassing. That misleading association originates with Diogenes (*c*.412–*c*.323 BCE), the first self-professed *kosmopolites* and a truly striking individual. It is worthwhile taking a brief look at his public life (for further discussion in a context of education, see Hansen, 2009). "The only true commonwealth," Diogenes proclaimed, is "that which is as wide as the universe" (Diogenes Laertius, 2005, 6.63, 6.72[5]). In the same breath he declared himself "a beggar, a wanderer . . . without a city (*apolis*), without a home, deprived of native land" (6.38). He was exiled from his native Sinope (on the Black Sea coast of modern-day Turkey) allegedly for defacing its coinage – an apt image for the life of harsh assault on convention he would go on to lead. Diogenes and his fellow Cynics treated local custom as narrow-minded and as out of tune with the simplicities and the spontaneity they saw as characteristic of nature. The Cynics rejected wealth, high office, and other conventional markers of success as barriers to genuine human flourishing.

Diogenes pursued his self-chosen destiny much farther than did any of his philosophical comrades. Upon his arrival in Athens, where he ended up residing for decades, Diogenes promptly intensified the iconoclastic practices he had initiated in Sinope. He publicly disavowed all local obligations and famously took to living in a large, discarded wine jar in the agora. There he relieved himself in plain view, ate his meals on the ground including raw meat (a real taboo to the Athenians), and in other ways strove to scandalize the people around him. At night he slept in the alcoves of temples, claiming they were built for the likes of him. He had no quarrel with those Athenians who time and again called him a dog or dog-like – *kynikos* (from the root *kyon*, dog) whence comes the modern term cynic. Diogenes admired that animal's naturalness and lack of guile in comparison with what he saw as the hypocrisies and pretentiousness of human society.

Diogenes railed against what he took to be his neighbors' narrow-mindedness, bigotry, and self-satisfaction. When they complained that what he did in public should be done in private, he replied in effect that what they did in public ought to be done in private – for example, demagoguery, putting on airs, and showing off about the religious offerings they make in the temple. At the same time, he refused to leave the bustling agora or to hide himself away like a hermit, no matter how disgusting he found the culture around him (and vice versa). He regarded his self-professed status as cosmopolitan as a credential for the office of permanent critic. He was a Greek chorus wrapped up in a single, hectoring voice. He mocked the desire for public acclaim while making a spectacle of his asceticism. He seems to have believed that people ought to see themselves as part of the larger fabric of nature rather than as the blinkered citizens of a particular political entity no more destined to last than Shelley's fabled Ozymandias. He had no sympathy with established religion, finding the multiplicity of gods and rituals distracting when compared with the grandeur of the cosmos and the task of dwelling in what he felt to be its moral light. Diogenes became a kind of hyper-Socratic gadfly, stinging people into awareness and self-criticism. In a remark that is at once both a tribute and a rebuke, Plato is alleged to have called him "a Socrates gone mad" (6.54).

Diogenes' reputation traveled well beyond the confines of Athens, in part because that city with its companion port, the Piraeus, was such a cultural crossroads in the ancient world, and in part because Diogenes often took to wandering from place to place and in fact ended up living part of his life in Corinth. His way of life exercised a mesmerizing effect on thinkers and teachers of all stripes and persuasions, regardless of whether they admired or were repulsed by him. References to his doings permeate subsequent Hellenistic and Roman philosophizing. His enactment of Cynic philosophy rendered it influential on Stoicism and other schools of philosophical practice touched on in this chapter. Moreover, his mode of life has continued to fascinate philosophers and social critics down to the present day. Many commentators seem to find in his life the reversal or transvaluation of values which Nietzsche later spoke of as a necessary step toward human freedom. Indeed, Diogenes Laertius suggests that the dogged Cynic sought "the recoining of values" in society (6.20, translation by Copleston, 1985, p. 120).

Diogenes' integrity toward a way of life is impressive and unusual in the annals of human conduct. As the eighteenth-century *encyclopédiste* Jean le Rond d'Alembert wrote: "Chaque siècle, et le notre surtout, auraient besoin d'un Diogène; mais la difficulté est de trouver des hommes qui aient le courage de l'être, et des hommes qui aient le courage de le souffrir" (Every age, ours above all, needs its Diogenes. But the difficulty is to find people with the courage not just to live his way but to endure the consequences that accompany it) (in Branham and Goulet-Cazé, 1996, p. vii; my translation). Diogenes shines a light on aspects of cosmopolitanism addressed previously: a willingness to question extant custom, seeing oneself as a participant in a larger world than that which one inherits from local culture, and courage to engage other people with different values and beliefs. As Gilbert Leung (2009) argues, Diogenes also reveals why cosmopolitanism can and at times must be provocative in tone and consequence. It can and at times must take its point of departure from the street, so to speak, rather than from formal institutions.

Furthermore, Diogenes demonstrates why cosmopolitanism does not depend upon a given material condition. His poverty mirrors that of Socrates and attests to the modest style of living characteristic of many figures in the tradition of philosophy as the art of living. His esteem for nature, combined with his relentless critique of what is today called consumerism, illuminates why cosmopolitanism reaches beyond an anthropocentric humanism, even while acknowledging the intimate overlap with humanism with respect to ethics and the moral life (more on this below).

It gives food for thought that the first person known in human history to have used the term cosmopolitan was an outsider – literally outside the center of established power and identity. This fact has marked the history of cosmopolitanism. As we have seen in this chapter, its voices and its practices emanate from the margins of society toward the center as much as the other way around (Fojas, 2005, pp. 5, 24–25, 59, 117–129). One might say they also emanate from the margins of the self where it meets the world. From that contact, they can work their way into a person's outlook through exercises such as dialogue with others, reading and study, reflection and contemplation, and shared labors.

It is also important to point out that cosmopolitan-minded people have been persecuted across history – for example, by the likes of Stalin, Hitler, Mao Tse-Tung and Pol Pot. They have been singled out as alien to an alleged national norm, in part because of their cultural versatility. On a less violent scale, at least in its physical sense, jingoists and cultural reactionaries have persistently singled out cosmopolitan attitudes as unpatriotic. In so doing they have failed to grasp that a mature patriotism necessitates criticism of one's polity when it goes astray from humane and just conduct. Diogenes' fearless and non-violent example triggers thought about the meaning of a cosmopolitan conscience.

However, while Diogenes gives the idea of cosmopolitanism an unforgettable jumpstart, his tossing aside of local obligations can be seen from the perspective of this book as counter-cosmopolitan rather than as merely counter-cultural. In severing his roots from the local Diogenes becomes not a citizen of the world but a citizen of nowhere. Cosmopolitanism implies roots even if they are flexible rather than set in concrete. The figures referred to previously – for example, Orwell, Rodó, and Woolf – did not cut themselves off from their traditions. They did criticize them and sometimes harshly so. However, at one and the same time they remained rooted and unrooted in a paradoxical, which is to say cosmopolitan manner.

Consider Rabindranath Tagore, who as a young, emergent poet and public figure in the latter part of the nineteenth century found himself at a cultural crossroads. In his view and that of others, artistic and other traditions in his native Bengal had ossified. "Our literature had allowed its creative life to vanish," he observes; "it lacked movement, and was fettered by a rhetoric as rigid as death" (1966, p. 81). He took heart from his contemporaries who were "brave enough to challenge the orthodoxy which believed in the security of tombstones and in perfection which can only belong to the dead" (p. 81). In part to re-imagine his poetic roots, he immersed himself in literary traditions from elsewhere, for example the Romantic tradition of poetry in Britain from which he drew a variety of motifs, ideas, and images.

While criticizing the traditionalism of his local artistic community, Tagore advocates not a break from it but rather a reconstruction. He suggests that attempting a radical break from the past implies not finding one's natal voice but rather becoming mute. A would-be poet, whatever her or his ambition, has always already inherited the very possibility of poetry from humanity and should be eternally grateful for it. Thus he criticizes colonialism (the British still governed in South Asia at the time) for implanting in some of his fellow artists contempt for their local traditions, a "distrust of all things that had come to them as an inheritance from their past" (p. 81). In his own poetic oeuvre, which became widely known in his era, Tagore remained deeply embedded in Bengali artistic tradition while allowing himself to be substantively influenced by traditions from elsewhere. He experienced what the literary critic Lionel Trilling calls "one of the significant mysteries of man's life in culture: how it is that other people's creations can be so utterly their own and so deeply part of us" (in Geertz, 1983, p. 54).

In sum, Tagore was critical of both traditionalists, who embrace local artistic values and methods so tightly they squeeze the life out of them, and aesthetes who look down their noses at local art practices as backward and ready to be buried. A reader can discern across his poetry a sense of genuine awe, pleasure, and tension in realizing the consequences of reflective openness to the new fused with reflective loyalty to the known.

Tagore's mode of being contrasts with Diogenes' relentlessly idiosyncratic, custom-defying manner. The latter is not a blueprint for a cosmopolitan-minded life. Cosmopolitanism is not a posture that elbows aside other dimensions of being a person. It is phasic. It emerges within and around the contours of a way of life. It finds expression in particular moments, spaces, and interactions. An analogy with another intensely debated outlook – namely, what it means to be moral – can shed light here. Dewey (1989, p. 170) observed that a sign of maturity is knowing when to raise the question of the moral: that is, knowing when to ask whether an act or proposal is just, fair, good, or worthy. To ask this question about every act or notion ("May I sneeze now?") would drive people mad and bring life to a halt. To never ask the question would render life a horror. In likeness, from a cosmopolitan perspective it is impossible to try to be open at all times to everything new, or loyal at all times to everything known. The former stance dissolves life, the latter petrifies it. Cosmopolitan artfulness involves discerning how and when to express openness and loyalty in the vicissitudes of everyday life. Such artfulness constitutes an educational way of being in the world, and this entire book is in process of coloring-in that way.

Educational Arts of and for Living

Stoic-minded practitioners sought an orientation attuned both to the cosmos in which they took humans to be deeply embedded and to the aim of dwelling humanely with other people. Consider Epictetus' *Handbook*, a set of his views on the art of living put together by one of his students. The handbook was meant to be carried around by the learner: to be held in hand, kept in hand, in order to be ready at hand. It was to be used as a source of guidance, what in Latin is called a *vade mecum*. As Epictetus himself wrote: "Let these thoughts be 'at hand' for you, day and night. Write them down and re-read them; talk about them, both to yourself and with others" (in Hadot, 1995, p. 195). The emphasis on the hand evokes work, labor, and task. Epictetus' handbook has a practical rather than theoretical intent. Thus its title has often been translated as *Manual* (as contrasted with, say, the *Thoughts* of Epictetus).

The handbook contains, among other things, commentary on conduct, examples of conduct, well-known quotations to ponder and inspire, and an array of tightly compressed arguments. As mentioned, its objective is to help a person lead a life rather than merely contemplate it or theorize about it. As John Sellars (2003, p. 130) reminds us, the original Greek term for handbook also meant a cutting instrument, calling to mind the use of tools in building and shaping. Practices of the self were to help persons build and shape their very being. As such they stand as an ancient precursor to the concept of *bildung* that eighteenth- and nineteenth-century writers introduced to capture their ideas about self-realization and human transformation through educative experience (for wide-ranging discussion see, for example, the essays in Lovlie et al., 2003). These echoes recall the fact that the Latin root for book is *liber*, a term that also means freedom. Epictetus' handbook, like others in the tradition, is intended to help people free themselves *from* envy, fear, and selfishness and to free themselves *for* the work of self-cultivation.

This notion of a handbook, of a-book-to-keep-in-hand, influences subsequent writers in the tradition of philosophy as the art of living. For example, Montaigne, Gournay, Emerson, and Nietzsche treat their favorite authors in a spirit comparable to how ancient readers regarded Epictetus. They look to them for both theoretical insight and for guidance on how to live. They hold their works in hand: Gournay, Emerson, and then Nietzsche in turn carry Montaigne's essays around for much of their lives. Nietzsche carried Emerson, too, and he arranged for the translation of the latter's essays into German. On his part, Montaigne refers routinely to what he calls "my moral guides" (1991, p. 172), among them Cicero, Seneca, and Plutarch. Montaigne's pioneering, still prescient view of the education of children (1991, Essay 26, pp. 163–199) pivots, in part, around his interpretation of the ancient arts of living that he found endlessly absorbing (Hall, 1997; Hansen, 2002). In the essay, he characterizes what it means to help children cultivate good judgment and discernment in juxtaposition with leading a humane life with others.

As suggested previously, the arts addressed by Epictetus and other ancient writers included deliberative ways of listening, speaking, and interacting with others. They involved *practicing* these ways, keeping at them until they formed the structure of habit and response in the world. This work involved reading and study, chiefly philosophy and poetry in addition to philosophically minded texts like the *Handbook* itself. A familiar contemporary comparison would be reading novels, drama, and the humanities writ large, based on the premise that such study can help sensitize people to the place of values in human life and deepen their moral awareness.

Another art was memorization of passages, poems, and aphorisms taken to embody wisdom and insight. The principle here was that a person could thereby "carry" fine words in mind and heart, just as he or she could carry a favorite handbook. This art seems to have been abandoned in a great deal of formal education today. Many educators seem to treat memorization of texts as a wooden, rote undertaking rather than as a universal, time-honored mode of substantiating the self. However, in various forms this art remains alive and well with many persons the world over. They could attest to the fact that the songs, poems, prayers, philosophical passages, and other words they memorize can penetrate and form the self. Here the selection of what to memorize becomes key, a fact that rendered this technique of great interest to various thinkers engaged in philosophy as the art of living.

Epictetus, who was born a slave, exerted a strong influence on another well-known Stoic thinker, the Roman emperor Marcus Aurelius. As Sellars (2003) notes, if Epictetus' *Handbook* constitutes a guide to exercises to be used by students, then Marcus' *Meditations* can be seen as a prime instance of a text "produced by a student engaged in such exercises" (p. 147) – a process we witnessed previously in Gournay's preface to Montaigne's *Essays*. Hadot (1995, p. 179) suggests that a better translation of the original Greek title of Marcus' book would be "Exhortations to Himself." They comprise not just theoretical musings *about* life but practical encouragement and admonishment *for* life. As in Epictetus' manual, Marcus' meditations feature a constant refrain of phrases such as "always bear in mind," "make come alive in you," "when you wake up each morning," "concentrate," "focus," and "stop drifting." "At dawn, when you have trouble getting out of bed," he writes, "tell yourself: 'I have to go to work – as a human being'" (2003, p. 53, Bk. V.1). Hadot remarks how invaluable it is that the *Meditations* survived since Marcus did not intend them for publication. "It is extremely rare," he writes, "to have the chance to see someone in the process of training himself to be a human being" (p. 201).

However, we can witness this process in a range of texts that embody the tradition of philosophy as the art of living. For example, Virginia Woolf (an accomplished essayist as well as novelist) offers the following remark about Montaigne:

> Once at Bar-le-Duc Montaigne saw a portrait which René, King of Sicily, had painted of himself, and asked, 'Why is it not, in like manner, lawful for everyone to draw [i.e., describe] himself with a pen, as he did with a crayon?' Off-hand one might reply, Not only is it lawful, but nothing could be easier. Other people may evade us, but our own features are almost too familiar. Let us begin. And then, when we attempt the task, the pen falls from our fingers; it is a matter of profound, mysterious, and over-whelming difficulty . . . This talking of oneself, following one's own vagaries, giving the whole map, weight, colour, and circumference of the soul in its

confusion, its variety, its imperfection – this art belonged to one man only: to Montaigne.

(Woolf, 1984, p. 58)

Woolf's artfulness allows her to sketch what she herself witnesses in Montaigne's visceral sentences. Montaigne's and Marcus' tasks differ in their emphases. The former aims primarily at self-understanding, the latter primarily at self-formation. Both would suggest that in actual thought and action the two emphases are interdependent – indeed, they are terms for dimensions of the very same process. "Know thyself" (from the Greek *gnothi seautou*) fuses with "cultivate the self" (Gr. *epimeleia heautou*).

While Woolf rightly signals how remarkable Montaigne's accomplishment is, any person, in principle, can take in hand diary or journal and attempt to ascend in insight and self-cultivation as best as circumstances allow. As one example among many, consider the diary Etty Hillesum has left us. Hillesum was a young Jewish woman residing in Amsterdam when the Nazis took over Holland during World War II. She was a university student and also a tutor. Her diary documents her ethical journey from a self-absorbed, often closed-minded person to one who becomes a public participant in pushing against the inhumanity of the Nazi occupation. She volunteers to work at the city's Jewish Council, set up to administer Jewish affairs. She helps refugees corralled in ghetto-like circumstances and eases their suffering. From the point of view of the art of living, what is striking to witness in the diary is her deliberative and mindful, if also halting and tension-laden, steps in transforming herself. She practices ways of paying attention to people and their concerns, of listening to others, of observing conditions in order to act. Hillesum's diary transcends the scope of what that genre of writing typically expresses. It takes on qualities of a handbook that others who seek meaning and courage can carry with them.[6]

Now back to the origins of the tradition – one which helped make possible, in both overt and circuitous ways, Montaigne's, Woolf's, and Hillesum's prose endeavors. In his *Meditations*, Marcus works on remembrance, on all that has shaped him as a person. He comments with incisive, poetic care on family, friends, associates, and others who have influenced him. He names them all, mindful of their *presence* in his life, of their impact on his thought, spirit, heart, and soul. With their influence in view, and informed by the reading he undertakes (especially of Epictetus), Marcus goes on to write of the arts of self-control, of regard for others, and of how to cultivate good judgment.

Another exercise is working deliberatively on one's perspective of things. Marcus experiments with modes of perception, trying to look "beyond" the self or with "more" than just the self. As Sellars (2003, p. 151) notes, Marcus refers continuously to "the point of view of the cosmos." He aspires to create reflective distance from the first-person perspective, which can also create distance from the first-person perspective in the plural ("our" point of view as well as "my" point of view). Marcus' attempt to obtain this distance does not imply a leap into abstract theory or metaphysics. It is not a project of transcending experience. Rather it is a way of looking deeper into the cosmos of which persons are already a part before they so much as begin to reason, to feel, and to choose. Dewey often evoked the value of building a mental observation tower so that one can distinguish the forest (life) from the trees (individual lives including one's own). But this tower is formed of organic materials – of concrete reflections on human experience rather than of fleshless abstractions – and it remains firmly rooted in the ground (cf. Dewey, 1988, p. 306).[7]

Still another art that Marcus practices is repetition, which has an affinity with the art of memorization. Marcus repeats again and again views and outlooks he hopes will guide his life. He wants not just to study them but to metabolize them, to absorb them into his being. He aspires to dye his soul with these precepts (2003, p. 29, Bk. III.4; p. 140, Bk. X.31), "to make himself so completely accustomed to [them] that they transform his character and thus his habitual behavior" (Sellars, 2003, p. 154). A crucial, dynamic aspect of this process is ensuring that what is repeated has been expressed as carefully and as appropriately as possible (cf. Hadot, 1995, p. 201; Foucault, 2005, p. 295) – yet another mirror to the art of memorization with its reflective selection of sayings to embody. Montaigne will later underscore this Stoic view of rhetoric: that how one says things is as self-formative as what one says.

Finally, still another exercise is conversing thoughtfully with others, a practice that brings together the tradition's focus on listening, speaking, considering, inquiring, and the like, and which flowers in the eighteenth-century salons in Paris, Berlin, and elsewhere. Recall that Epictetus encouraged his students not just to read his handbook but to talk about it with others. He did not mean they should regard his words as writ in stone. Like other Stoic-minded figures, Epictetus esteemed the ideal of the sage but did not presume to be one. Rather his intent was to provoke thinking, itself understood for these writers as a mode of "internal" dialogue or dialogue-with-the-soul. Conversation opens that process into public thinking. Once again the example of Socrates loomed large for these figures. Socrates: drawn to conversation like a bee to flowers whose nectar it converts into honey to sustain life, just as people addressing questions in dialogue convert words into understandings that sustain life. Socrates: hungry to examine any topic, with any person, that might make a difference in how people lead their lives, whether it be the meaning of virtue, the nature of the good, the contours of a just social order, or the limits of knowledge.

Writers in this tradition were also taken by the fact Socrates never published a single word. For him writing incarcerated thought. It froze words into manikins. He believed the purpose of the *logos*, the word, was to unleash thought and keep it mobile, supple, and responsive. Consequently Epictetus and other figures return again and again to the arts of dialogue, which they conceived like the other practices touched on here as a cardinal element in fashioning a humane life.

While Stoic-minded writers took inspiration from Socrates' passion for dialogue, they did not aspire to follow his example on all counts, any more than they sought to mimic Diogenes' radical break with convention. For one thing, they *did* write and often at length. For another thing, they were not always agitators or "gadflies" like Diogenes or Socrates, stinging the body politic into critical self-awareness (Plato, *Apology*, 30e). Though Socrates cherished serious philosophical conversation, there seems little doubt he took a devilish delight in publicly showing up puffed-up politicians as ignoramuses. Epictetus' approach, like that of Socrates in other instances, was that of the patient teacher whose influence emerges piecemeal, over time, in sometimes unpredictable ways. It is an unannounced influence, not the subject matter of public demonstrations.

On Inhabiting the World

Readers can discern in Seneca, Epictetus, Marcus, Montaigne, Gournay, Emerson, Woolf, and other writers associated with the tradition indices of withdrawal, of resignation, and of self-cocooning to ward off the harshness of an uncontrollable world. They would concur, in certain moods, with the Roman emperor Hadrian's remarks in Marguerite Yourcenar's novelistic rendering of his life:

> Life is atrocious, we know. But precisely because I expect little of the human condition, man's periods of felicity, his partial progress, his efforts to begin over again and to continue, all seem to me like so many prodigies which nearly compensate for the monstrous mass of ills and defeats, of indifference and error.
>
> (Yourcenar, 1990, p. 293)

These figures' tendencies to retreat dwell in tension with their cosmopolitan impulse to participate, to respond, to engage life as it comes in all its diversity and difficulty.

Rather than contradicting cosmopolitanism, I regard the quiescent aspects of the tradition as natural. For one thing, withdrawal into solitude from time to time *is* salutary, if not essential, for self-replenishment. It can also be an experience of sublime joy in being alive. For another thing, these writers were acutely aware of human limitation and weakness. In the face of incessant war, violence, injustice, cruel caprice, and the constraints imposed by humanity's biological makeup, they harbor few illusions about the possibility of constructing a heaven on earth. Confucius' observations on political breakdown are as sharp and devastating as any that can be found in the writings these figures have left us.

However, their posture does not imply pessimism, itself a luxury affordable only to those who can step outside the stream of human interaction (cf. Hadot, 1995, pp. 180–186). These writers provide an enduring cosmopolitan complexion to the arts of living. In contrast with the stereotype of a "stoic" retreat from the world, perhaps in order not to feel suffering or confusion, they put forward arts that strengthen a person's capacity to dwell efficaciously in an unpredictable cosmos. Such practices are meant to assist people to *inhabit* life in the most substantial meaning of that term.

Thus, from this point onwards in the book I shall take the term cosmopolitan to denote not "citizen of the world" but "inhabitant of the world" – a translation of *kosmopolites* that I take to be warranted by the philosophical tradition under review here. In this respect the term becomes that much closer to the teacher. The term asks the teacher (and teacher educator, head of school, and others involved in the enterprise): How are you inhabiting your world? How are you inhabiting your school and classroom? How do you carry and conduct yourself? How do you encourage your students to engage in ethical work – to carry themselves in ways that draw out their aesthetic, moral and intellectual capability? As teachers work their way toward responding to such questions, they become more fully *in* and *of* the world. They move into the conjunction featured in the title of this book: the teacher *and* the world.

Such is the view of teaching when seen through a cosmopolitan prism. The next chapter illuminates background or what might be called existential conditions in which all educators work. The ensuing chapter then takes up foreground conditions, which is to say contemporary ways of communicating and interacting that demonstrate the vitality of a cosmopolitan orientation toward teaching and education.

3 On the Human Condition and its Educational Challenge

As mentioned at the start of Chapter 2, philosophy as the art of living encompasses reflections on what has often been called the human condition. One feature of this condition that forces itself to the front today is the sheer speed of globalization. This acceleration (cf. Halevy, 1948; Piel, 1972; Scheuerman, 2004) began, in earnest, some two hundred years ago with the economic upheaval known as the Industrial Revolution, and with the simultaneous political earthquakes known as the American and French Revolutions. Their positive and negative effects can be seen everywhere today. Values such as respect for the individual and for the distinctiveness of human cultures have endured, despite the fact that they continue to be trampled upon in various parts of the globe. Democratic practices come and go, but not the democratic impulse. Countless economic initiatives arise and then collapse, but not the spirit of economic innovation. Cultural styles and products bloom and then wither, but behind them abides a passion to create.

Side by side with these fruits of globalization are bewildering and painful losses. The social, economic, and political tsunamis set off by revolution two hundred years ago have washed away many traditional modes of life around the globe, often leaving in their wake bewildering conditions. "Cosmopolitanism has always been a way of being in the world, however confusing the world is," writes Ackbar Abbas, adding that "nothing so far is as confusing" as what can be summarized under the term globalization (2000, p. 786). The incessant demands of contemporary economic life, the press of population growth and movement, the ever-expanding overload of information, the spread of intrusive modes of entertainment: to many people, or so it seems, these and related phenomena undermine stable forms of human association and with them a sense of control and direction. They appear to distract people from contemplation, from reflection, and from questioning, as well as from the values of both generative solitude and sustained engagement with others. In the wake of the acceleration of globalization, crucial human values, like much of the physical environment on the planet, sometimes suffer and degrade.[1]

People are naturally rattled by the speed of these changes and worried about their consequences. They rightly wonder how to respond to them. Although philosophy as the art of living arose in comparatively calmer conditions, appearances can be deceiving. The figures mentioned in the previous chapter were, in an important sense, "just like us." They were universally struck by the facts of change in the cosmos and by the uncontrollable and unpredictable nature of the process. They observed that humanity cannot control its own imagination any more than it can control the movement of the sun. Humanity cannot predict its own next steps any more than it can anticipate nature's sure-to-come evolutionary steps. Humanity cannot stop itself from changing and transforming, since the very endeavor to do that would itself constitute a mode of change.

However, these conditions do not mean people ought to throw their hands in the air and simply hunker down and look after their own. Thinkers conceived the art of living, in part, as a method for taking one's head out of the sand and responding with all the resources at one's disposal to the facts of an aleatory universe. This method provides not a theoretical explanation of events but a way of enacting an efficacious response to feelings of hope, uncertainty, and despair. To transfigure a metaphor from Plato, it is a method for turning the soul: for reconstructing one's perceptions of and conduct in the world.

This fusion of perception and action constitutes an orientation. In that orientation, as we saw in Epictetus and other writers, seeing and acting become mutually formative. They work together, albeit in unwieldy, unscripted, and sometimes fruitless fashion. A cosmopolitan compass does not provide a fixed moral latitude and longitude. Rather it points to ways of moving in the world responsive to the facts of incessant change and of endless human diversity. The practices of self-improvement addressed previously constitute an attempt to respond to these uncontrollable conditions in which human beings reside. This perspective provides yet another reason why these arts, which at first glance can appear privatistic, are educational and social in their significance. They provide ways of moving further and further together through difficulty and opportunity. They bring people closer and closer apart as they recognize how uniquely each person speaks, listens, responds, and interacts with the strange and the familiar in life.

Cosmopolitan views of the human condition boil down to (1) a belief in the inevitability of change combined with cultivating a balanced response to change, and (2) a critical appreciation for the unfathomability of human disposition, outlook, and conduct. In what follows I will feature the tone and range of how thinkers on the art of living characterize these conditions, both of which underlie the work of teachers everywhere and at every level of the system today. The discussion will also take up questions of home and belonging which form a related backdrop to educational work in our time.

Life is Change: Cultivating a Sense of Stability

Nothing is permanent. Persons, communities, nations, arts, technologies, trees, rocks, rivers: all come and go. Summarizing some two thousand years of Stoic reflection, Emerson writes in his essay, "Circles": "permanence is but a word of degrees" (1983, p. 403).[2] Permanence is a matter of the temporal and spatial perspective one provisionally adopts. This evident fact about the world is unsettling. It seems to undermine or even sunder the sentiment of stability without which it is difficult to fashion a coherent human life. The difficulty is recognizable today in the oft-cited anxieties, touched on above, about the pace of contemporary life under the pressures of globalization. Everywhere, it seems, one witnesses and experiences the consequences of acceleration. For two hundred years observers have been noting how the increasing speed of change has brought in its train countless reactions, some quite violent, with regards to economic, cultural, political, religious, and other modes of life. Many of these reactions can be understood as attempts to stop the press, so to speak – to cling to something of value that can provide stability.

One claim discernible in the long conversation on cosmopolitanism and the art of living is that it is not possible to "choose" stability. A person cannot wake up one day and declare, as if it were a speech act, "Starting today my life will be stable." Nor can a community or nation choose stability, especially now under conditions of wholesale change. And yet, for many if not most people there appears to be an ineradicable need for a sense of stability, of control, of direction.

That word "sense" is where philosophy as the art of living, in its cosmopolitan expressions, offers a generative response to change. A "sense of stability" is not the same thing as a money-back guarantee about social reality that can put the mind and spirit at ease. Rather, it is a disposition or sensibility that propels people to think about change, including the forces triggering it, rather than merely flinch or pull back when faced with differences from the norm. This distinction recalls the fact that humanity everywhere, at all times, often seems driven as much by curiosity in the new as it is by the need for a stable way of life. Appiah (2006) emphasizes how ubiquitous human movement and interaction have been since the time when humanity first began migrating out of Africa. "[T]he way of segregation and seclusion has always been anomalous in our perpetually voyaging species" he writes. "Cosmopolitanism isn't hard work; repudiating it is" (p. xx).

I take from Appiah's provocative claim the idea that a sense of stability does not necessitate self-enclosure or self-cocooning, whether on the part of a person or community. However, at the same time this notion does not imply simply opening the doors and shutters wide and letting in come what may, which would be a recipe for dissipation. Recall Gandhi's perspective touched on in Chapter 1 (see p. 18), in which he combines reflective openness to new ideas and cultures with a refusal to be "blown off his feet" by them. Dewey echoes this point in describing why being open-minded is not the same thing as being empty-minded (1985, p. 183). To open the mind is like opening a door: it takes an effort, a conscious gesture to engage what is on the other side. This reflective hospitality constitutes a hallmark of a cosmopolitan outlook. An empty mind, in contrast, is an empty space in which one thing that comes along is as good as any other. Many if not most people appreciate this difference as well as the challenge it can present. They either feel, intuit, or learn that every new human contact is potentially unsettling or destabilizing, even while it may also appear intriguing or even compelling.

The alternative to a condition of unsettlement is not a reified, frozen, rigid mode of life. In contrast to stability or instability cast as dichotomous conditions, *a sense of stability* can be cultivated through recognizing the permanence of impermanence.[3] Put less paradoxically, the sense of stability can emerge from an education that assists people in seeing that when Emerson states that permanence is a word of degrees, he is not offering a negative, much less a despairing, comment on the human condition. Quite the contrary. The key is in the term "degrees." From the point of view of an individual person, Mt. Kilimanjaro is immortal even though we know from geology that it is destined to shift in the future. From the point of view of an individual citizen of the United States, the country may also seem immortal even though we know that it will likely be something different centuries from now, when it may have become a dozen associated regions or part of a larger configuration. Long ago people thought Rome was eternal, just as today's nation-state structure seems timeless.[4]

To contemplate the longevity of a mountain or of a nation can make the individual feel not only mortal but like a mere speck of dust, no more stable than the grit on city streets blown hither and yon. But it is a matter of degrees: there is *matter* that fills every moment of a human life, however taken for granted or oblivious to this primordial fact most persons are most of the time. To gloss the familiar adage, one can picture the whole world in a sparkling human action – a spatial image – and the whole of time in a meaningful moment – the complementary temporal image. This idea recalls Stoic-minded esteem for the present which is, literally, the only time in which persons can think, feel, and act, albeit mindful of past precedent and future possibility. In a quote discussed previously, Epictetus urges the student to "set up right now" – that is, in the present moment and in each succeeding present moment – "a certain character and pattern for yourself" (1983, p. 22, No. 33). Marcus Aurelius writes: "Give yourself a gift: the present moment" (2003, p. 110, Bk. VIII.44). In his essay "Experience," Emerson opines: "Since our office is with moments, let us husband them. Five minutes of today are worth as much to me, as five minutes in the next millennium. Let us be poised, and wise, and our own, today" (1983, p. 479).

The sense of stability, for all its fragility and lack of guarantees, can potentially turn every moment and place into a possibility rather than a passing, empty void. As Elizabeth de Mijolla writes (1994, p. 62), space and time can be full rather than merely fleeting. While this accomplishment will often be hard-won and temporary, it is just as real or substantive as any rock, tree, river, or mountain, which are also temporary, given the fact of change.

Human beings feel, intuit, or learn that every contact in life may necessitate a change in outlook or habit, however subtle or casual it may seem. A person's encounters with others and with the environment leave effects, some hard to detect, others as striking as a radical change in the weather. Dewey expressed the point by suggesting that as a person takes up an activity and then moves on to another, the person continuously loses her or his self and finds another. He did not mean one's entire being is continuously overturned. As the saying goes, that happens only on the road to Damascus. Dewey meant that nobody is unaffected by life's contacts, however minuscule a particular effect may be (1985, pp. 133, 361–362). For the tradition of philosophy as the art of living, one task of education is to become mindful of this existential condition and to work to make one's contacts with the world as fruitful as circumstances permit. The self and its relation with the world are always in question, and the answer finds expression in how a person responds to the passing moment. Put another way, while the relation between self and world is permanently unstable, it is possible to cultivate a pattern or web of conduct motored, in part, by a sense of stability.

Teachers are well-positioned to work with young people in this spirit. They are, or can be, on the proverbial frontline of how students encounter the world. For example, it is a cliché that today's youth often exceed their elders in knowing how to manipulate the ever-changing landscape of communications technology. Moreover, there is an undeniable thrill and seductive quality to the speed that this technology facilitates, such that talk of stability may sound odd. However, as the Greeks argued *techne* – technical or skilled know-how – is not synonymous with *phronesis* – practical wisdom and insight into the consequences of technique and skill. Teachers can play a dynamic role in helping students appreciate why technology that feels liberating may in other cases overwhelm or even undermine their aesthetic, moral, and intellectual sensibilities. Teachers can model uses of technology that do not substitute for spontaneity, imagination, and thinking, but are appropriately supportive of them. The arts of living discussed here come into play since it requires *reflective* rather than *uncritical* openness to keep technology in service of distinctively human ends rather than of ends the technology itself willy-nilly throws on the table, some of which are determined by profit-seeking rather than by educational considerations. The positive and negative consequences of technology dwell in tension, and it is not easy to tell whether the pro outweighs the con. Once again, teachers at all levels of the system are well-placed to help students think of specific contexts, uses, and ramifications (see Hull et al., 2010, for an example of creative, cosmopolitan-minded uses of online technology). It seems wise to keep in view the longstanding human habit of pushing every technology it invents to the limit, for both good and for ill.

On Human Diversity: Not Foreign but Unfathomable

Has every human being who has ever walked the planet felt the questions, Why am I here? What is the meaning of life? Philosophers on the art of living are variously credited and criticized for posing such questions. But might it be true that everyone in some way or another has *felt* them? Perhaps in looking up to see a rainbow, or watching one's crop wither in the brutal sun, or hearing a loved one laugh, or kneeling beside a dying friend or comrade, or running gleefully through the rain, or witnessing the destruction of a city. Why am I here? What is the meaning of all this? It seems that many if not most people feel, intuit, or learn that life is unfathomable, that there is no end to questions of life's purposes and meanings because there is no end to joyful and painful experience. From one point of view, this claim is no different than saying life is change. But the idea of unfathomability emphasizes the fact of the new, that, as the early Greek philosopher Heraclitus contended, life is never mere repetition. In a sense, there is nothing new under the sun because *everything* is new, however infinitesimal or modest its novelty may be, such that the very idea of "newness" is redundant – or at any rate, *pace* Emerson, is a matter of degree.

This notion recalls a recurring theme in the long tradition of philosophy as the art of living that runs alongside the idea of permanent impermanence. That theme is diversity, whose very existence on the planet gives rise to the cosmopolitan idea in the first place. The cosmopolitan understanding of diversity does not presume unbridgeable axiological, ontological or epistemological divides between groups of people or between individuals. Mutual understanding is not easy or assured, but there are no barriers that render such understanding permanently impossible.

Moreover, as Montaigne adroitly illustrates, the cosmopolitan perspective suggests that the diversity or variability *within* any community is likely to be as great as that *between* any two communities, and that the diversity or variability *within* any person is likely to be as great as that *between* any two persons (1991, pp. 380 (II:1), 887 (II.37), 1207 (III.13), 1220 (III.13), *passim*). Montaigne's insight brings to mind the familiar aphorism of the Roman poet and playwright Terence (*c*.190–159 BCE): "I am a man; I deem nothing that is human to be foreign to me." Terence's assertion (to which I will return in Chapter 5), that nothing human is foreign to me since I am myself human, encompasses the notion that nothing within me is foreign either. This claim does not mean I must approve of what I find. But everything within is human, which is one reason why Montaigne, in the recurrent editions of his essays, rarely edited out a previous word or phrase. That practice jibes with his provocative rejection of the idea of repentance (though not of regret), understood as casting out a part of his being as alien or sub-human. To take all features of one's person seriously, Montaigne came to believe, will soon enough show up their deficiencies. He demonstrates how the same approach will sooner or later render stark the flaws in one's community, and yet without necessitating a moralistic rejection of those features as contrasted with a thoughtful reconstruction of them. Montaigne illustrates how human beings can most richly inhabit life, and most humbly interact with one another, through a critical embrace of their multifaceted humanity.

Montaigne demonstrates that the variability within and between persons is conjoined with an inconstancy in human conduct that would be startling to us were it not so ubiquitous. No doubt every person could provide her or his version of what Montaigne says of himself:

> Every sort of contradiction can be found in me, depending upon some twist or attribute: timid, insolent; chaste, lecherous; talkative, taciturn; tough, sickly; clever, dull; brooding, affable; lying, truthful; learned, ignorant; generous, miserly and then prodigal – I can see something of all that in myself, depending on how I gyrate; and anyone who studies himself

attentively finds in himself and in his very judgement this whirring about and this discordancy. There is nothing I can say about myself as a whole simply and completely, without intermingling and admixture.

(Montaigne, 1991, p. 377, II.1)[5]

This marked inconstancy, as characteristic of cultures as it is of individuals, fuses with what Montaigne argues is a human propensity to borrow, absorb, try out, mimic, and ponder things that other individuals and communities embody as their ways of life. Differences mushroom as exposure to the new alters people's relation with the familiar.

These characteristics, in turn, cohere with the remarkably different ways in which individuals and sub-communities within the same collective remember past events. It is not just historians who come up with contrasting interpretations of the past. This feature saturates human life on every plane and dimension. The phenomenon is widespread in families, friendships, schools and other institutions, and adds yet another layer to the diversity of the human tableau (cf. Halbwachs, 1992; Wineburg et al., 2007).

Consider also the highly distinctive networks that individuals from the same collective can develop today thanks, among other things, to the internet and other media – a process in fact initiated five hundred years ago with the invention of the printing press, which fueled a ballooning diversity of interests, styles, and tones of human expression. Walter Feinberg captures a lesson that can be drawn from these facts:

> I am uncomfortable with the idea that people belong to cultures in the sense that culture determines their horizons of values and understandings. My own view is that human beings are engaged in networks of meaning, and that each of us differs somewhat regarding the various strands that form our particular nodes within those networks. For any two individuals the strands may be relatively thick, requiring limited explanation, or relatively thin, requiring a lot of explanations or gestures. I suspect that an approach that views culture not in terms of epistemological or axiological constraints but rather in terms of networks of meaning and value could result in a stronger dialogical approach to cultural difference.

(Feinberg, 2003, p. 78)[6]

Such a posture, because of how attuned it is to the contours of people's actual experience, can support a cosmopolitan ethic and morality.

In parallel with the sense of stability's abandonment of an either/or world – "you either have stability or you don't" – the platform of unfathomability does not presume an either/or philosophical anthropology – "either the person or community has a fixed essence, or it has nothing upon which to build a meaningful and distinctive life." The assumption here is that it is precisely the presence of different people and groups that can provoke fuller forms of aesthetic, intellectual, and moral realization. This process can yield a deeper, more luminous grasp of the values in local tradition. Put another way, to appreciate human unfathomability turns one away from a homogenizing universalism and from a humanism that would at all points privilege similarity over difference. To adopt a cosmopolitan orientation is to expand the differences and similarities in view.

There have always been multiple ways of life, on the part of both communities and individuals, within the way of the world. There appears to be no end to them, just as their beginnings and endings are often uncertain and difficult to pinpoint. Moreover, the evolving or sudden expression of new modes on the part of communities and individuals will always outrun the capacity to interpret or explain them through theory, philosophy, science, or the arts. I am presuming that the worldwide presence of art, of thought, of inquiry, can be viewed, in part, as an ongoing attempt to respond to and understand the facts of unfathomability. All such attempts are no more terminal or exhaustive than are attempts to bring change to a halt. The cosmopolitan idea envisions no "final" descriptions of individuals or communities. Every new person who enters a given community – whether by birth, marriage, immigration, training, or whatever route – complicates the human scene (cf. Fuller, 1989, p. 16), just as every new contact an individual has complicates, however subtly or microscopically, her or his self-understanding and ways of moving in the world. All these complications derive from the world in which humanity dwells, and a cosmopolitan philosophy urges people to engage and learn from them. This posture of educational solidarity does not entail agreeing with or embracing the new, but it does entail not fleeing from it as if change and unfathomability were foreign to the cosmos itself.

Dwelling in an Uncertain World

Change accelerates as a consequence of technological developments, the pressures of population growth and movement, expanding modes of communication, and other factors. Today as in the past people strive to build institutions – law courts, schools, legislative arrangements, and the like – to control the effects of transformation. Moreover, many argue for institutions that are just and equitable, that distribute fairly the fruits as well as the costs of change. As touched on in Chapter 1, political and economic cosmopolitanism can be seen as an effort to support this process.

The sheer facts of change and unfathomability have been experienced for millennia. They accompany ways of living, now and in the past, like the other side of a coin. And they will always do so, unless humanity establishes a perfectly planned, rationalized, and predictable world (no doubt a picture of a true dystopia). The arts of living articulated by the critical tradition reviewed here constitute, in part, a response to these conditions. As arts of education, which they all are, they conjure emergent solidarities based not on a common ideology but on a shared set of ethical and moral activities. Deliberative ways of listening, speaking, waiting, reading, writing, memorizing, repeating, and judging: for the tradition of philosophy as the art of living, these activities can cultivate any person in her or his relation with the world.

Put another way, such arts can help fuel the ideal of a fused ethic and morality that the tradition evokes. Recall once more Epictetus' evocative urging: "Set up right now a certain character and pattern for yourself which you will preserve when you are by yourself and when you are with people" (1983, p. 22, paragraph 33). This "character" and "pattern" emerges through practice, through exercises of the self. The process takes time, effort, and is never completed. Its outcomes can be invaluable. For Epictetus, they include a deeper sensitivity to different points of views and a more patient approach to conflicts of interest and concern. While these achievements are all provisional, they can be improved over time and can be more fully integrated into the ethos of the person's and community's orientation and life.

Self-control remains a key virtue to philosophers of the art of living. Against a backdrop of an unpredictable world, Epictetus and other writers refer to "the things within our power," that is to say the things that a person can influence. Much of life is not subject to a person's power: storms, sunshine, mortality, and so much more. Nor can a person control other people's opinions, values, feelings, and insights, regardless of what appearances might suggest. Epictetus and other thinkers conceived the care of the self as an approach toward guiding that which they claim is within the individual's purview: her opinions and views, her decisions to act one way or another, and her desires if brought into awareness by juxtaposing them with her aversions (cf. Epictetus, 1983, p. 11, No. 1). In their view, self-control and self-improvement move hand-in-hand.

This concern for self-control is not built upon an atomistic or individualistic sense of self. For thinkers like Montaigne, self-control makes possible richer, more engaged, and more just association with other people. In "On Cruelty," "On Coaches," and in other essays, he emphasizes avoiding harm to others – avoiding acts of *inhumanity* which are the mirror opposite of what Confucius conveyed in his pioneering idea of humaneness. However, this apparently "negative" approach of *not* being cruel constitutes at one and the same time a profoundly "positive" approach toward social and political life. For one thing, it remediates suffering. For another, it can form, in Epictetus' terms, the character and pattern not just of my life but the lives of others, thereby making possible humane ways of dwelling together.[7] Self-control on the part of individual and community become mutually dependent. We see again the aspiration toward fusing ethics and morality the tradition strives to effect.

The acceleration of change in our time has placed the questions of ethics and morality, if not in so many words, on the doorstep of virtually every community if not every person on the planet. How shall I/we live? How shall I/we regard and treat others? Even cultures where such questions have no linguistic equivalent confront, in actual experience, some version or form of them. To be sure, as both life in our time and the historical record demonstrate, people can deflect the questions and instead assume or assert that the answers are already there and require no examination. They can limit their contacts precisely through recognizing, however inchoately, the permanence of impermanence. One can see this impulse at its most extreme in today's economic, political, and religious fundamentalism.

Their proponents mime the hope to freeze movement. Their claims to absolute truth express the desire for absolute stability. Cosmopolitanism presumes that this urge can never be realized, and that one of the illusions that seems to recur continuously in the human imagination around the world is that one or another attempt just might do the trick and bring change to a halt.

However, from a spiritual, emotional, and practical standpoint that illusion is understandable. It speaks to a human need for stable meaning that is anything but illusory. An experienced, cosmopolitan-minded person or community may appreciate the new. They may venture without fear, albeit with anxiety, into the space of questions about values and purposes. They may seek to learn from new contacts in life, a process which in its fullness embodies a readiness to engage ethics and morality. However, a wise cosmopolitan-minded person or community will grasp why such a posture may in fact be hard-won and provisional, why it may presuppose a long personal or communal journey of transformation, and why it may appear frightening to those without such experience. It may appear so because of histories of war, of conflict, of the materially stronger exploiting the weaker and enforcing a one-sided permeability, all of which needs to be factored into the equation. Cosmopolitanism generates moral and ethical reciprocity: a willingness to move further and further together even while moving closer and closer apart. Part of this fundamentally educational process is recognizing and acting upon shared conditions of instability and unfathomability.

Tensions between Home and Movement

Tension is a two-sided concept. On the one side, it denotes unsettlement and anxiety, sometimes even fear. Consider tense moments in a battle, in a political election, and in a marriage, where the future itself seems at stake. But consider also tense moments in a football game, in trying to land the fish on the line, and in cooking multiple dishes at once. Here the stakes, while vivid, are less weighty than in the previous examples. Tension appears to come in many degrees. The other side of tension has to do with fascination in the new. Consider the familiar, compelling qualities of narrative tension in novels, paintings, music, and other arts that lead people to open their sensibilities and understandings to them. In their most absorbed encounters, people give themselves over and ride this tension as if it had no beginning and no end.

Home is also a two-sided concept. On one side it has been culturally understood as a precious place to raise a family, to express intimacy, and to share values and beliefs. Home is a safe haven, a place to relax, to let down one's guard, and to be at ease and in company with familiar faces. People in various cultures have also treated home as a hallowed sanctuary, as a place of ritual and ceremony, linked up with community, religious and cosmological ideals and images. Home becomes an analogue to the home in the world created by the community, or by a deity or deities, or by the cosmos itself. The other side of home is its analogy with a fort, a castle, and a prison. Home becomes constituted not by a generous-minded quest for meaning and purpose. Rather it is the domicile of fear, isolation, and rejection. Its office is to keep the world out, not to invite it in. It can become a place of suffering, of diminishment, of arbitrary and unilateral action, even a nightmare.

From a cosmopolitan perspective, persons are always leaving *and* remaining at home. On the one hand, a cosmopolitan outlook implies leaving home in the closed, walled-in sense of the term. This movement entails an ongoing loss of a certain innocence and comfort (cf. Tuan, 1996), in the sense of dissolving the mystique of the given, that "the ways things are" is the way they must be – or is the way in which others must see them. As emphasized above, cosmopolitanism presumes the permanence of change even if the alteration in custom, outlook, and belief may be modest and hard to detect. Moreover, in a globalizing world such as ours a "pure" home, uninfluenced in any way by the larger world, seems chimerical.

At the same time, to abandon an Edenic, or fortress, image of home can mean remaining at home in a generative sense. By reflecting on the very meaning of home, people position themselves to discern, appreciate, and realize in their conduct the distinctiveness and values of home in an always changing world. In the recognition of the very real values *of* home, rather than solely the values of *this* particular home, a person immediately perceives that there are many ways of being at home in the world, and many ways of leaving home, too. The sense of home need not be absolute and unchanging in order to remain meaningful.

William Connolly (2000, p. 603) deploys the concept "rhizomatic roots" as a perspective on these themes. A rhizome can be characterized as "a form of plant life stabilized by a dense network of connections close to the ground" (p. 617). The plant sends out roots horizontally, sometimes above ground; examples of rhizomes include potatoes and many grasses. Rhizomes contrast with arboreals like trees which in many cases send roots deep into the ground. Connolly frames what we will witness in the next chapter: that many people in today's world, from all walks of life, evince a capacity to find new ways to communicate and grow through differences and, thereby, to transform their ways of life however modestly in the larger scheme of things. They generate new roots in the never-ending human task of creating a dwelling, understood not just as having a roof over one's head (profound as that can be) but as a place of meaning. They do not do so *de novo*, nor wholesale. Their often spontaneous, intuitive doings are not necessarily in conflict with their prior roots although they are necessarily in tension with them.

For example, André Aciman (1994) portrays how roots can become looser *and* stronger, in a paradoxical sense that illuminates the idea of home in cosmopolitan perspective. Aciman's artful memoir recounts the life, over several generations, of a Jewish family in Alexandria, Egypt, from the late nineteenth century through the nationalistic expulsion of all non-Egyptians in 1956. The family is astonishing in its cast of personalities and dispositions: some individuals are pinched and fearful, others joyous; some close-minded, others hungry to engage the world; some bigoted, others tolerant; some parochial, others cosmopolitan in their fusion of openness and loyalty. Through his account, the picture of Aciman himself that emerges is of a figure secular in outlook and practice but respectful of religious tradition; a figure insightful about human weakness and yet humane in his rendering; a figure nostalgic for natal home (the tone of the book is often elegiac) but also free of it as evidenced in the reflective distance in his authorial voice. He has loosened his ties to many aspects of his family heritage. At the same time, he has rooted himself more deeply in them than ever before, precisely through perceiving their formative power in conjunction with grasping the many-sidedness of being at home in the world. He has culti-vated a dynamic sense of tradition he could not have articulated before, although it was clearly growing in him through the days of his upbringing.

Home has often meant a specified place or location with longstanding traditions and cultural roots. "My home is Chicago," "my home is on the south side of town," "my home is on the coast," "my home is the Fiji Islands." However, Aciman's memoir sheds light on the fact that home can denote a space not determined geographically but rather ideationally, spiritually, and imagi-natively. A person may feel more at home in an arena of the arts, of religion, or of a profession or vocation, than in a particular longitude and latitude. A person may feel equally at home on several platforms; consider the science teacher who feels deeply at home both in the realm of science and in her or his school and surrounding community. Either home can be intensely social, interactive, spontaneous, and fulfilling, even if also accompanied by tension, by an unsettled aspect given the unceasing tide of events, changes, voices, and implied questions (such as those about ethics and morality touched on above) that pour over the threshold of any home, anywhere today, in any place or space. In short, either home can generate a bounded though permeable locality, and thus ground a sense of reflective loyalty toward the local which is a necessary condition for a cosmopolitan orientation.[8]

In the previous chapter I touched briefly on Rabindranath Tagore's capacity to remain rooted and unrooted at the same moment – to leave and remain at home, in the terms of the present discussion. He was clearly at home in the universe of poems, no matter where they originated on planet earth. His love for poetry opened doors to interact with other poets from near and far (most famously, with W. B. Yeats), and he seems to have derived an extraordinary sense of fulfillment from dwelling in this realm of words, ideas, and emotions. He had other homes, too, such as his pioneering work as a founder of a well-known school that focused on aesthetic and what we would today call environmental education (O'Connell, 2007). As poet, educator, novelist, public speaker, and more, Tagore was able to cultivate a large horizon of hospitality to other people.

But the hypothetical science teacher mentioned above has a large horizon, too. If we were to ask her: where do you come from? she might reply: from many places. A family, a community, a nation; a school and community to which she is wedded; a love for science and for teaching it; a sense of teaching itself as a deep source of meaning and fulfillment; a set of longstanding human interests, perhaps film and sport, in which she loses herself in a spirit of trust and enjoyment; and perhaps more. In short, the teacher comes from the world, and brings that world with her. Even if two teachers, close colleagues and friends, say they come from the same places, still they do not do so in an identical way. Home and belonging have distinctive qualities for every educator, just as they do for every student. The possibilities for reflective loyalty to the local are no more preordained than are those for reflective openness to the world writ large.

Home and belonging also remain, for the teacher as for everyone else, subject to change, to pressure, and to unsettlement whether physical or spiritual in nature. In cosmopolitan perspective, the dual sides of tension and of home continually intersect. Anxiety and contentment, being adrift and being moored, fear and hospitality, vertigo and stability: a cosmopolitan orientation does not banish these conditions of risk and safety, of loss and gain. Instead, it highlights modes of generative response to them. Cosmopolitanism constitutes a longstanding response to the facts of mutual human influence that are impossible to prevent today, just as they were thousands of years ago when different groups first became aware of one another and instantaneously began to change. Cosmopolitanism embodies an attempt not just to accept this human situation but to turn it to creative, humane account.

The Teacher in the World, and the World in the Teacher

A thin line separates cosmopolitan thinking from romanticism. The former can move unawares from analysis, description, and inquiry into idealized, perhaps even utopian yearning. However, the most articulate expositors of philosophy as the art of living, from Confucius through Gournay and beyond, have struggled with a quite different thin line: that between complete despair and a realistic sense of hopefulness. They are appalled by the violence, injustice, stupidity, bigotry, and indifference they perceive in the world. While they do not generate a unified voice – one of their recurrent motifs is the danger of uncritical attempts at unity – they express their thought in ways that suggest it does make a difference how one responds to events, how one interacts with others, and how one dwells with oneself. In a sense, they take their point of departure from one of Marcus' paradoxical formulations: "Although everything happens at random, don't you, too, act at random" (Bk. X.28, quoted in Hadot, 1995, p. 212). A critic wants to reply: if all happens at random, surely my acts do too! But for Marcus, philosophy's power shines through here. Rather than conceiving life as a toss of the dice he means the direct opposite. The very fact that I can conceptualize randomness implies a space of freedom from determination and from caprice in the universe. It is not random that I can take up, or drop, the question of randomness.

This posture is not rationalistic. Marcus is not a precursor in any direct sense of René Descartes' famous claim that "I think, therefore I am." In philosophy as the art of living, the claim would be more along the lines of: I think, feel, wonder, fail, succeed, dream, analyze, owe my very being to nature and to my fellow humans, and do not know what will happen next – therefore I am. What the ancients conceived as practices of the self can help persons play a role in their own formation as well as participate that much more fully in life, however modest the local scale may be. Put another way, such practices can render life into a work of art, not in the sense of a finished product to put on display, but rather in Dewey's (1989) sense of an ongoing transaction with the world that can be marked by broader awareness and deepening insight into conditions and possibilities. For Dewey, "the work of art" is precisely that: a form of ongoing work, of effort, of interaction, of making sense, and of beginning again. There is nothing idealized in this perspective. It emerges from a penetrating, critical, and sympathetic examination of what people in any walk of life are capable of doing within the circumstances that prevail. For Dewey, art and artists (in the familiar sense of the terms) happen to show in a particularly instructive manner how persons can appreciate and participate creatively in all the phases of living. He would be the first to agree that countless teachers have shown the way here, too.

In this and the previous chapter I have highlighted the cosmopolitan accent in philosophy as the art of living. This focus illuminates why deliberative, responsive modes of listening, speaking, interacting, writing, and the like can assist people in realizing their personhood and in engaging others whose views and values may differ. These modes constitute an educational posture in the world, whether so-described or not. As such they are not merely a means to an end, though they serve that function, but rather enact a cosmopolitan orientation. They position people not just to tolerate others, as significant as that accomplishment is, but to learn from them, which means to permit them to influence one's life. This open door, or port, to their worlds does not mean abandoning outright previously held outlooks and values, nor does it mean blindly welcoming whatever comes through the door. Rather it means grasping the fact that those influences can never be halted. In the terms of this chapter, there is no end to change and unfathomability in the human. The very forms of resistance people put up attest to the reality of ceaseless external influence. Cosmopolitan arts of living assist people to play a role in determining the meaning and consequences that such influences will have on their lives.

Can people today really adopt such an orientation? Aren't the arts and practices addressed here for people with the leisure and resources to work them out? Aren't they necessarily reserved for an elite, as in some cases they were in parts of the ancient and early modern world? As we will see, the answer to these questions is firm if qualified: it is possible for anyone to enact them – a fact that gives rise in the first place to these arts and practices – but people will need support and one another to do so.

What about the reality of today's schools with their top-down accountability and bureaucratic structures that seem to render education into social sorting and job preparation, rather than human cultivation? What difference can pursuing the arts of living make to this state of affairs?

Very little has ever been made easy for teachers, today or in the past. At the same time, the historical record attests to the efficacy of every succeeding generation of teachers: many have made a marked difference in students' lives. The arts and outlooks examined here can, crucially, strengthen teachers' agency, an accomplishment with dynamic and endless ramifications for their continued influence in schools and other settings. Nothing has ever succeeded in smothering the human impulse to make and exchange meaning, which is another way to describe the work of all who educate. These remarks do not mean teachers can or should go it alone, so to speak. I intend my emphasis on their creativity – itself easy to overlook – to complement the important work researchers, policy-makers, reformers, and teachers themselves are doing to improve the concrete conditions in which they work.

What about the facts and methods that comprise the subject matter of education, from art to history to science? Where do the practices illustrated here fit into the teaching of these disciplines? Can they in any meaningful way become part of formal education? Chapter 5 responds to these questions also in a firm if qualified manner: any teacher and group of students, in any subject and at any level, can bring these practices to life. But doing so will involve becoming mindful of what it means to imagine life as an art – as a quest for meaning and as an appeal to develop people's possibilities. I believe these practices and arts are in fact alive and well on the ground, if not in so many words, including in many schools and classrooms. The challenge is learning to see them, which is a first step toward sustaining them. Taking the cosmopolitan prism in hand can help in this task.

4 Cultural Crossroads and Creativity

This chapter addresses ways in which people enact in their lives, if not in so many words, reflective openness to the new fused with reflective loyalty to the known. The account can benefit educators by providing a picture of what cosmopolitanism looks and sounds like in contemporary experience – including, perhaps, in their own. This picture can serve educators, in turn, in working toward the cosmopolitan-minded pedagogy this entire book is in process of framing. I also hope the chapter can be of use to researchers interested in teaching and education in a globalizing context, whom I encourage to take seriously the history and current trajectory of cosmopolitan studies.

Before beginning the inquiry, however, I must address a serious challenge to the very possibility of cosmopolitanism as an orientation.

Has Diversity Been Eclipsed in our Time?

To some observers, globalization undermines the conditions that render cosmopolitanism viable. Given today's mobility and migration patterns, they argue, concepts like "home" and "local" are losing their longstanding traction. The sheer momentum of physical movement, critics contend, combined with the psychological and cultural movement available through the internet and other media, are transforming human consciousness, its sense of time and place. To the extent that these claims are warranted, they may pull the rug out from under talk of cosmopolitanism and the local, as well as talk of a creative, meaning-making space between the local and the global. The global has infiltrated almost all localities today, or so some argue, dissolving not only traditional concepts of home and place – such as those addressed at the end of the previous chapter – but with them an authentic sense of diversity.

Cornelius Castoriadis conjures the prospect that genuine human diversity has faded away in our time:

> If we look at the life of the thirteenth century, passing from Chartres to Borobudur and from Venice to the Mayas, from Constantinople to Peking and from Kublai Khan to Dante, from the house of Maimonides at Cordoba

to Nara, and from the *Magna Carta* to the Byzantine monks copying Aristotle; compare this extraordinary diversity with the present state of the world, where countries are not really different from each other in terms of their present – which, as such, is everywhere the same – but only in terms of their past. *That* is what the developed world *is*.

(Castoriadis, quoted in Mehta, 2000, p. 636)

In a study of cultural transition in Hong Kong and Shanghai, Abbas (2000) pushes Castoriadis' view further by suggesting that many communities today appear to be converting their pasts into a commodity. They (or in some cases multinational corporations) develop what Abbas calls a "heritage industry" (p. 781) – theme parks, museums, spectacles, and historical districts to attract tourists and business – and meanwhile global economic forces work their will with respect to how people on the ground live. So-called "cultural diversity" boils down to the use of local languages – but infiltrated everywhere by English and other idioms thanks to the internet and related media – differences in food, a handful of old-time customs of greeting people, and the like.

These perspectives appear to render moot inquiry into cultural variability today, including through a cosmopolitan prism, as the world succumbs to an apparently unavoidable, homogenizing wave of globalization. Cultural pasts do differ markedly, but the cultural present, Castoriadis and other critics claim, with its world-saturating consumer products, internet services, factories and transport systems and more, has become "everywhere the same." As the writer Paul Morand remarks, commenting on the acceleration of history in our era: "La vitesse tue la couleur; le gyroscope, quand il tourne vite, fait du gris" (Speed annihilates color. The gyroscope, when it spins rapidly, turns everything grey) (quoted in Bruckner, 2000, p. 21, my translation). The prism of globalization, so it seems, flattens everything out.

One problem with such claims is the sheer difficulty of self-assessment. We are all too close to current trends to judge them and their consequences comprehensively. Furthermore, any student of the past that Castoriadis evokes knows that history is uncanny and cultural change not easy to diagnose. In my view, recent research on cosmopolitanism challenges fatalistic, death-of-diversity outlooks by revealing that cosmopolitan permeability both generates and sharpens expressions of variability. Some of the latter may lack the constancy of the traditions that Castoriadis highlights. But that fact does not mean they are by definition shallow and superficial, though many surely are ephemeral. This claim takes on added weight if we conceive culture – at least in some of its iterations – as an embodiment of creativity, whether at the familiar anthropological level wherein communities reconstruct practices or ideals, at the level of cultures of art (medicine, teaching, architecture, etc.) in which new forms and techniques evolve, or at the level of the individual person endeavoring to cultivate ("culturate") her or his life as meaningfully and seriously as circumstances permit. Later in the chapter I will suggest that culture so understood constitutes at all three levels an educational as well as creative experience.

It may be true that to perceive genuine cultural variability and creativity is harder today than in the thirteenth-century tableau Castoriadis picturesquely paints. Indeed, perhaps it is more difficult today than a mere fifty or even twenty-five years ago. Consequently, it comes as no surprise that commentators on the cosmopolitan urge a careful, nuanced look at the quotidian. For example, in remarks on the work of Clifford Geertz (an exceptional scholarly artisan of fine-grained renderings of culture), Tobin Siebers writes:

> As the world grows smaller, we may expect examples of ethnic diversity not to be isolated in remote jungles or on exotic islands but to be *growing* in our midst, whatever "our midst" comes to mean. This fact, Geertz explains, will require more imagination on our part, not the imagination to make up diversity but the imagination required to pick out subtle examples of it.
> (Siebers, 1993, pp. 43–44, my emphasis)

Nikos Papastergiadis (2007) argues that "to grasp the forms of cosmopolitan agency and community we need a different perspective on identity. One that is more attuned to subtlety" (p. 145). Ulrich Beck (2004, p. 447) adds a moral shading to this counsel when he writes that the research community, through detailed field-based studies, can help enhance global consciousness of the manifold, often low-key, always transforming manifestations of cosmopolitanism as it appears on the ground.

Furthermore, one could argue in response to Castoriadis that some of the very places he cites, from Borobudur to Constantinople, themselves featured vibrant cosmopolitan practices in the thirteenth century (not to mention in even earlier eras). Historical research has demonstrated a similar phenomenon in places as different as Alexandria (Egypt) from ancient times through the Ottomans (Jasanoff, 2005a; also see Aciman, 1994) and Odessa (Russia) under the long reign of the Czars (Richardson, 2008). It is simply not the case that the human past constituted a universe of pure cultures that has given way to a mongrel, superficial cultural present.

To this argument a critic might reply that the mere presence of a cosmopolitan ethos implies a dilution of distinctive culture, perhaps even its dissolution. The latter worry has triggered paranoid tribalism and nationalism across history. In response one could cite the experience of many Africans and Jews in diaspora. Time and again numerous individuals have enacted cosmopolitan sensibilities, at once retaining significant features of tradition, roots, and cultural continuity, and yet at the same time not just borrowing but deeply absorbing – and, indeed, sometimes championing – cultural traditions of the places in which they found themselves. In so doing, they also *influenced* those traditions in substantive, enduring ways.

Consider the experience of people of African descent in the Americas, which has resulted among other things in imaginative, reconstructed, and renewed forms of art, of music, of religious practice, of community life, and more, all of which added significantly to local cultural creativity (Du Bois, 1987; Nwankwo, 2005;

Wardle, 2000). The fact that these contributions were sometimes met with indifference by the majority (depending on locale) does not gainsay their enduring significance, discernible today across cultural life in the region and beyond. In addition, although often dwelling under oppressive conditions – for example, slavery – people nonetheless conceived *their* sense of the local, *their* sources of meaning, which ultimately can never be determined from without.

Consider the experience of many Jews in Germany, in which over the centuries they often became deeply engaged in Germanic literary, artistic, philosophical, and other traditions and contributed vitally to them – even as they were rejected as "un-German" by many "natives" whose grasp of those very traditions was shallow and fragmented (Elon, 2002; for an analysis of the experience of Jews in the United States, with their often complex journey of straddling longstanding tradition and cosmopolitan openness, see Heilman and Cohen, 1989). The dissident writer Georg Konrad captures the complexity and ambiguity in these experiences in the title of his autobiography: *A Guest in My Own Country: A Hungarian Life* (2007). As a reader senses before turning to the first page, "guest" need not imply "being welcome," a point which Konrad sure enough demonstrates repeatedly and painfully. And yet, he describes his account not as a Jewish but rather as a *Hungarian* life that unfolded in *his* rather than someone else's country. Despite numerous opportunities, some invitational, others coercive (the Communist regime wanted him out of its hair), he never emigrated from his country.

The fact that people of African descent and Jews in diaspora have historically been discriminated against or oppressed mirrors the recurring, sometimes violent persecution of cosmopolitan-minded people everywhere, whether at the hands of a Hitler, Pol Pot, Stalin, or Mao Tse-Tung, or at the hands of regional tribalism. The experience of these targeted people highlights the contrast between cosmopolitanism *and* the local, considered in symbiotic relation, and parochialism *and* homogeneity. As argued throughout this book, cosmopolitanism conflicts not with local culture as such but with the view that culture can only survive inside a bubble.

As also emphasized repeatedly, there are dynamic tensions, and real losses and gains, that accompany the movement of reflective openness and reflective loyalty. Not only is this cultural ledger hard to tabulate, but the ledger itself keeps transforming. What was at one time considered a loss – of a particular belief, practice, or ideal – morphs into a gain, an encounter with the larger world for which one is now grateful. The opposite appears to happen just as often. Perhaps what is most typical is the realization that most changes embody aspects of loss and gain. There is no halting this experience but there are, as highlighted here, better and worse ways of responding to it.

Cosmopolitanism casts light on why the idea of culture does not in itself denote the walled-in or the self-contained. To be sure, at any place and at any time, and without exception as far as I can determine, culture can operate in a closed manner especially when pressures from without increase. This point holds for culture understood at all three levels: sociolinguistic communities, social practices, and individuals. But this trajectory is never preordained. Furthermore, as emphasized in Chapter 2 cosmopolitanism is not a totalizing ideology. As an orientation it dwells itself in tension with countless other modes of allegiance. Its expressions are not pre-scripted, its ethos not fixed in form, and its responsiveness to the world not predetermined.

The first section that follows discusses historical precursors of today's modes of inquiry into the cosmopolitan. These literary precursors, most of them multi-lingual and well-traveled, demonstrate how longstanding has been cosmopolitan curiosity about the world. Their focus complements time-honored cosmopoli-tan concerns of philosophy as the art of living. The second section links results from recent field-based, anthropologically minded research with the philosophical anthropology characteristic of reflection on the art of living. Current research documents why expressions of the art of living and their associated, ever-dynamic practices can emerge spontaneously and organically. They do not require prior ideological commitments such as the particular view of humanity's place in the cosmos that marked some ancient Stoic thought. At the same time, their very spontaneity can render them vulnerable and fragile, which is where formal educational development and support come into play.

The third and final section builds on the previous analysis in order to clarify the notion of cultural creativity that underlies cosmopolitanism. We will see that cosmopolitanism is not an identity per se. That term can conjure images of unchanging sameness. Cosmopolitanism refers, instead, to the continuity across space and time of individual and community integrity. Integrity denotes not fixity but, in figurative terms, an ever-permeable membrane that retains bodily whole-ness even while undergoing transformation (the latter typically subtle and piecemeal). To achieve continuity implies creative effort that is responsive to changes in the world.

Cosmopolitanism invites a reconstruction of the idea of culture itself. It generates a view that can do justice to the porosity of individuals and groups alike. Thus, in the course of the discussion I will respond to the criticism that as a concept cosmopolitanism lacks sufficient definition to function as a serviceable interpretive frame in fieldwork and, by extension, in educational work. The fact it lacks an airtight definition does not mean it constitutes an empty conceptual cell. On the contrary, the plasticity of the concept reveals its analytic strength and potential, or so I will argue.

Precursors to Contemporary Research on Cosmopolitan Practices

Appreciating Critically "This Great World of Ours"

Today's field-based research on cosmopolitanism on the ground has a rich ancestry it can draw upon with respect to both cultural substance and research methodology. Consider anthropologically minded writers such as Herodotus (*c*.484–*c*.425 BCE), Ibn Battuta (1304–*c*.1368 CE), Ibn Khaldun (1332–1406

CE), and Michel de Montaigne (1533–1592, whom we met in previous chapters). The first three named were born and raised in cosmopolitan settings in, respectively, what are now Turkey, Morocco, and Tunisia. Herodotus was a polymath, interested in culture, geography, politics, natural science, and more. He traveled widely throughout the eastern Mediterranean world. On the basis of his experience and knowledge he wrote the famed *Histories* which center around the Persian-Greek wars of 490 and 480–479 BCE and which contain extensive, absorbing accounts of customs and traditions from throughout the then vast Persian Empire.

Ibn Khaldun was born in Tunis to a family that had for many generations lived and flourished in the Andalusia region of Spain. He voyaged extensively across North Africa, the Middle East, and Spain, often in the employ of various political authorities. On the basis of his experience as well as sustained scholarship, he wrote his renowned *Muqaddimah* (Prolegomena) which is the first volume of his *Kitab al-Ibar* (Universal History). The text fuses anthropology, sociological analysis, economics, historical research, pioneering reflections on historiography and philosophy of history, and more, and includes a particular focus on the history of the Maghreb. It is regarded as one of the most trenchant versions of what are today called the social sciences published in the medieval world (Issawi, 1987, pp. ix–x, 1–2; Zubaida, 2002, p. 33). Ibn Khaldun's published autobiography, *Al-Ta'rīf bi-Ibn Khaldūn wa-Rihlatihi Gharbān wa-Sharqān* (Voyage from the West and East – the conjunction "and" triggering in itself cosmopolitan overtones), contains a wealth of information about the cultural world of the Mediterranean during his era.

Ibn Battuta, born in Tangier, was a scholar, judge, and one of the pre-modern world's greatest all-time travelers. Over a roughly thirty-year-long period he voyaged some 73,000 miles (Dunn, 2005, p. 3) by sailboat, horse, cart, and foot through North Africa, West and East Africa, Eastern Europe, the Middle East, across Asia through India, and all the way to China. He detailed his observations in his *Rihla* (Travels), which remains a priceless account of cultural life in much of the "known" fourteenth-century world, an era that Castoriadis evokes.[1]

As with Herodotus and Ibn Khaldun, for Ibn Battuta virtually every aspect of human affairs becomes an object of curiosity and reflection. The temper of all three authors is difficult to categorize, not unlike the human diversity they encountered. In their individualized ways they are worldly, parochial, tolerant, judgmental, amused, aghast, and above all taken with the varied expressions of what it means to be human that they witnessed.

Montaigne did not travel as widely as these figures, although like them he was sometimes heavily involved in politics and practical affairs. For example, he served both Catholic and Protestant kings of France by negotiating several peace treaties during the religious wars that plagued the country (and Europe writ large) in his era. His service echoes that of Ibn Khaldun. Among other things, Ibn Khaldun served as an ambassador to the Christian court of Pedro the Cruel in Spain (at a time of near permanent warfare between Muslims and Christians for control of the peninsula), and later helped directly in negotiations with the dreaded warrior Timur, at that time besieging Damascus. Montaigne published his finely attuned observations derived from an extensive journey through Germany and Italy. He was a voracious reader of the likes of Herodotus, as well as of numerous other traveler-scholars (a category difficult to define, or even conceive, from the perspective of today's academic specializations). Montaigne drew heavily upon these writers' insights about cultural difference to fashion his cosmopolitan viewpoint.[2]

For example, his essay "On the Cannibals" (1991, pp. 228–241) constitutes a formidable critique of so-called civilized society – to wit, in Europe and especially his native France – but also of so-called uncivilized society – in this case, sixteenth-century Brazil. For Montaigne, civilization denotes not a particular level of material or artistic culture but rather the systematic absence of cruelty (Bouriau, 2007, p. 77). Thus the "simplest" society can be more civilized than the most economically protean and expansive. Montaigne pummels French pretentiousness and artfully shows how, through the eyes of a Brazilian, the inequity in French society can be seen as abominable. At the same time, he does not romanticize or idolize the tribes who dwell, as some would put it, close to nature (a quintessential romantic trope). He points out that they are unable to question and thereby alter their violent customs such as incessant war, torture and killing. In metaphorical terms, Montaigne takes a page from his anthropologically minded precursors in emphasizing that no culture is a mirror of heaven. All are characterized by complexity, by tensions among various internal values, and by an ability to change juxtaposed with head-in-the-sand tendencies (a point underscored in Chapter 1, p. 13, in the discussion of Achebe's *Things Fall Apart*). This perspective applies to culture at the level of sociolinguistic communities, social practices, and individuals. Montaigne is unsparing in his condemnation of stronger material cultures who seek to dominate others, referring specifically to the notorious conduct of the Spanish conquistadores (see his essay "On Coaches," 1991, pp. 1017–1037). He regrets that the first, inevitable contact between Europe and the Americas did not occur in the days of the ancient Greek philosophers, who he argues "would have appreciated them better than we do" (p. 232).

The writings of Herodotus, Ibn Battuta, Ibn Khaldun, Montaigne, and others of their eras have been criticized for being larded with hearsay and conjecture. Rather than being proto-anthropologists or proto-historians, critics have alleged that they are unreliable reporters and as such their writing cannot be of service to scholarship. One suspects that Herodotus et al. would find the charge amusing, as did, it seems, the Parisian authorities who determined the location of the statue of Montaigne on the Rue d'École. Montaigne appears lost in thought with a contemplative smile on his face – and he is placed *across the street* from the Sorbonne. The passer-by is left to ponder whether the deliberate gap implies scholarly exile for Montaigne (who certainly does not seem in a resentful mood) or a loss for the academy. Stephen Toulmin's (1990) provocative answer is that philosophy and social inquiry took the wrong turn when they chose to follow, metaphorically speaking, the methods of Descartes rather than those of Montaigne. Green (2008) suggests the wrong turn in the academy occurred when what he calls Thucydides' positivism ousted Herodotus' cosmopolitan historical-anthropology.

As we will see later in the chapter, the criticism leveled at these precursors mirrors questions raised about the utility of today's research on cosmopolitanism. Their responses to such criticism remain as pertinent as their distinctive inquiries. They understood and respected scholarly standards. Herodotus addresses directly in the *Histories* the evidential distinction between witnessing (Greek *opsis*) and hearsay (Gr. *akoé*) (Flory, 1987; Green, 2008). Montaigne takes pains at the beginning of "On the Cannibals" to establish the reliability of his sources, to such an extent that, as Caroline Locher (1976) demonstrates, the essay can be read as a sustained meditation on the nature of evidence and sound argument. Subsequent research has borne out most of the myriad details in Ibn Battuta's accounts (Mackintosh-Smith, 2002, pp. xvi–xviii; Dunn, 2005, pp. 313–318). Ibn Khaldun writes in detail about questions of historiography. He elucidates sources of error such as partisanship, over-confidence in one's sources, a failure to look at context, and a propensity to exaggerate (in Issawi, 1987, pp. 27–33).

These writers reflected seriously about the meaning and place of evidence, judgment, critical balance, and the like. They were aware of deploying, at times, suspect accounts and tales. But they also show that these very sources reveal human sensibilities and hopes that mark a particular era. In the hands of a thoughtful observer, the sources open up truths about the human that can enhance the interpretive lens brought to bear on hard facts. Stewart Flory (1987) remarks of Herodotus: "[He] knows the difference between truth and falsehood, but he attempts to demonstrate, often in a playful way, that what actually happened – the truth – was trivial compared with an admittedly fictional story that expresses a deeper kind of truth" (p. 21). Herodotus often juxtaposes seemingly contradictory reports. At one moment he describes Themistocles as a wise general; in the next the man comes across as a real rascal. At one moment King Xerxes laughs with pride and joy at his vast army marching by to invade Greece. In the next, he weeps uncontrollably at the thought that in a hundred years not one soldier will still be alive (in Flory, 1987, pp. 17–18). Herodotus consistently discloses human inconsistency.

Taken together, the highly detailed reports of these figures reveal the ubiquity of "the fluidity of mixture" (Papastergiadis, 2007, p. 140): the fact that from the very dawn of culture people in many parts of the world have interacted with and absorbed ideas from other groups. In some cases the process has been voluntary, in others it has been the outcome of conquest from without, and in still others it is not easy to isolate causes from the sheer momentum of events. In the swirl of these processes can be seen the fusion of what I have called reflective openness to the new and reflective loyalty to the known. This cosmopolitan experience goes back a long way in time and space.

The symbiotic relation between the local and the cosmopolitan can be discerned in these writers themselves. At no point, as far as I am aware, do they call themselves cosmopolitan. What *is* cosmopolitan about them is precisely their ability to traverse the space between the far and the near, the general and the particular, the universal and the neighborhood. They neither deprecate nor disguise their local sensibilities – sometimes, warts and all (see, for example, Montaigne's essay "On Experience," 1991, pp. 1207–1269). They are loyal to home, to all that gave them their start in life, to all that allows them to have a reflective standpoint in the first place. But their respect for tradition does not render them traditionalists. They are able to take seriously different perspectives, mores, and philosophies of life – so much so that Herodotus, for example, was chided by some of his contemporaries as a "barbarian lover" (i.e., admirer of non-Greek speakers) for his sympathetic treatment of various Persian customs (Flory, 1987, p. 21; Hartog, 1988, p. 204). In their writing, these figures dwell in the world educationally: in varying degrees they learn *from* and *with* the world they observe, interact with, and read about. They are neither parochial nor universalistic in their ethos, despite the all-too-human fact that at times they are judgmental and dismissive (they are not saints). Each of them, in a distinctive and cosmopolitan fashion, holds in hand the local and the global.

Novelistic Enactments

Alongside these historic accounts, the arts provide helpful instruction for today's field-based and educational work on cosmopolitanism. For example, Montesquieu's *Lettres Persanes* (Persian Letters, published 1721) is a novel-in-letters featuring two Persian noblemen, Uzbek and Rica, who travel from modern-day Iran to Europe and take up residence in Paris. They write home kaleidoscopic, moralistic reports of what they see and hear, expressing disgust and admiration for various French customs. They also use these letters to question and comment upon the cultural, political, and religious traditions of their native land. While Montesquieu clearly intended to lampoon what he saw as his countrymen's foibles and weaknesses, he also makes plain his sense of the culture's abiding strengths – and all of this while doing the same with regards to seventeenth-century Persia. In cosmopolitan fashion he uses ideas, ideals, and customs from one culture as a standpoint to criticize those of the other. He moves back and forth in an interpretive dialectic and, through the voices of his two Persian commentators, demonstrates what it can mean for people from different traditions to move closer and closer apart as well as further and further together. The reader, in effect, is invited to become Persian and French, French and Persian, Persian-French, French-Persian – as well as none of the above, while in moments of transition and uncertainty as to what to think.

   At the same time, Montesquieu makes plain that understanding self and other does not come easily and in fact is difficult to achieve. The letters are replete with finely rendered cultural misreadings as well as signs of how hard it can be to grasp one's way of perceiving the world. At many points, and in many ways, the two chief letter-writers seem unable to perceive their own attitudes – much as Montesquieu's very project expresses his recognition that *he* cannot easily discern his own cultural outlooks. Paul Gilroy (2004, pp. 77–79) argues that these and other steps position Montesquieu to avoid what today might be called orientalism or eurocentrism (also see Venturi, 1972, p. 11). For Gilroy, Montesquieu's imagination carries him beyond the bounds of his own or indeed of any culture. He does not achieve a neutral or view-from-nowhere stance but rather one in which he can see culture for the shaping force that it is in human lives. It is a force not to be condemned or extolled but rather to be reckoned with.

Neither Montesquieu nor any of the writers mentioned in this chapter presume to be final authorities on their or any other culture. Their aim is not to defend or disparage but to hold in relief, in the spirit that such a project can be educative – and also funny. No doubt in their day as in ours much talk of culture lacked a sense of humor, as if humor is superficial or dismissive rather than miraculous – where do people get the spirit of humor in the first place? – and expressive of the human – comedy being the other side of tragedy. Malcomson (1998) concludes on the basis of his observations of humanity that "an attractive cosmopolitanism would have to have a sense of tragedy, a sense of humor, and a sense of limits – that is, a strong sense of history" (p. 244). Immanuel Kant expresses all three aspects in his writing on cosmopolitanism. For example, he prefaces his influential *Perpetual Peace* (1963b) by recalling that he took his title from a Dutch tavern sign upon which a burial ground had been painted. Kant pokes fun at his own project (he evidently enjoyed tavern life) – while also symbolizing the fundamental truth that without peace, war will send people to a premature death.

Montesquieu illuminates in his *Lettres Persanes* the symbiotic relation between the local and the cosmopolitan as well as how that relation can help steer one away from their parochial and universalistic alternatives. His orientation evokes the truth that I can only know myself if I come to know others, just as a community can only know itself if it comes to know others. His widely read book inspired a number of like-minded social commentaries in which authors enacted the cosmopolitan method of deploying multiple cultural perspectives for the purpose of mutual criticism and understanding. Like Montesquieu these writers made use of the dialogical form of letter-writing, to such an extent that he remarked later in his life that "mes *Lettres Persanes* apprirent à faire des romans en lettres" (My *Persian Letters* showed others how to write letter-novels) (Montesquieu, 1991, p. 513, *Pensées* no. 1621). There are, for example, Boyer d'Argens' *Lettres Juives* (Jewish Letters, published 1738) and *Lettres Chinoises* (Chinese Letters, 1739), and Poullain de Saint-Foix's *Lettres d'une Turque à Paris, écrites à sa sœur* (Letters from a Turk in Paris, Written to his Sister, 1730) which was reprinted several times in conjunction with Montesquieu's text. Another pioneering example is Françoise de Graffigny's *Lettres d'une Péruvienne* (Letters from a Peruvian Woman, 1747). The chief protagonist in the text is an Incan captured and sent to Europe, who writes letters addressed primarily to her future husband back in Peru. The letters contain often biting critiques of local French customs including the treatment of women, juxtaposed with the protagonist's increasing awareness of the limitations in traditional life back home (for discussion see Mallinson's introduction to Graffigny, 2002). Once more the lesson appears to be not that some cultures have better traditions than others but that all *have* traditions and that these traditions, in principle, can both limit and liberate.

In the same time period, writers on the other side of the English Channel developed cosmopolitan modes of social inquiry and commentary. They, too, took inspiration from Montesquieu's oeuvre, as can be seen in Oliver Goldsmith's *The Citizen of the World* (1760–1761, and quickly translated and published in France). Goldsmith's text contains the letters of a fictionalized Chinese philosopher, Lien Chi Altangi, who writes home from London with detailed accounts of English mores and customs, ranging from what he sees as the ridiculous to the impressive. Like Montesquieu, who read deeply in the available sources on Persian history and culture, Goldsmith did the same with regards to China. He jokingly refers to himself, in a letter about his book, as "the Confucius of Europe" (in Smith, 1926, p. ix). He aspires to frame Lien Chi's sensibility through the lens of his reading rather than uncritically convert him into an ersatz Englishman. Thus the letters also contain various critical observations, pro and con, about Chinese culture (Smith-Ponthieu, 1971). Smith (1926, pp. 132–148) provides an annotated summary of works in this genre that likely were known to Goldsmith and perhaps to Montesquieu before him, such as the influential book of pseudo-letters entitled *The Turkish Spy*, written and published by Giovanni Paolo Marana in 1687.[3]

Goldsmith's accomplishment, like those of the other worldly writers mentioned here, raises educational questions. For example, how *do* people learn about – or "take in" – the lineaments of another tradition or cultural inheritance? How were Herodotus, Ibn Khaldun, and Montesquieu able to see the world from contrasting perspectives, even if imperfectly? From a cosmopolitan perspective, this education can become as natural as learning about one's own natal roots. Such a process would be particularly true in settings where multicultural interaction is everyday, peaceful, and indeed expected. In some cases persons can autodidactically enter into other viewpoints and inhabit them in thoughtful, serious-minded ways. This experience can result, for example, from intensive, long-term reading in another tradition of thought and life, or from living and working in a part of the world new to the person. In still other cases formal education – a combination of rich curriculum and thoughtful teachers – may be necessary. These familiar processes do not imply a person must abandon original orientations even though they do necessitate a degree of metamorphosis.

A related question is: On what basis can one meaningfully deploy another person's or culture's viewpoint to criticize one's own, or use one's own to criticize those of others? From a cosmopolitan perspective this basis is ever dynamic. It is incomplete and imperfect, but also wondrous and efficacious. There are countless instances across historical time and space, such as those touched on above, of an "outsider" offering incisive, right-to-the-nub insights about another person or community (or era). Commentators as different as Alexis de Tocqueville (for example, in his writing on the culture of the United States) and Rabindranath Tagore (for example, in his essays on cultures of the West) come to mind.[4]

Moreover, it appears to be the case everywhere that from the moment two or more viewpoints intersect, the process of taking different standpoints becomes unstoppable. For many persons, at least in a variety of instances, it seems to become spontaneous, organic, and as natural as breathing. Some people just do try to see themselves through the eyes of others rather than solely the other way round, even if they may not acknowledge the impulse. Their motivation may be curiosity, anxiety, compassion, or fear; it may express sheer habit. From a cosmopolitan perspective, it is possible to become more deliberative and focused in this process. Put another way, the process can be enacted in better and worse forms, which introduces again the issue of education.

Cosmopolitanism urges us to remember the fact that people have *reasons* for their thoughts and ideas (cf. Oakeshott, 1989, pp. 20, 35). It will be impossible to access those reasons, be they weak and shallow or be they wise and insightful, if the assumption reigns that ideas merely have *causes* (whether sociological or biological). A better operating procedure is to consider the possible relations between reasons and causes, or between reasons and contexts. Ideas always emerge from particular settings but cannot be exhaustively explained by them. Thomas Schlereth (1997) notes that "not only are ideas acted upon, but also they act on the society in which they are operative" (xiv). The point holds for cosmopolitan ideas as much as for any others.

Cosmopolitanism on the Ground Today

Method and the Cosmopolitan Prism

As mentioned in Chapter 1, research on cosmopolitanism is proliferating today as scholars examine the concept and deploy it to make sense of various features of contemporary social life. Kleingeld and Brown (2006) provide a helpful heuristic for approaching much of the literature. They refer to political, moral, cultural, and economic cosmopolitanism. While their framework is useful theoretically, a broader conceptual and methodological tableau is needed to do justice to cosmopolitanism's diverse expressions on the ground. In this section I show why by considering concrete, particularized studies of cosmopolitan views and practices. However, before examining them let me address several methodological questions the answers to which may make a difference in how one approaches the research literature.

In some of its longstanding versions, cosmopolitanism foregrounds human similarities as a springboard to transnational and trans-cultural solidarity. Commentators spotlight universal features of culture: the ritualized observance of matters pertaining to birth and death, to relations between men and women, to interaction between the young and the old. They point to the worldwide prevalence of religion, however diversely expressed, as well as of the arts of dance, song, painting, sculpture, and film. They emphasize human vulnerability to violence, environmental degradation, and economic shocks that reverberate around the globe. They point out that every human being shares a common biological lineage reaching back to the very instant when life began on the planet. These and other features of humanity constitute a basis, or so some argue, for establishing cosmopolitan solidarities in a world marked by injustice, war, and persistent uncertainty.

In contrast, other commentators suggest that cosmopolitanism implies that solidarity between peoples depends upon acknowledging cultural variability. Rather than highlighting shared conditions, practices, or predicaments, these critics conceive cosmopolitanism as a way of establishing deeper recognition and respect for fundamental differences. Rather than dissolving or overlooking distinctiveness, cosmopolitanism creates productive distance from values, which in turn allows, or so some argue, for more authentic modes of mutual dwelling.

Costa (2005) rightly observes that there exists "no precise set of normative claims that unify all cosmopolitan positions" (p. 258). A reader of the literature also discovers that there is no hard-and-fast descriptive agreement about the concept's scope. These facts help account for why scholars in the field deploy so many different qualifiers to capture their foci and questions. The distinctions range from "actually existing" (Malcomsom, 1998) and "rooted" cosmopolitanism (Appiah 2005, 2006) to "discrepant," "environmental," "layered," "realistic," "aesthetic," "embedded," "postcolonial," "situated," "banal," "abject," and "vernacular" cosmopolitanism. Such qualifiers differ from possible theoretical constructs such as "Buddhist cosmopolitanism," "Polynesian cosmopolitanism," or "Western cosmopolitanism" – all of which in fact obfuscate if not contradict what is distinctive about the core idea.[5] Unlike these neologisms, qualifiers such as "vernacular" and "embedded" spotlight specific relations between the particular and the universal. The terms hold in generative tension reflective loyalty to the familiar and reflective openness to the strange, accenting evolving modes of permeability and porosity.

Within many of today's qualifiers are further gradations of meaning. For example, scholars refer to "strong" and "weak," "thick" and "thin," or "strict" and "moderate" versions of cosmopolitan thought and action. As indicated previously, the problems as well as possibilities cosmopolitanism is said to address are also multiplying today, ranging from the political to the cultural, economic, artistic, and educational.

At first glance, these facts might render the concept suspect as an analytic tool. In Lewis Carroll's tale, *Sylvie and Bruno Concluded*, several characters consider the ingredients of what they think the most useful map of all would be. They conclude that such a map would have to be literally as big as the world itself. Their experience mirrors the difficulty of mapping the literature on cosmopolitanism. It also haunts the history of the concept: in its impulse to consider humanity in both its generality and particularity, its gesture may turn out to be vacuous.

Montaigne glossed this danger in his quip that French education produces people who know a little about everything and nothing about anything (1991, p.163). A fellow countryman, Honoré de Balzac, suggested some centuries later that this outcome bottoms out in indifference. "The Parisian is so interested in everything," he wrote, "that he ends up being interested in nothing" (in Fojas,

2005, p. 50). Analogues to Montaigne's and Balzac's barbs can be found in many cultures and eras, and they foreground today's debates about cultural cosmopolitanism (see Chapter 1, p. 11). Tzvetan Todorov contrasts what he calls a genuine "dialogue of culture" with a superficial "eclecticism and comparitivism" marked by "the capacity to love everything a little, of flaccidly sympathizing with each option without embracing any" (in Mehta, 2000, p. 638). In a related vein, Pascal Bruckner (2000) contends that the celebrated World Wide Web, despite the enormous window on the cosmos that it opens, can erode rather than substantiate moral sensibilities. It can become "la forme la plus désincarnée de la communication. D'où l'étrange jubilation que procurent ces machines: n'être avec personne tout en étant avec n'importe qui" (the most disembodied mode of communication conceivable. From that fact wings the weird thrill these machines provide: to be with *anyone* but not *with* someone) (Bruckner, 2000, p. 25, my translation). In brief, cosmopolitanism stretches its hand out far and wide only to find, or so it may seem, that it is grasping air.

Some researchers express frustration with what they perceive as intellectual disorder in the field. For example, Zlatko Skrbis and co-authors (2004, pp. 115–116) criticize what they see as vagueness and slipperiness in their peers' use of the concept. Among other things, this feature entrenches in their view what Beck (2002, p. 97) identifies as a problem of comparability across studies. The authors take issue with James Clifford's claim that no "coherent cluster of experiences" could ever be neatly ascribed to cosmopolitanism, which by its very nature (or so Clifford argues) will have many "discrepant" expressions (in Cheah and Robbins, 1998, pp. 362, 365). Skrbis et al. criticize Pollock and his colleagues for their view (2000, p. 577) that it would be "uncosmopolitan" to try to cement the terms of cosmopolitanism. Skrbis et al. dub this posture "anti-empirical" (2004, p. 118). They describe what they see as several limitations in the empirical and theoretical literature. These include: (1) a continued indeterminacy in the concept's meaning, (2) the lack of a clear identification of who is and who is not cosmopolitan in outlook and conduct, and (3) the absence of a fleshed-out taxonomy of cosmopolitan dispositions. They agree that the concept has a necessary "fluidity and complexity" but that it is susceptible to greater precision through careful empirical work (p. 118). They point to how social science has succeeded over time, in their view, in refining complex concepts such as social class and ethnicity, and that there is no prima facie reason for presuming such success cannot be had with cosmopolitanism.

Other critics fuse their concerns about a perceived lack of scholarly precision in the field with political complaints. For example, David Harvey (2000) argues that cosmopolitanism "has acquired so many nuances and meanings as to negate its putative role as a unifying ethic around which to build the requisite international regulatory institutions that would ensure global economic, ecological, and political security in the face of an out-of-control free-market liberalism" (p. 529). Harvey's remarks echo criticisms alluded to previously: that cosmopolitanism, like the fashion magazine that bears its name, constitutes a shallow, aestheticized, and politically disengaged posture.

In the face of such concerns, why do scholars persist in deploying the concept cosmopolitanism? Why are there more and more inquirers joining them? Why do they continue to coin new qualifiers to accompany the concept? A number of possible explanations come to mind. For one thing, some inquirers worry as much about the drive for what Harvey calls "a unifying ethic" as they do about run-amok capitalism. As a contrast to the latter they posit not unifying postures but rather terms like communication, interaction, dialogue, modesty, patience, faith, and hope. The issue is not unity, they suggest, but literally remaining in touch so that people address problems as well as possibilities mindful of others whose values, customs, and yearnings may differ. In the terms of this book, the challenge is to learn to move closer and closer apart and further and further together. This dynamic process requires not unity in values as much as it does recognizing the very fact that all human beings are valuers. They share the capacity to value and, through education, can come to share the capacity to reflect upon value.[6]

Many scholars in the field appear to be drawn to cosmopolitanism by its long-standing hospitality to intellectual, moral, aesthetic, and cultural diversity. The term presupposes variability in individuals and communities. It would vanish like difference itself were homogeneity to rule in human outlook and practice. Thus these scholars challenge the claim that cosmopolitanism is synonymous with universalism. As we will see below, they appear to deploy the concept because, for them, it allows for a supple, nuanced approach to the complexity and richness in human modes of life. Some scholars are so impressed by the historical vicissitudes yet also sheer endurance of the concept that they find, as Camilla Fojas (2005, p. 6) notes, that adding a qualifier is the best way to negotiate the concept's semantic challenges. Other writers do not want to dissolve the term's ambiguities but rather seek means for representing and expressing them. Bruce Robbins suggests that many contemporary novelists are focusing on the "tone" of cosmopolitanism in human affairs (1999, p. 79). In this light, the proliferation of qualifiers reflects not confusion but sensitivity to context, that to get things right matters more than taxonomic regularity.

The use of qualifiers also mirrors the fact that scholars from many disciplines and interdisciplinary configurations are examining cosmopolitanism. It may not only be unrealistic to expect them to reach unity in theoretical outlook but also limiting, as new aspects of the concept and of its applications continue to emerge and require theoretical creativity. It also bears adding that the field of empirical research remains sufficiently new and unmapped that scholars quite naturally struggle to conceive suitable concepts and language to frame what they are seeing, hearing, and thinking. Some clearly appreciate what they perceive as an open-ended dimension to the concept, since this creates intellectual space for framing new forms of human interaction for which nobody, or so it seems, has yet developed a description, much less an interpretation. In short, if the phenomena are in transition, then so must the concept be that trails behind them.

I sympathize with critics who point out that the term is sometimes employed as no more than a catch-all for an astonishing array of conjectures and hypotheses.

I agree that some of the debates seem to generate more heat than light – more "din than sense" as Montaigne (1991. p. 192) remarked about some of the writing in his era. Perhaps it is not appropriate to refer at all to a field of research on cosmopolitanism, but rather to an ever-shifting, often ill-fitting assembly of inquiries.

For me the unsettled quality of the concept feels invitational and true to life. It seems to me that the richness of the writing that can be found in the literature renders it sufficiently robust to facilitate the sort of work investigators are trying to undertake. The concept provides the non-ideological precision that Aristotle long ago advocated with respect to concepts and their relation to the objects of inquiry. In his view, a concept ought to embody that degree of specificity and boundedness, which also means of generality and openness, necessary to do justice to the phenomenon in question. Aristotle himself, were he to reappear miraculously among us, might criticize the field's handling of its core term. But he would reject the alleged priority of theory over lived reality, with its consequence that scholars should not look at the world and try to understand it until they have "finished" their theoretical work. Furthermore, many concepts today continue to carry the weight of contrasting if not competing meanings and yet have remained useful for purposes of research, understanding, and teaching. Consider concepts such as moral, artistic, and democratic, as well as concepts such as education and curriculum. Echoing Aristotle once more, a key factor in the intellectual vitality of a field appears to be whether scholars characterize their uses of core concepts sufficiently well, which is a matter among other things of capacity, preparation, temperament, and tenacity.

Tales from the Field

The recent field-based studies I will touch on in this section do not deploy the idiom of the art of living which formed the structure of Chapters 2 and 3. All the same the studies illustrate a cosmopolitan orientation in ways that mirror these ancient perspectives. The analysis here will be suggestive rather than conclusive. It would take a larger canvas to do justice to each study as well as to the range of current research on cosmopolitanism. My hope is to portray images of cosmopolitanism on the ground that can illuminate for educators some of the experiences circulating in their classrooms, schools and communities.

The research commented upon below could be productively viewed through broad political, sociological, juridical, and other theoretical and programmatic lenses. However, what can be learned from the studies cannot be accounted for solely through these familiar modes of classification and explanation. Put another way, it is certainly possible to treat cosmopolitanism as a proposed solution to contemporary problems generated by globalization and other large forces. This defensible approach allows one to deploy cosmopolitanism as a tool or instrument for analysis and reform. But it is also possible to regard a cosmopolitan outlook not as a solution to anything – as if, to pose the matter polemically, life were solely an engineering problem – but rather as a way of living, or way of being, that answers to life's unimagined possibilities as well as its all too determinant predicaments. Accordingly, my accent in the remarks that follow will be on the artfulness of people as they respond to varying circumstances, conditions, and tensions.

For example, Huon Wardle (2000) undertook extensive ethnographic study of the philosophies of life and daily experience of economically downtrodden residents in a neighborhood in Kingston, Jamaica. Although leading an often uncertain, hand-to-mouth material existence, the residents enjoy a highly creative cultural life pivoting around rituals of birth, death, friendship, and religion. At the same time they exhibit, in highly diverse ways, an awareness of and openness to influences from elsewhere which they creatively incorporate into their own quotidian repertoires of face-to-face interaction. Many families have one or more members who have gone "to the world" – migrated to the United States or the United Kingdom to work for some years, sending back funds and eventually, in many cases, returning to restart their lives in the neighborhood. Wardle is struck by the residents' capacity to cultivate a sense of "extraterritoriality" in the face of a weak, almost nonexistent local political structure that provides them with virtually no supportive resources. They do not conduct themselves as if they came from a nation – a notion that holds little meaning for them – but rather from the world.

Wardle abandons the anthropologist's stock-in-trade concept, "belief system," because he discerns that rather than possessing a store of shared meaning as such, the residents are vibrantly engaged in an ongoing *quest* for meaning, to make meaning, to be heard and to hear others. They enact a highly stylized, performative mode of communication though which they inhabit the present moment artfully. It is an intensely social, open-ended mode in which persons constantly modify ritual forms for purposes of self-expressivity and connectedness. Wardle takes care not to romanticize what he witnesses and participates in; he does not downplay the costs of an unpredictable material life, of a lack of political stability, and of local biases and prejudices of which the residents – like residents of every other neighborhood on earth – have their share. Nonetheless, he discovers that their cosmopolitanism finds expression, among other ways, in their capacity to re-form continuously their sense of home and place without becoming undone, existentially speaking, by the process.

Daniel Hiebert (2002) illuminates the "cosmopolitan ecology" that he argues constitutes some of today's changing urban environments. He draws upon an extensive field-based project investigating immigrant experiences and perceptions in Vancouver. He considers everyday experiences such as diverse people establishing a backdoor, neighborhood gardening culture in which they exchange practices from the world over. On a broader scale he considers the dynamics of immigrant interaction on a communal basis. The data indicate ways in which immigrant communities integrate newcomers, even as the newcomers sometimes branch out in their social relations in novel, unanticipated ways. This process seems especially apparent among youth, who often cultivate ever-shifting transcultural friendships and networks (not always to the pleasure of their parents).

Hiebert identifies what might be called a seasoned cosmopolitanism. He describes young people from various ethnic communities who gravitate back to them as they enter adulthood – for example, re-immersing themselves in natal languages – and yet who do not abandon their previous transcultural selves (pp. 220–221). In so doing they illustrate what it can mean to dwell in cosmopolitan space. Their experience demonstrates that the cultivation of a cosmopolitan orientation is not linear or unidirectional but rather dynamic and evolving. It depends on contexts and experiences, and on hopes and expectations. On the basis of his research Hiebert characterizes a cosmopolitan outlook as "a way of living . . . associated with an appreciation of, and interaction with, people from other cultural backgrounds" and which can bring into being settings "where diversity is accepted and is rendered ordinary" (p. 212). "Ordinary" does not mean insignificant. Quite the contrary. Like simplicity and grace, it signifies a remarkable human accomplishment often rooted deep in humanity's past.

Chan Kwok-bun (2005) argues that many Chinese immigrants in Canada, Thailand, and Singapore eschew at one and the same time what he calls traditionalism, assimilation, and multiculturalism. Based on systematic interviews, he suggests that many individuals lead a genuinely experimental life, in the sense that they are constantly negotiating affinities to their original homeland, to their local immigrant compatriots, to the majority and other local cultural groups, and to their selves. They reside in shifting space between the new and the old, the familiar and the strange. They find this space variously fascinating and unsettling, attractive and repellent, welcoming and hostile.

Kwok-bun is struck by the cosmopolitan confidence he hears in numerous voices, which he suggests has a more substantive or transformative quality than what the concept "transnational" typically conveys. For example, a resident of Bangkok explains his orientation as follows:

> It is like milk and coffee. When you pour milk into coffee and stir it, they mix. It is very difficult to distinguish the milk from the coffee. But, they are still two different things. I can speak Thai like any other Thai, but I am Chinese. To be Thai is not to deny my Chineseness. To stress Chineseness is not to deny my Thainess.
>
> (Kwok-bun, 2005, p. 33)

Halfway around the world, the Peruvian writer José Carlos Mariátegui illuminates this person's comment in the following remark about Argentinian poets of the 1920s who were experimenting with new forms. "Despite their being saturated with cosmopolitanism," writes Mariátegui, and "despite their universalist vision of art, the best of these avant-garde poets *are still the most Argentinian*. The Argentinism of Girondo, Guiraldes, Borges, etc. is no less obvious than their cosmopolitanism" (quoted in Salomon, 1979, p. 104, emphasis supplied).

Bronislaw Szerszynski and John Urry (2002) conclude from their focus-group interview project, undertaken with a diverse sample of adults in Britain, that it is possible to discern in everyday thinking today "a reflexive awareness of a culture of the cosmopolitan" (p. 461). Their informants characterize this culture as a fusion of mutual awareness and solidarity based on a fundamental feeling that people are "in it together." A retired man remarks: "I think we are living in a shrinking world now, aren't we. I think you can't do anything without having a, you know, an environmental effect on everybody else" (472–473). A professional woman says: "I am a global citizen because I am aware of people, I'm aware of culture, I'm aware of other countries and to a certain extent the impact that I have on it as well" (473). Respondents expressed moral solidarities that extend beyond national borders. Rather than remaining numbed or "immunized" from feeling (cf. Masschelein and Simons, 2002) by the sheer range of moral tragedies which the media pour over the transom, they imagined quite specific ways of being helpful. These included aiding a particular child or group rather than contributing to a large, impersonal charity, and participating in a locally organized boycott to assist workers on the far side of the planet (pp. 475–476).

Many of Szerszynski and Urry's informants appear to envision this emerging culture of the cosmopolitan as a contrast to an ethos of fear and suspicion of others. Gilroy (2004) sheds light on their remarks in his analysis of the "cosmopolitan attachment" he sees as emergent in various urban neighborhoods. Such attachment, he writes, "finds civic and ethical value in the process of exposure to otherness. It glories in the ordinary virtues and ironies – listening, looking, discretion, friendship – that can be cultivated when mundane encounters with difference become rewarding" (p. 75; see also Erskine, 2000, for a comparable analysis of the pacific outcomes that can flow from cosmopolitan interaction).

In a study of the meaning and possibility of "cosmopolitan citizenship," Audrey Osler and Hugh Starkey (2003) administered a questionnaire to six hundred young people (10–18 years old) at four schools in Leicester, England. They followed up with a series of focused, discussion-based workshops with youth at each school. They sought to understand how young people interpret and respond to today's often rapidly changing local and global circumstances. Their core finding jibes with what Szersznski and Urry (2002) dub a culture of the cosmopolitan that features not just awareness but critical appreciation for how differently people dwell in the world. "The young people in our research," Osler and Starkey write, "demonstrated multiple and dynamic identities, embracing local, national and international perspectives" (p. 252). The authors show that the youths' self-reports and views cannot be straightforwardly ascribed to or captured by their class, ethnicity, race, religion, sense of nationality, or other familiar factors. The authors conclude, among other points, that "an education for national citizenship is unlikely to provide a sufficiently comprehensive context for [youth] to integrate their own experiences and identities" (p. 252). Osler and Starkey regard cosmopolitanism as pointing toward that more "comprehensive context."

In a comparable study, Katharyne Mitchell and Walter Parker (2008) conducted focus group interviews with youth in a city in the western United States in order to plumb their responses to 9/11 and subsequent world developments. One of the authors' aims was to examine the tenability of the view that people must choose between either a national or cosmopolitan outlook because the two cannot, or so some have argued, be reconciled or balanced. They draw especially upon a significant debate between Martha Nussbaum (2002) and an array of note-worthy critics (among them Kwame Anthony Appiah, Judith Butler, and Hilary Putnam) regarding the very possibility of a cosmopolitan orientation in a world still defined by the nation-state and its claims to loyalty. (For useful commentary on this debate, see Bader, 1999 and Waldron, 2000, 2003.) In this book, I have remarked on the alleged gap or irreconcilability between the cosmopolitan and the local, and have claimed that rather than opposites the two can be symbiotic. The relevant contrast is between cosmopolitanism and the local, on the one hand, and parochial or universalistic outlooks, on the other hand.

Mitchell and Parker report that some youth in their study have adopted – without any prior, formal civic education on cosmopolitanism – what the authors characterize as "multiple, flexible, and relational" points of view toward the local and the global. The youths' moral, political, and cultural allegiances cannot be contained within any preordained framework, whether called multicultural, pluralist, or national. The authors conceive cosmopolitanism as, among other things, a useful lens for understanding and appreciating the youths' evolving perspectives. Like the other studies reviewed here, their research discloses the value of fine-grained attention to *how* people respond in a cosmopolitan mode to experience on the ground.

June Edmunds and Bryan Turner (2001) also examined the question of nationalism "and/or" cosmopolitanism. In an interview-based project involving seven publicly active, professional women in Britain, they discern what they call "cosmopolitan nationalism" as an emergent contemporary outlook. Based on their informants' views, the authors characterize cosmopolitan nationalism as a dynamic interweaving of local commitments such as solidarity with the Welsh or Scots, broader affinities such as feeling themselves part of both a multicultural society and of Europe, an ironic sensibility marked by a sense for the dynamic nature of personhood, a posture of being against both militarism and paternalistic modes of nationalism, and last but not least a deep engagement in trying to practice more open-minded points of view. Mariátegui, a writer mentioned previously, provides a background perspective to this analysis when he writes:

> Contemporary history constantly teaches us that the nation is not an abstraction or a myth; but it also teaches us that civilization and humanity are not myths either. The fact of the reality of the nation in no way negates international reality. In short, nationalism is valid as an affirmation, but not as a negation.
>
> (quoted in Salomon, 1979, p. 104)[7]

Michele Lamont and Sada Aksartova (2002) undertook focused interviews with working-class white and black American men, in parallel with systematic interviews with a sample of working-class white and Maghribi men in France. They examined how what they call "different ordinary cosmopolitanisms," each informed by a particular language of moral universalism, enable people to resist racism in their everyday lives (p. 18). The ordinary cosmopolitanisms to which they refer find expression, in part, in the differing tropes the men employ to describe their sense of self, other, and world. The Americans emphasized that hard work, demonstrating competence, and making a steady income lend one cross-cultural legitimacy, voice, and solidarity. The French shared these values about how to lead a life but also stressed socialist and republican ideals of fundamental human dignity as undermining racist presuppositions. All spoke unhesitantly in a universal register, in which they underscored their belief that all people seek a meaningful life and that there are good and bad persons in every community. They also strongly esteemed an attitude of moral seriousness toward life (cf. Duneier, 1992).

Lamont and Aksartova are struck by the contrast between the cosmopolitan outlooks of the men and what they see as the focus in the academy on cultural relativism, the celebration of difference, and multiculturalism, all of which they found notably absent in their sample's voices. They recommend that researchers who study racism as well as responses to it shift their focus from identity to what they call "boundary work" (p. 18). They treat cosmopolitanism as a name for life in those ever-shifting boundaries in which persons artfully seek forms of solidarity that substantiate their sense of personhood and give them strength in living justly. Their project sheds light on what scholars have called rooted cosmopolitanism, which features moral allegiance not just to "one's own" but to a broader horizon of people.

Pnina Werbner (1999) undertook systematic interviews with two groups of working-class Pakistani immigrants in Britain. One group, whom she calls "transnational," more or less transplanted wholesale from Pakistan their ethnic culture, eliding significant interaction with the cultural environments they found upon arrival (cf. Hiebert, 2002, p. 215). This self-cocooning, Werbner reports, was at times centered around religious views and at others around marriage patterns. This approach contrasts with other working-class immigrants who partook, sometimes liberally, in new cultural forms of expression and identification. What Werbner characterizes as their cosmopolitan patterns of life sometimes put them in tension with those who elected a more self-contained mode. The author describes cases in which individuals found ways to lead a meaningful life whether in self-enclosed or in experimental form, or in which they in effect emigrated from one group to the other. She reports that people were keenly aware of these disparate choices and options, such that a truly sheltered posture was impossible.

My focus in this book has been on people who experiment, with that term understood in its down-to-earth Deweyan sense of human beings trying seriously to respond to life situations in which blueprints and prescriptions fall short or simply do not exist. Cosmopolitanism as I am approaching it refers not to the person who cuts the chord with the past as well as with all prior roots – the wanderer "whose only real place of belonging is movement itself" (Skrbis et al., 2004, p. 117). Rather the concept characterizes the person who engages the larger world and finds *in* that engagement a renewed, revitalized, and creative mode of enhancing the integrity (though not fixity) of the local, either directly through concerted action or indirectly by virtue of a visible way of being. Such conduct, in turn, can support more artful, more humane, and more peaceful interaction.

Werbner criticizes the often unexamined assumption that cosmopolitanism constitutes merely an elite aesthete's attitude toward the world (for related critiques see, for example, Beck, 2004; Cheah and Robbins, 1998; and Waldron 2000, 2003). She argues that the cosmopolitanism of the working-class men and women in her study features both knowledge of and openness to other cultures, and that it has a suppleness and range that is more dynamic than what can sometimes be seen among the privileged classes. Werbner also echoes what research has characterized as cultural cosmopolitanism when she concludes that cosmopolitanism "does not necessarily imply an absence of belonging but the possibility of belonging to more than one ethnic and cultural localism simultaneously" (p. 34).

Harri Englund (2004) undertook several years of field-based research among Pentecostal Christians in Malawi, almost all of them materially impoverished in comparison with the rest of the world. Englund's framework derives, in part, from theoretical debates about the place of home in human sensibilities, particularly under conditions of globalization and considerable migration. This literature echoes the debate between Nussbaum and colleagues touched on above regarding cosmopolitanism and nationalism. However, here the two camps are (1) those who consider the cosmopolitan homeless and rootless, and (2) those who regard home and roots as creative, dynamic outlooks of mind and place, rather than a natal fixture from which any movement *ipso facto* condemns one to an alienating exile. Englund found that the Pentecostal Christians with whom he lived retain a fluid sense of home. They have migrated to a city – they have *left* home in an authentic sense. They are at all times absorbed in what the author describes as their cosmopolitan project of learning to dwell interactively where they now find themselves.

However, they do not reject their roots, usually in rural villages to which they periodically return, even as these become intertwined with new sources of meaning and value. The author reports that in general they do not find useful in their self-understandings binaries such as village vs. city, traditional vs. modern, us vs. them, or near vs. far, even though they are keenly aware of value differences. The only binary they embrace is that between heaven and what they see as a devil-saturated world in which humans are driven time and again to distraction and loss. They employ a universalized discourse of a suffering humanity, though not one of "believers" to be elevated and "nonbelievers" to be punished. They shared with the author their wish to send missionaries to Europe, if only they had the funds, not to convert people there into Pentecostals but to help them grasp what they regard as the source of conflict and unhappiness. Compassion informs their lives and positions them to enact a rooted cosmopolitan morality toward others in the urban mélange in which they reside.

Fuyuki Kurasawa's (2004) study of the "alternative globalization" movement illustrates another mode of current field-based inquiry into the cosmopolitan. Kurasawa characterizes the movement as "a loose constellation of transnational 'subaltern counterpublics' giving birth to progressive aspects of a fledgling global civil society" (p. 235). These "counterpublics" range from the Zapatista movement in Mexico which supports local economic autonomy for poor people, to organized protests at meetings of the World Trade Organization, to the World Social Forum launched in 2001, to organized protests against the United States invasion of Iraq, and to various anti-sweatshop, environmentalist, and other activist undertakings. In distinctive ways the groups work against what they see as the cultural, environmental, and political depredations of globalized capitalism.

Kurasawa examines media accounts, websites, interviews, publications, and more to sketch a portrait of what he calls "cosmopolitanism from below." He does not endorse the aims of particular groups in this movement. Rather he seeks to contrast their efforts with what he sees as an undue emphasis on trickle-down theories which presume global solidarities depend first and foremost upon universal principles, such as participatory democracy and human rights, which must be entrenched in international laws and institutions in order for effective change to occur. Kurasawa acknowledges the value of such laws and institutions. But he finds extensive evidence in alternative globalization movements that people on the ground are not waiting for top-down initiatives but are enacting what he calls "practice-oriented" cosmopolitanism (p. 234).[8]

According to Kurasawa, people in a wide array of activities appear to be establishing networks with a "web-like character" that nourish cosmopolitanism from below (p. 235). Echoing Gilroy's (2004) reminder that many people esteem cultural difference, Kurasawa writes of the playful dimension of this interaction on the ground – with play understood as a quite serious if less planned form of work (cf. Dewey, 1985, pp. 202–214). "The acts of sharing these sorts of ludic public spaces and moments with others, of discussing matters of common concern with them, or yet again of being in a crowd that marches through the streets of a city, can cultivate transnational relations of solidarity" (p. 251). With continued proximity, he suggests, transnational relations can morph into cosmopolitan ones.

A final study I will mention is Nikos Papastergiadis' (2007) richly attuned examination of what he calls "the cosmopolitan hospitality of art." He describes an internationally collaborative art exposition housed in an old building in Thessaloniki, Greece, that had at various points in history served as a mosque, a synagogue, a hostel for refugees, and a museum. He was interested, among other things, in understanding the reaction to the exhibit on the part of various visitors, whether fellow artists or local working-class, professional, or elderly people who came to look. He discerns in their responses what he calls "glimpses" of the cosmopolitan. He quotes a local woman who came up to him to comment on the exhibit: "What all humans have in common is their mixture. It is this mixture that precedes and outlives any narrow national identity" (p. 140). Papastergiadis is struck by the modesty and "meekness" (a far from passive term, which he takes from Norberto Bobbio) that he hears in the woman's words. Their very ordinariness affects him more than strident calls for global political or economic concords undertaken in a cosmopolitan spirit, not because the latter are unimportant but because they lack the everyday spontaneity and organicity of the former (cf. Waldron, 2006). Papastergiadis is moved by this and other down-to-earth glimpses of the cosmopolitan because they open the door to a fundamental insight he gained from the project: "What is it that art does that is so exquisite in its execution of the political that differentiates it from politics? I have been arguing that artists do not deliver documents which reveal the condition of cosmopolitanism, but rather that they take an active role in the mediation of its emergence" (p. 149).

Learning with Others

In casting an eye back on these various studies, one could argue that working-class people, retired people, youth, highly prepared professionals, recent immigrants, activists, deeply religious persons, and many others – including teachers and heads of schools – can all play mediating roles in bringing cosmopolitan sensibilities to life, which is to say in their own lives and in those around them. Put another way, we see in these studies indices of cosmopolitan artfulness, of on-the-ground practices of listening, speaking, and interacting, of being receptive toward the new and yet not in a way that negates the known. Indices are not airtight demonstrations. Scholars across the disciplines who are conducting fieldwork on cosmopolitanism typically underscore the provisionality of their findings, if only because this line of research remains fresh and open-ended. Nonetheless their efforts are helping to clear a terrain for giving the cosmopolitan idea a thoughtful hearing.

To me the research is fascinating, in part, because its outcomes articulate dynamically with longstanding traditions of philosophy as the art of living. This interlacing of philosophical and field-based anthropology generates, in turn, a rich outlook for teachers to bring to bear in their work. That outlook consists of questions such as these:

- What would it mean to perceive one's students as engaged, if not in so many words, in an ethical project of self-formation?
- What would it mean to provoke and help them to treat their lives in an artful way – as we can picture the men and women in the studies recounted here doing?
- What would it mean to perceive students as potentially creative cultural beings in the substantive sense characterized in this book?
- What would it mean for students to perceive themselves as having these capacities and acting upon them?

Once more, the notion of culture at play here works at three levels: socio-linguistic community (the familiar focus of anthropology) which undergoes change through the initiatives, however microscopic, of individuals and sub-groups; communities of art ranging from doctors to teachers to airline pilots in which, again, any participant can have an impact on how its practices evolve; and the individual human being "culturating" himself or herself as fully as circumstances permit, a process that brings the person into the world and the world into the person, and that indirectly positions him or her to contribute to larger communities.

Cosmopolitan cultural creativity (pardon the awkward phrase) is readily discernible in the literature featured in these pages. Cosmopolitanism is not a synonym with multiculturalism not only because of this reconfigured framing of culture but because its focus is not on cultural identity as such. Rather it is on cultural continuity and integrity, themselves entirely dependent on cultural creativity: that is to say, on what communities and individuals are in process of becoming through the experience of reflective openness to the new fused with reflective loyalty to the known.

I appreciate that connecting Epictetus' focus on ethical practices of self-cultivation in the second-century Mediterranean world with the conduct of Pentecostals in Southern Africa in the twenty-first century seems like a stretch – perhaps even fanciful and anachronistic. However, I do not mean to imply sameness in their outlooks and actions. Rather the point of the comparison is to highlight how their cosmopolitan orientations reflect a conscious concern to conduct themselves in deliberative ways. Those ways reside at the intersection of the strange and the familiar, the surprising and the expected. They emerge at the crossroads of change and stability, of unfathomability and recognition. They prompt people to consider how they talk with others, how they listen to them, interact with them, regard and treat them. In short, they move people to think about the practices and artfulness which, if not in so many words, constitute their ways of living. Formal education, the topic of the next chapter, can play a dynamic role in helping people cultivate their awareness of these artful practices as well as of their consequences.

Like all persons, Epictetus' students and the Malawian Pentecostals have (or had) their partialities and moral blind spots. But partiality does not imply exclusion. It constitutes a necessary ground for any inhabitable way of life, and it is requisite for making meaningful contact in the first place with others who are different. Without this local rooting – which can be in the soil of a geographical location or of a spiritual, professional, or vocational endeavor – it becomes that much more problematic to adopt a cosmopolitan orientation. To judge from the literatures addressed in these chapters, a holder of Epictetus' *Handbook* and a holder of the Pentecostal's *Bible* can find these sources of teaching to be openers of doors to other people rather than the materials for building walls between them.

Such may not be the case with everyone who deploys them. The *Handbook* and the *Bible* can be treated, on the one hand, as instruments for withdrawal from life or, on the other hand, for brow-beating others into mimicking a particular code of conduct. Recall that the original Greek meaning of handbook included the idea of a cutting instrument – and the latter can be used to destroy as well as to construct. The difference has to do with the quality of presence in life, of responsiveness to its vicissitudes and challenges. The cosmopolitan-minded people portrayed across these chapters differ in countless ways in their values, beliefs, hopes, and the like. But it seems to me they *hold* their values and beliefs in ways that keep them open to the concerns and perspectives of others. It is not mere romance to imagine that Mediterranean Stoics and Malawian Pentecostals would have substantive things to say to one another, that their posture would be one of considering rather than of dictating, and that they would be willing to alter their conduct however modestly as a consequence of their listening.

As such, their conduct incarnates, as I have sought to show, the creative dimension in culture discernible through a cosmopolitan prism. Whether at the level of sociolinguistic communities, social practices, or individuals, cultural life can incorporate a reflective openness to the new, the other side of the coin of reflective loyalty to the known. Life can become educational in both formal and informal terms. People can broaden, widen, and deepen their ways of thinking and acting at the various crossroads of difference they come upon. As Samuel Scheffler argues, people with a cosmopolitan orientation "demonstrate," at whatever local or larger plane of life they occupy, "the very capacities that make it possible for human beings to create culture in the first place, and they enrich humanity as a whole by renewing the stock of cultural resources on which others may draw" (2001, p. 113). Scheffler's remark echoes the claim (see Chapter 1, pp. 9–10) that it is shared human capacities such as thinking and telling stories that form a ground for cosmopolitan-minded relation. Cosmopolitanism is not an identity in the familiar sociological sense of the term, nor is it a badge or the name for an exclusive club. It is an orientation that assists people in sustaining their cultural integrity and continuity – but not fixity or purity – through change.

Skrbis et al. (2004, p. 117) suggest that the research community has failed to provide a clear definition of who is and who is not cosmopolitan in outlook and conduct. To me that "failure" is a redeeming achievement. It acknowledges a hard-won insight emergent through millennia of cosmopolitan reflection, namely, that everybody and nobody "is" cosmopolitan. I would hazard the guess that most persons, at least at some significant moments, are open in a reflective way to the new and willing to be influenced by it – whether the new comes in the form of a new person, idea, or custom from another culture. These same persons, at other important moments, are close-minded, in effect covering ears and eyes and withdrawing from touch. I have difficulty picturing a human as contrasted with saintly or devilish exception to the rule.

As we have seen, it is quite possible to characterize and esteem a cosmopolitan orientation, as numerous studies and this book attempt to do. An inquirer can circle around the concept and can walk the world, so to speak, with the concept in hand. Throughout, the inquirer continually clarifies uses and applications, but without trying to master the concept or to own it. Correspondingly, inquirers can retain a reflective distance from the concept so as to avoid being warped out of their orbit by it, to echo a trope from Emerson. Any concept can take on a power of its own and subtly turn persons away from what may have led them to it in the first place. Thus the inquirer develops a transactive, intimate relationship with the concept. He or she dwells with it, reflects upon it, and imagines the questions the concept itself would pose if, like Socrates' daemon, it suddenly took on a voice.

When the practice of working the concept cosmopolitanism metamorphoses into trying to define it in a terminal manner – and, especially, to define "who is" and "who is not" cosmopolitan – we have left the terrain of cosmopolitanism itself. It should be emphasized that Skrbis et al. (2004) call for constructing a prototype in theory, which they argue can be used to analyze empirical data. They are not being moralistic. All the same a serious danger lurks here. If not careful we may find ourselves – if not in so many words – playing with moral scorecards, counting up a person's dispositions that we deem cosmopolitan and weighing them against those we deem non- or anti-cosmopolitan, and then dividing the world into cosmopolitans and those excluded from its dispensation. What humane outcomes would issue from this game of moral mathematics? Who is the human being wise enough, and all-seeing enough, to orchestrate the game? To be sure, criticism of bigotry, narrow-mindedness, and cruelty are ever-vital, a point amply documented thus far. But this criticism is most sagely undertaken, it seems to me, with a mirror in one hand (and perhaps a handbook like that of Epictetus in the other).

"You think because you understand one, you can understand two, because one and one makes two. But you must also understand *and*" (ascribed to an ancient, unnamed Sufi teacher and quoted in Starmer, 2009, p. 1). At the methodological center of these chapters has been the attempt to reside in the conjunction "and" – as in cosmopolitanism *and* education, cosmopolitanism *and* the local, leaving *and* remaining at home, receptivity to the new *and* loyalty to the known. It is not easy to conceive this conjunction philosophically, and it is not simple to occupy it in day-to-day life. Social, political, cultural, economic, and other pressures from without, and psychological pressures from within, constantly push people toward one end or another of the continua that mark human affairs. "Or" rather than "and" often seems the operative condition. "You are with us *or* against us": how endless is the grim history of this expression. "You are with us *and* against us": here is a provocative adage closer to the cosmopolitan ideal. It means persons do what they can to support one another as they strive to cultivate lives of meaning. It leads me to say: I am against stasis. Given the way of the world in our time, and "given the given itself" – *the gift of being here at all* – I am against the "you" that would unthinkingly reject learning, growing, and participating. I am with your right and your effort to move creatively in the world, whatever the scale may be as teacher, parent, friend, neighbor, or newcomer.[9] The conjunction "and" proliferates in the cosmopolitan: with *and* against, closer and closer apart *and* further and further together, the teacher *and* the world.

As we have seen, cosmopolitanism comprises something other than utilizing an environment strategically and something other than adapting to change (as useful as both capabilities will always be). Cosmopolitanism means *participating* in pluralist change as an agent, as an actor, rather than remaining passive or merely reactive to events. "Unlike 'globalization'," writes Bob White, ". . . cosmopolitanism is not something that happens to people, it is something that people do" (2002, p. 681). Among the voices that can be heard in the literatures cited here are those of people, young and old alike, putting their foot forward both figuratively and literally. They engage the world at whatever level their resources and strength permit. They think about their settings and the world writ large. And their porosity to the environments in which they move differs from that of certain rocks in which water merely passes through.

5 Curriculum and Teaching in and for the World

We have seen in previous chapters that society contains multiple agencies for educating. They include homes, schools, books, other print media, the World Wide Web, email, radio, and television. They encompass associations, clubs, and countless other groupings. The ubiquity of such agencies that deliberately seek, as Lawrence Cremin puts it, "to transmit or evoke knowledge, attitudes, values, skills, and sensibilities" (1970, p. xiii) demonstrates why education and schooling are not synonyms (also see Varenne, 2007). The former occurs on a broader scale and is more ongoing, although it may often be less structured and systematic than what school can provide.

Although other institutions are important, schools, universities, classrooms, and teachers continue to play an extended role in the lives of young people the world over. Accordingly, in this chapter I will focus upon curriculum and teaching in such settings. I will endeavor to show how processes of formal education in them can fuel a cosmopolitan orientation.

The term "cosmopolitan orientation" metamorphoses another concept, moral sensibility, that I deployed in a study of the moral significance of teaching (Hansen, 2001). In that project I sought a term that would capture the fusion of attentive thoughtfulness, emotional sympathy, and dedication to education that one can discern in some teachers at all levels of the system, across all disciplines and fields of pedagogy. The notion of a moral sensibility brought these elements together, and I sought to illustrate it through an array of examples. The idea of a cosmopolitan orientation is a natural extension of the previous concept. It echoes the claim of Chapter 2, that cosmopolitanism embodies an attempt to fuse the moral and the ethical – that is to say, to merge the cultivation of self (ethics) in its humane relation with others and the world (the moral).

A cosmopolitan-minded education does not require a radical overhaul of what is taught in primary, secondary, or university settings. It does not imply doing away with or downplaying art, history, mathematics, science, and other subjects – quite the contrary. Nor does this modality of educating depend upon or necessitate a formal program modeled, say, after those in civic, global, or moral education. A cosmopolitan orientation is not necessarily in conflict either with programming in general or with these specific programs in particular. However, a cosmopolitan education emerges within and alongside the typical school curriculum that features multiple subjects taught sequentially and in different time periods of the day and week. As we will see, the idea does call for some shifts in emphasis as well as, from time to time, the addition of new curricular elements, with some of these planned and others unanticipated. A cosmopolitan outlook spotlights ways of working *with* curriculum.

Put another way, the approach accentuates perspective understood as a method. It is a way of seeing that illuminates how curriculum constitutes a potential and dynamic inheritance to all persons. Curriculum embodies more than merely a body of facts and theories, as important as they are. Whether in art, literature, or science, it also mirrors recurring, time-honored human attempts to understand and to make a home in the world. In this light curriculum "addresses" teachers and students, calling upon them to respond to these prior attempts at meaning-making as they engage in their own.

In the first part of the chapter, I employ the idea of an address as a springboard for examining the meaning of an inheritance. There are in fact two meanings here, one rooted in socialization, the other in education; I try to indicate how the two processes are not synonymous. Then, to illustrate the reception of inheritance – what it means "to take it in" – I sketch with a refreshed palette the idea of a cosmopolitan orientation. This term becomes another way to capture the fusion of reflective openness to the new and reflective loyalty to the known illuminated in previous chapters. A cosmopolitan orientation accompanies moving closer and closer apart with others as well as further and further together with them. The ways in which teachers and students engage curriculum can generate such an orientation. I will also return to the discussion from Chapters 2 and 3, pointing out exercises teachers can undertake to fashion themselves into educators in, of, and for the world they inhabit.

Responding to the World's Address

The cosmopolitan idea invites the teacher to draw out from curriculum the ways in which subject matter expresses the human quest for meaning. This quest suggests something more than the pursuit of knowledge in its instrumental and scientific senses, though these undertakings can be juxtaposed in the same moment. The notion of a quest reflects the idea of curriculum as a living response to experience: as an expression of attempts to make sense, to understand, to appreciate, to become at home. The quest for meaning is neither spectatorial in its posture nor acquisitive in its aim, although it can lead to wondrous new insights, tools, and methods for life. It is participatory in the sense of openness to being formed, not merely informed, by what one sees and learns.

In figurative terms, the quest for meaning opens a growing person to the address of the world, as if the latter were asking her or him:

• What do you make of me? How is it for you being *in this place* rather than in some other kind of cosmos?

- In what ways are you dwelling here? What relations do you have, and what relations are you creating, with the world around you?
- Why do *you* ask questions? What kind of being are you *that poses questions?* Do rocks pose questions? How about the stars? Has a frog ever posed a question to the cosmos? We know that humans do. You do. Why is that?

These questions resemble those posed in Chapter 3 (p. 51) in a context of the unfathomability of human diversity, and those framed toward the end of Chapter 4 (p. 85) in a context of learning from others. The questions mirror the idea of philosophy as the art of living. In this outlook, life constitutes an active response to experience. Human life is not mere existence, nor mere replication of what has gone before. Individuals and communities alike can give shape, substance, and meaning to their lives, as indeed people have done since the dawn of culture. Cultural creativity pertains to the level of society, of particular practices, and of individuals. We have seen how the quest for a meaningful life is bound up with arts, or artful methods, of speaking, listening, participating, interacting, and the like, all of which can be fostered in the course of working with any educational subject.[1]

Along with a cosmopolitan outlook, teachers would continue to work with students to develop skills of reading, writing, numerating, learning new languages, and inquiring. They would encourage students to gather resources to pursue particular interests and to attend to particular needs. In the cosmopolitan, however, curriculum serves more than the familiar functions of socialization, knowledge acquisition, and preparation for economic life, as important as they remain. It also constitutes a world inheritance of meaning-making bequeathed to all human beings. As such it casts the cultivation of academic skills in a new light. It gives them reconstituted depth, significance, and social reach.

Picturing an Educational Inheritance

Curriculum as world inheritance is something other than a sum of the parts. It differs from pluralist approaches, as seen for example in global and multicultural curriculum. A pluralist approach can be taken as a necessary educational beginning although not as a final or self-sufficient ending. It is important in today's world to inform students of cultural and community histories with their distinctive characteristics, purposes, and aspirations. It is equally important to educate students to esteem tolerance. Some critics might argue that these aims add up to a cosmopolitan education (Heater, 2002; Nussbaum, 1997a, 2002). However, in my view this conclusion obscures the issue by casting the cosmopolitan as a solution to a predetermined problem, rather than as an invitation to a yet-to-be-determined experience. Recall the point from Chapter 1 (pp. 8–9), that in cosmopolitanism the point of departure is not the individual or community as such – as it is in liberalism and multiculturalism, respectively – but what they may be in process of becoming through a reflective reception of the new fused with a reflective handling of the known. Thus in the cosmopolitan the difference with pluralism is not one of curricular content per se, but rather one of perspective or orientation as it influences people's engagement with content. I will elucidate this idea by considering the term "inheritance."

A preliminary point, also touched on in Chapter 1, is that education and socialization are not synonyms. Socialization is the time-honored process of drawing the young into a way of life and equipping them to sustain it. Without socialization (other terms include acculturation and enculturation), human ways of life would perish. Socialization will remain a required activity of humans for as long as culture subsists. Through it, the young learn ways of understanding, communicating, and interacting, along with a body of evolving cultural knowledge, that together are constitutive of their way of life. In the context of socialization, an inheritance means precisely this: an element in an established way of life. It is taken on uncritically not in the sense of unreflectively or unimaginatively but rather in the sense that socialization makes it possible to be critical in the first place – i.e., to be in a position to stand back existentially from ideas, values, beliefs, and practices and to consider them rather than merely enact them. No such standing back, no such experience of being critical, is conceivable without having been socialized into a way of life. Without the latter there is nothing to stand back from, just as there would be nothing to stand upon. An unsocialized human being would find it as impossible to engage with people as they would with him or her.

The idea of a cosmopolitan education recognizes the necessity of socialization, which entails, in turn, recognizing the place of the local in human life. Education depends upon socialization, on having entered a way of life and become a part of it. However, from a cosmopolitan perspective education has to do with new forms of understanding, undergoing, and moving in the world. These modes may be in accord with processes of socialization but they do not simply replicate them. They often accompany socialization and at times may be hard to distinguish from it. However, the differences between them can create tensions and difficulties when the requirements of socialization butt up against the concerns of education. At all times education is a standing back as well as standing in. In the experience of education the student maintains a degree of detachment or distance from the object of study even while being immersed in it. Put another way, the student is aware it is an object of study rather than just a passing object; and it is an object of study because the student has rendered it so, often through the prompting of the teacher and the curriculum.

The student's awareness mirrors the fact that education is purposive rather than merely functional. Socialization is entirely functional: its aim is to sustain culture and, in what amounts to the same thing, to equip human beings to inhabit it. Education is purposive as well as functional: its aim is to contribute creatively to culture understood at the three levels featured in this book. In education a person responds to questions, pursues interests, and acts upon curiosity in ways that are unscripted rather than predetermined. Oakeshott argues that:

> [Education] has no pre-ordained course to follow: with every thought and action a human being lets go a mooring and puts out to sea on a self-chosen

but largely unforeseen course. It has no pre-ordained destination: there is no substantive perfect man or human life upon which he may model his conduct. It is a predicament, not a journey.

(Oakeshott, 1989, p. 23)

Unlike a problem that can be solved or a journey that can be completed, a predicament is a condition, a feature of life to be engaged in one way or another. Oakeshott also characterizes education as an unsettling and unrehearsed "adventure" (p. 23) to places nobody has been before, in the sense that no two human beings understand the world and its elements in carbon-copy ways, and in the sense that the experience of education involves at important moments genuine surprise, the disconfirmation of expectations, and the unpredictable. In contrast, socialization is a marvelously well-rehearsed if evolving system of inhabiting the known and the familiar.

Thus in an educational context an inheritance takes on a different character than in socialization, even if the vehicle may initially be the same. That is, the vehicle in both cases can take the shape of what we call books, methods, equipment, exercises, activities, and so forth. It can take the form of what is called carpentry, mathematics, physical education, etc. However, in education an inheritance is not like being bequeathed a piece of property or a cache of goods. It is not something a student can pull out of a pocket when asked for an accounting. It is not something a student can easily describe, even after a long immersion – or, perhaps, especially after a lengthy involvement.[2]

For example, the longer a person studies, say, art or philosophy, the deeper, richer, and more perplexing it may become. What are the boundaries of art? When does art "begin"? Does it commence the moment a person takes brush in hand? Or does it only start when the person turns a corner, figuratively speaking, and realizes (not necessarily in words) what is calling her or him to paint in the first place? What counts as philosophy as contrasted, say, with theory or ideology? How can we distinguish philosophy from rhetorical manipulation, or can we? When does philosophy "happen"? Whenever we think? Whenever we question? Or does it highlight particular kinds of thinking and questioning?

In education an inheritance is a dynamic amalgam of questions, values, ideas, practices, doubts, and yearnings. To assimilate an inheritance educationally constitutes a process whose shape and substance are always in motion. That process encompasses thinking, imagining, inquiring, contemplating, studying, and deciding. Students *participate* in an educational inheritance rather than merely ingest it or glance at it like a museum visitor idly strolling by one object after another. In this light, an inheritance is always something other than the visible or official curriculum (or "vehicle" as touched on above). It is also something other than what have been dubbed, respectively, the "enacted" and "hidden" curriculum, though it could be understood as instantiated through them. Scholars have characterized the enacted curriculum as the work with subject matter that teachers and students in fact do rather than what they may have intended to do or had prescribed for them (Bussis et al. 1976, Snyder et al. 1992). The hidden curriculum denotes understandings, outlooks, habits, and the like that are, in turn, an unintended outcome of the enacted curriculum (Jackson 1968).

Curriculum as cosmopolitan inheritance is an educational idea. It denotes a dynamic, purposive, if also unpredictable transaction between student and what has given life in the first place to the subject matter at hand. Consider a student in science class. Science metamorphoses from object to object of study when the student begins to ask about her or his experience of it rather than merely getting through it. The object in question is, say, Copernicus' demonstration that the solar system is heliocentric. It becomes an object of study, and more, when the student feels and thinks questions such as "How could Copernicus come up with this idea in the first place? What led him there? What education did he undergo? Why did he care about the solar system at all? How did he describe his discovery in his own terms? What were his emotions as well as his ideas, questions, conjectures at that time? With whom did he communicate about it? What was their critical response? Did he have any regrets about the approach he took? How has what he did influenced the way people look at the earth and its place in space and time? How has it influenced the way I look at such things? Shall I become an astronomer too?" Copernicus' effort half a millennium ago is on the road to becoming an inheritance for this student. Rather than merely acquiring information about him and the solar system, the student is taking on modes of questioning, wondering, being perplexed, and so forth, also illustrated above in the examples of art and philosophy. The student is responding to an address from the world embodied, in this case, in Copernicus and astronomy. The process has ongoing social and communicative elements.

The idea of responding to an address helps distinguish curriculum as cosmopolitan inheritance from the familiar idea of curriculum as "cultural literacy" (Hirsch, 1987). The latter idea emerged in a particularly outspoken form in the 1980s and 1990s as a reaction to multiculturalism in the United States. Critics were concerned that without a shared background of facts and understandings – ranging from the names of poets and playwrights to the names and workings of political institutions – the nation's political culture would unravel and lose a sense of unity. The idea also became bound up in a longstanding debate about instruction: namely, whether students should be required to learn relevant facts (understood as a mode of literacy) before being asked to think through problems and projects, or whether they should be drawn immediately into problems and related processes in the course of which, or so advocates have long argued, they can acquire the pertinent facts.

Cultural literacy falls squarely within the process of socialization. As such there are good reasons for taking it seriously, not just in the United States but in any polity that aspires to retain a sense of integrity. But there are equally good reasons for criticizing it when it dominates *educational* thinking. For one thing, when it does so it can lead people to assume that the bounded cultural knowledge they have acquired is all that is necessary in a globalizing world (cf. Gaudelli, 2003). It can thereby potentially weaken their motivation to seek out new cultural knowledge, the latter characteristic of a cosmopolitan outlook. For another, it bears emphasizing that curriculum conceived as an educational inheritance constitutes more than a store of information and something other than a process of cultural acquisition. As Laura DeSisto (2007) points out, an inheritance "is something to be studied rather than acquired" (p. 104). Her point calls to mind Oakeshott's reminder (1989, p. 45) that one can purchase (i.e. acquire) a painting but one cannot buy an understanding of it. Understanding involves *a change in the self* however modest in comparison with the totality of one's character, experience, knowledge and outlook. Understanding entails questioning, inquiry, and wonder. It can lead one to "dis-acquire" aspects of what one initially absorbed. In the terms of this chapter, understanding entails rendering oneself the subject of an address from the world, as contrasted with conceiving oneself as a pre-shaped vessel awaiting filling. These points echo the claim first made in Chapter 1 (p. 11), that a cosmopolitan-minded education has transformative rather than merely additive or quantitative consequences.

The idea of curriculum as cosmopolitan inheritance suggests that the questions the student enunciates in the example above, or ones comparable to them, can be those of any student, anytime, anywhere on the planet. Thus while the study of Copernicus and astronomy is part of many national, regional, and local curricula the world over, as cosmopolitan inheritance it always reaches beyond such formal, institutionalized markers. It is always something other than what they can denote. Moreover, all the conceivable ways in which this subject is taught and undergone by students cannot capture the student's experience described above. In other words, no two students however enamored of Copernicus and his achievement will respond in an identical, point-by-point manner. No student's unrehearsed, unpredictable adventure in education will be duplicated by another.

Education and New Voices

Curriculum as cosmopolitan inheritance is therefore not a traditionalistic or universalistic notion. It does not mean regarding accomplishments from the past uncritically and simply absorbing without remark their ideational content. Nor does the cosmopolitan prescribe which human achievements, from what eras, and from what parts of the globe, ought to be included in the curriculum.

In the chapters of this book I have been contributing to an ever-evolving and yet substantive cosmopolitan canon for research, teaching, and teacher education. It includes writings by Plato and Marcus, Montaigne and Gournay, Tagore and Dewey. I picture a canon as that which a person in quest of meaning esteems. It encompasses texts or text-analogues (e.g., musical works, paintings) which educate in a sustained manner. They are creations that continuously yield insight and understanding to those who dwell with them. These creations are edifying; they deepen, broaden, and enrich the person's outlook. The person reveres them in the familiar way that certain poems, novels, songs, and sayings become beloved and life-guiding to people.[3]

José Enrique Rodó (1988) provides an instructive, cosmopolitan-minded example of this perspective in his book, *Ariel*. Published in his native Uruguay in 1900, the book is difficult to classify. It fuses fiction, history, philosophy, and cultural commentary. Like the Shakespearean character from *The Tempest* after whom it is named, the book seems to swirl and fly. It is marked by deep feeling for the promise in a cosmopolitan orientation, and by sober-minded analysis of the many parochial attitudes and customs that can block its emergence. It is also at times highly opinionated and seemingly one-sided; it is replete with moments of tension for the reader. Rodó is especially concerned with the drive toward materialism and the abandonment of "poetic" modes of living under the weight of economic imperatives. He conveys his account through the voice of an elderly teacher named Prospero – inspired, again, from *The Tempest* – who, at the close of the academic calendar, is giving his final remarks to students. (Rodó dedicates *Ariel* itself "To the youth of America," meaning in both the south and north.) The elderly teacher slowly and patiently conveys to his students what it means to regard the world's creativity as a shared human patrimony. A community's creativity captured in art, literary work, social institutions, and more are not private possessions but can inform the outlooks and practices of people anywhere. As I have emphasized in these chapters, such a posture does not imply possessing other people's creations. Nor does it imply that it is a simple matter to hear their address and respond to them.

Prospero documents these points through his extensive commentary on a wide array of European novels, histories, philosophies, essays, and other works of art. He speaks with love about them, illuminating what he sees as their strengths as well as limitations. He demonstrates that to engage such objects necessitates careful study, critical receptivity, and a commitment to dialogue with them and about them. In between the lines, so to speak, he acknowledges that the attachment to some works – on the part of individuals as well as of entire communities – will ebb. They will fall by the wayside, at least until someone perhaps hears them again one day. Through the often beautiful voice of Prospero, the elderly teacher who seems to be giving his Socratic swan song rather than end-of-year benediction, Rodó captures what it means to generate a canon of meaning-makers: an evolving constellation of works that teach, that inspire, that accompany a person or community through its own creative endeavors to dwell in the world.[4]

Every group of teachers and students, and every individual therein, can continuously form and re-form canons as they work their way through subjects of study. Much of their content will rightly come from the school or university curriculum. Teachers and students will bring in elements from their experience elsewhere as they see fit. The ongoing process of conceiving worthy objects of study is endlessly rewarding – and challenging. A canon is much richer, deeper, and more complicated than what provides mere entertainment or passing fancy. Put another way, a canon mirrors the discussion of handbooks in Chapter 2. Recall that these are works to carry in hand, to keep at hand – works so valued that it is as if they take the person herself or himself in hand, and guide them through life's confusions, doubts, and possibilities. I will return later in the chapter to why teachers might wish to reopen continually the question of what canon, or what "handbooks," matter to them and can help them avoid the institutional feeling (doubtless familiar to teachers the world over today) that they are billiard balls being knocked around the pool table.

The cosmopolitan dispensation would encourage as much diversity in curricular selection as possible, so long as the engagement is in-depth and systematic. The latter requirement necessitates selecting achievements or objects – poems, historical events, scientific inquiries, a new sport – that hold promise for extended, ever-provocative involvement: that can constitute a meaningful rather than shallow address to students and teacher alike. The objects must have weight. Put another way, they must have sufficient richness to frustrate a facile or glib response but, instead, call upon teachers and students to rise aesthetically and intellectually to meet their address. In this light, curriculum as cosmopolitan inheritance highlights the process of thoughtful receptivity rather than a predetermined body of content per se. Through a cosmopolitan prism teachers and students can see why, as DeSisto shows (2007), "the object of a tradition [i.e., an inheritance] does not represent a definitive statement on the world; instead, it is a response to that world" (pp. 115–116).

A vital element in education is learning *how* to respond to other people's responses to the world. How shall the class respond, figuratively speaking, to all those scientists over the generations who have bequeathed us that which we call biology? This receptive capacity entails cultivating methods of listening, contemplating, considering, and articulating framed in Chapters 2 and 3 through philosophy as the art of living. There is art in learning how to converse with others: literally, as the root term suggests, to speak "with" them rather than at or past them. Thus the approach here aspires to provide all students with opportunities to experience local and broader traditions educationally rather than solely from the point of view of socialization. This engagement *means* dialogue. Students should be able to raise questions, to wonder about origins, and to compare their undertakings with other traditions, all in ways that derive as much from their reactions as from those of their elders (cf. Burtonwood, 1995). It would be a disservice to students to smother and leave undeveloped, unarticulated, and unshared their fundamental responses to human experience as embodied in the curriculum. As we will see, their responses can be productive beginnings. The teacher and the curriculum can help mature them into educational realizations.

At first glance, the outlook here may conjure an image of endless tension if not actual strife with established belief and custom – in a word, with the trajectories of socialization. In my view it calls instead for the kind of experienced insight that dedicated teachers develop through confronting these very tensions. If a child asks why people believe in religion, democracy, or science, there is no reason to reply "Because the world is so and that's an end to it," or "What a profound question, let us abandon our traditions and start over." If heeded, the child's query could, however minutely in the scheme of things, lead to wiser ways of thinking about religion, democracy, or science. Put another way, the child's query could help her or his community reaffirm its integrity – its belief in religion, democracy, science – and yet in a way that positions it to subsist more efficaciously and justly with the larger world with its unfathomable diversity of values.

Thus to silence the child would be to inflict harm not only on her or his dignity but on the community itself. More than ever, given contemporary world developments, it is impossible for the child not to know about the reality of human variability. Merely walking down the street of almost any town or city today exposes the child to an ever-changing cultural kaleidoscope of sights, sounds, smells, and other expressions of the human. Thus to advocate giving the child's response a hearing does not imply individualistic ethnocentrism, i.e. that doing so is "more human" or is "the morally superior posture." Rather it constitutes an attempt at cosmopolitan common sense: the intuition that in this great world of ours people must continually renew tradition and practice if these are to survive. To pretend the child has no response to experience and consequently to suppress it constitutes a loss to humanity because it would deprive it – whether at the local or global level – of always needed new and reconstructed cultural resources. To move beyond the blind hold of custom is not to move beyond the life of custom.

Inheritance and Pedagogy

As an educational orientation, cosmopolitanism can give rise to a richer consciousness of the creative legacy and capacity of people everywhere. That consciousness, as we saw in Chapter 4, can give rise to important, dynamic modes of interaction and mutual support.

The practice of curriculum as educational inheritance can fuel the emergence of a cosmopolitan orientation. An orientation denotes a fusion of emotional and rational responsiveness to experience. As suggested previously it resembles the familiar term "sensibility." People refer to a vibrant, alert, active, and finely-tuned sensibility. They also point to a deadened, closed, passive, and narrow sensibility. At first glance the term may connote an atomistic psychology, as if each person struts around with a self-contained, private, unreachable mind-set or mentality. But the French root for the concept, *sens*, encompasses among other things "meaning" and "significance." Such things are not privatistic but depend upon social interaction. The idea of a purely private criterion for meaning is as non-sensical as the idea of having a private language. The emotion, the reasoning, the degree of openness and responsiveness, and the intuition that comprise an orientation form through interaction in the world. They are not determined causally by the world but nor are they self-generated.

A cosmopolitan orientation finds expression at the crossroads of reflective loyalty to the known and reflective openness to the new. It has no pre-given, embodied form and cannot be educated directly. It cannot be forced into being nor produced according to a preset curricular blueprint. And yet, it can be cultivated. In this section I will draw on results from previous chapters to further colorize the meaning of a cosmopolitan orientation, and then turn to a classroom example to illustrate its emergence.

Contours of a Cosmopolitan Orientation

Two familiar utterances will help set the stage. The Roman playwright and poet Terence gave voice to the first, which we heard in Chapter 2: "*Homo sum; humani nil a me alienum puto*" – "I am a man; I deem nothing that is human to be foreign to me." The quote (translation by Norton, 1904, p. 175) comes from line 77 of his play *The Self-Tormentor (Heauton timorumenos)*, written *c.*166–160 BCE. The American philosopher John Dewey (1985) expressed the second utterance in his closing line to *Democracy and Education*, first published in 1916: "Interest in learning from all the contacts of life is the essential moral interest" (p. 370).

Terence's turn of phrase prompts the idea that in enunciating one's humanity – in whatever idiom deployed – a person enacts the idea that nothing about other humans, who are also enunciating their humanity in their words and works, is alien. In polemical terms: there are no foreigners. People may find other persons, and themselves, to be strange, off-putting, enigmatic, and opaque. But that response differs from regarding those features as beyond the pale of the human rather than as marks of its character. This posture does not necessitate endorsing, much less adopting, other customs and beliefs, whether those of individuals or communities. However, it does mean not recoiling from others' lives as if they were creatures from another cosmos.[5]

Dewey emphasizes learning from *all* the encounters in life, not just those which are familiar, pleasant, and confirming. This "interest" is moral, in his view, because it concretizes and thereby sustains the very possibility of meaningful contact across and within differences. The willingness to learn from every encounter does not mean such learning will be easy or always possible. Understanding self and other is seldom guaranteed and is in any case always incomplete. But this interest does presume that there are no impermeable walls that permanently prevent people from moving further and further together even as they move closer and closer apart. People can learn to discern the values at play in different forms of life (cf. Mei-lin Ng, 2006), as well as learn from the often quite different ways in which people hold values, even the same ones.

Though penned over two thousand years apart, and in milieus strikingly different, the utterances from Terence and Dewey converge in a cosmopolitan orientation. As I have suggested, this term crystallizes modes of receptivity and communication that can be seen both in philosophizing on the art of living and in recent field-based research on cosmopolitanism on the ground. Let me put forward two additional realms of human conduct where one can witness the enactment of a cosmopolitan orientation. One is the world stage occupied by well-known and respected public figures. The other is the far less public setting of the classroom.

When I picture such widely admired, global-sized figures as Mohandas Gandhi, Nelson Mandela, and Eleanor Roosevelt (there are many others), I witness in action a capacity to respect and to acknowledge publicly, in one and the same moment, one's own cultural traditions and the reality of other traditions. I observe in their doings a profound interest in people, not just in "their own" but in people everywhere, an interest that expresses itself among other ways in a visible capacity for patience, reflection, articulate responsiveness, and self-criticism. I witness what it means to absorb and to make one's own ideas and values from other people's inheritances. These figures enact in an often bold fashion a living, dynamic conviction that as individuals they are not mere ciphers of internal or external material forces but rather are beings with a substantive degree of agency and autonomy, i.e. of freedom. At the same time, in their wondrously visible display of agency, they express a conviction that all of their listeners, all of their interlocutors, indeed all of their fellow humans are also agentive beings capable of influencing in better rather than worse ways the affairs of life.

So much for a brief look at extraordinary manifestations of a cosmopolitan orientation. Its brush strokes include a visible interest in and respect for the reality of other people and their traditions, inheritances, and concerns. They include a willingness to speak publicly about the things one cherishes even while listening, waiting, considering, pondering, and engaging those whose commitments may differ. And it incorporates a disposition to metabolize new ideas and values, albeit reflectively rather than thoughtlessly.

However, this summary of the cosmopolitan orientation that I see Gandhi, Mandela, and Roosevelt expressing in their lives does not capture *in toto* either the persons they were, or are, or their actions. I make this obvious point in order to underscore the fact that an individual's overall sensibility is impossible to pin down or taxonomize in a final, complete way. As suggested, these figures illuminate in striking ways constituents of a cosmopolitan orientation such as respect for the moral and ethical reality of other people, a respect that reaches beyond what can be contained by any national, regional, ethnic, racial, class, religious, or other boundary that comes to mind. But we also know that these extraordinary persons were at times parochial and defensive of "their own." Moreover they were at various moments strongly judgmental. They brought grief to some persons close to them; they were sometimes irresponsible and negligent in their policy-making; and they were at various junctures confused or wracked by doubt about their direction.

The upshot of this observation is that it is important not to reify the idea of a cosmopolitan orientation. Put in a more positive way, another constituent of a cosmopolitan orientation is a recognition, however inchoate or inarticulate, that there would be something amiss, awkward, untrue to life experience for a person to proclaim, "I am a cosmopolitan," or to say about his or her community, "We are cosmopolitan." As emphasized previously, a cosmopolitan orientation is not a possession, not a badge, not a settled accomplishment or achievement. It depends fundamentally upon the ongoing quality of one's interactions with others, with the world, and with one's own self. Like education – or like democracy, or like being a moral person – it is ever incomplete, ever emergent, and ever vulnerable to dissolution.[6]

Exemplars of a cosmopolitan orientation can be found across the universe of arts and letters. These persons do not approach others and the world writ large as consumers or spectators but rather as students in the richest sense of that term. I have in mind, for example, the enduring sense of being a student that one can argue was enacted by Confucius and Socrates. If we ponder more recent candidates for this ever-changing and enjoyably controversial list, it would likely include figures (a few of whom were mentioned previously) such as Jane Addams, Hannah Arendt, W. E. B. Du Bois, Sigmund Freud, George Orwell, W. G. Sebald, Susan Sontag, Rabindranath Tagore, Virginia Woolf, and Stefan Zweig. These are persons who, on the one hand, were deeply steeped in and knowledgeable about the culture of a particular community or nation. They had a profound sense for the local. On the other hand, they seemed to embrace Terence's invitation not to regard anything human as foreign. They heeded Dewey's urging to be receptive to all the contacts of life, which means being open to their potentially transformative influence. Moreover, these figures reveal how it is possible to retain spontaneity of response to the new – and more, to render this quality mature and to trust in it over the course of a life. This perhaps counter-intuitive process – the idea of *educating* spontaneity – helps account for why these persons cannot be categorized or pinned down from the perspective of a particular ideology. Like the youth interviewed by Osler and Starkey (2003) and by Mitchell and Parker (2008) (see Chapter 4, pp. 80–81), these figures show why cosmopolitanism points to a dynamic space between the individual, the community, and the world that is not subsumable to any one of them taken in isolation.

Educators could nominate their own list of individuals who in one form or another exemplify a cosmopolitan orientation. Among their suggestions would likely be figures such as John Dewey, Maria Montessori, and A. N. Whitehead. Like other cosmopolitan-minded exemplars, these diverse figures were deeply rooted in a particular constellation of tradition and inheritance. However, through the course of their education and experience they incarnated broader horizons, such that they were able to traverse familiar categories of person, place, and idea. It is noteworthy that, like the other figures mentioned previously, their influence cannot be contained within any specific national boundary but has percolated far and wide.

Research reviewed in previous chapters suggests that cosmopolitan exemplarity can in truth be found anywhere, however modestly expressed, including within the ethos of many people who might be surprised to have such an historically rich concept associated with them. Recall the working-class men whom Lamont and Aksartova (2002) interviewed, or the local people whose word and demeanor taught Wardle (2000) the meaning of the cosmopolitan. As we have seen, cosmopolitanism is not a badge or mark of identity but rather a heuristic for a dispositional, agentive orientation toward life characterized by receptivity, expressivity, and transformation. This way of moving does not operate in terms of outsider/insider, foreigner/compatriot, or other fixed divisions, even though the very same persons who embody the outlook will on countless occasions also think and act as insiders in any number of communities (familial, national, professional, religious, etc.). Cosmopolitanism describes a spirit of openness to learning from the contacts of life, especially those that are new and which, for that reason, can seem odd, unsettling, disquieting, perhaps even frightening. Given the inevitable tensions and ambiguities that accompany such a posture, cosmopolitan expressions will often be low-key, sporadic, inconsistent, and unpredictable.

These facts do not undercut cosmopolitanism's promise but rather attest to its inhabitability. They are why it is important to focus not just on the lives of well-known exemplars such as those named above. These persons are indeed universally fascinating and helpful to contemplate. They provide invaluable frames for criticizing present human arrangements and they generate hope in possibilities. Because their large accomplishments are rare, their example becomes all the more precious. As Sissela Bok cogently notes,

> an exemplary life is one we find astonishing, not because it is in some sense perfect from a moral point of view but because it is lived in the belief that it matters to think through how one should live, what goals one should strive for, and what it would mean to take them seriously.
>
> (Bok, 2006, p. 259)

However, the same individuals mentioned here might be the first to say that their affecting examples distort the scene if they push everyday life into the shadows. Cosmopolitanism on the ground, including in the school and classroom, does not require global-level heroism although it does necessitate effort and imagination. Moreover, as we saw in Chapter 4 it does not depend upon wealth, privilege, and power, even though increasing resources always position people to adopt new activities. "Ordinary" working-class people, recent immigrants, urban youth, and others can express a more cosmopolitan disposition than the most well-heeled and advantaged individuals. So can teachers and students in their everyday interaction.

Educating an Orientation

The classroom example I will offer here respects the claim put forward by Iris Murdoch (1970), Elaine Scarry (1998), and others that imagining or grasping the *reality* of other people can be a formidable task. The web of fantasy, the gravitational pull of self-interest, the siren call of ideals that become more important than persons, and the lingering force of disappointment can fog one's vision of others or even blind it. For Murdoch, this outlook leads her to advance humility as a core virtue in the moral life. For Scarry, it leads her to be highly skeptical of the sort of argument I am making in this book on behalf of cosmopolitan education. She implies that education has a minimal as well as fragile capacity to form moral imagination, and urges attention instead to establishing strong international institutions to advance human good. As emphasized in Chapter 1, that focus is invaluable, given the scale of contemporary problems and concerns. But the issue is not either/or. International commitments to the good will have no soil in which to grow without steady, patient, dedicated, and ongoing educational work the world over.

In what follows, I will presume that humility constitutes a dynamic condition as well as outcome of authentic learning about world, other, and self (Hansen, 2001, pp. 167–191). I will part company with the presumption that successfully imagining the reality of other people and their concerns is an uncommon occurrence. This imaginative achievement is not the preserve solely of the moral heroes of the world. A close look at the everyday indicates that it happens more often than meets the eye, perhaps especially an eye primed to be pessimistic by the all-too-comprehensible view that misunderstanding and violence dominate human affairs.

Consider a music teacher and music students in a local school anywhere in the world.[7] The students enjoy listening to music from all round the globe. At one point several are so taken with the flamenco strains in a particular track that they want to incorporate its sound in their own budding compositions. If asked why, they might simply reply, "Because we like it!" The teacher endorses their decision but at the same time poses a range of questions they must slowly but steadily consider, some technical, some philosophical. What is the history of this form of music? What kind of instruments does it deploy and what are their histories? Of what materials are these instruments made? Who makes them? With respect to the origins of flamenco, to what in human life or in nature might it be a response? In what ways – call them ludic, if you will – do traditions of flamenco respond to particular human joys, sufferings, values, aspirations, and the like? How do those responses, in turn, help us think about how we express our own joys, sufferings, concerns, and hopes through music and perhaps art in general? Might the responses embedded in flamenco tradition suggest ways of reconceiving or even reconstituting our cares and desires?

In short, through questioning, coaching, suggesting resources, and the like, the teacher helps students move from what could become a merely passing fancy, or a consumerist, spectator-like, or acquisitive sampling, to a participatory inquiry in which meanings and outlooks are explicitly at play. The teacher does not, to be sure, pose all these questions at once. That staccato approach would overwhelm students and doubtless squelch their curiosity. It might cause them to stare back at the teacher, perplexed about what sort of terrain or place she is describing.

The teacher's task is to help them travel there. Thus, her questions are crucial, for education sometimes necessitates discomfort, unsettlement, and friction. In the age of the internet it is all too easy to simply "click again," literally or mentally speaking, when one is pushed to think in a new key. Marcus Aurelius contended, in words that also echo Confucius' outlook, "The impediment to action advances action. What stands in the way becomes the way" (2003, p. 60, Bk. V.20). Thus the teacher speaks, listens, waits, and acts as if the students' initial spark of delight can, if nurtured and prodded with care, ascend into a higher, richer, more enduring mode of aesthetic, moral and intellectual meaningfulness. Put another way, the teacher conducts herself or himself as if the musical traditions of flamenco are not only emblematic of aspects of Spanish culture but are also a world inheritance bequeathed to persons everywhere – including in that teacher's local classroom far removed in space and time from flamenco's origins.

Moreover, imagine for a moment a whole train of encounters like the one described here that this teacher helps make possible for students. This teacher's approach expresses in an everyday, ongoing manner a visible conviction that her or his students dwell someplace other than "only" in the local – or "only" in the global – and that they are something more than "only" the persons they appear to be at the moment. Rather, this teacher's actions imply that the meanings of the local, of the global, and of personhood are always in motion and capable of enrichment. Put another way, a sustained engagement with curriculum as inheritance makes it possible for students to re-imagine and re-embrace the meaning of being at home in the world – or to come to grips with this meaning for the very first time. That meaning has to do with responding, participating, and creating.

In Chapter 1, I anticipated the use of metaphors – such as a "crossroads" – to elucidate cosmopolitanism as an educational orientation. In a commentary on this orientation, Luise Prior McCarty writes:

> The crossroads is thus an apt metaphor for the contemporary classroom or school in which individuals and groups with different backgrounds interact. Crossroads are temporary spaces in which we can look back at the familiar places from where we came and these crossroads point toward uncertain and unknown paths. Such a place might prepare us for this journey into the future by supplying us with nourishment and equipment, such as maps, as well as good wishes and encouragement. We meet strangers there, and we are cautious and curious, vulnerable to the risks we are about to undertake.
>
> (McCarty, 2009, p. 16)

The students in the music classroom have arrived at a crossroads where their knowledge and experience intersects with a significant cultural inheritance. They share that crossroads with their teacher and with one another, each of whom brings to it a distinctive aesthetic and reflective sensibility. The crossroads constitutes a scene of dynamic interaction, confusion, and discovery.

The students enter the crossroads as they are: they have been intrigued by a piece of music. But they travel someplace else: they have incorporated into their orientations a response to a human inheritance that has percolated through the world. However modest this transformation may be in the totality of their evolving humanity, it is noteworthy not only in its technical and musical senses – the students and teacher now know more about flamenco than they did before – but in the accompanying philosophical, moral and ethical senses of their experience. The students still live *in* their local world, but they are no longer merely *of* it. They have the same names and are the same ages but their orientations are now different. They have had an opportunity to cultivate a deeper intimation of what it means to take the world seriously, to learn from the reality of its offerings, and to appreciate it. To recur to the language I employed previously, they dwell someplace between the local – that which they were and are – and the global or universal – that which they can in principle take in and become. If they could speak like veteran artists or physicists, perhaps they would say they are no longer quite sure how to delimit the local and the universal.

Furthermore, what these students have learned, and what they have become as persons with respect to their evolving orientations, will affect the local world in which they move because they will carry those orientations everywhere they go. This claim reflects the fact that in engaging the philosophies of life and of art embedded in flamenco they did not abandon their own musical traditions and accompanying values, even if these were subjected to influence. Their learning was not a matter of all or nothing. It was a transaction between the new and the familiar such that both have been infused with new dynamism (Dewey 1991, Rosenblatt 1978). Thus their learning will also affect the ever-changing shape and substance of the cosmos, namely because these students' creativity and undergoing are unprecedented and irreproducible, and not just for them. They have expanded, deepened, and enriched the human tapestry in ways that matter, however infinitesimal all this may seem. As they consolidate their experience through subsequent encounters, their ever-evolving achievement can itself contribute, in microcosm, to a potential inheritance for others.

Educational Cosmopolitanism Revisited

Curriculum as cosmopolitan inheritance reflects an orientation in its own right toward cultural creativity understood in its sociolinguistic, practice-centered, and individual senses. The teacher does not regard flamenco as a purely bounded inheritance whose significance is a priori contained or exhausted within a particular frame of meaning. The teacher does not presume that to learn something authentic from flamenco traditions is reserved *ipso facto* only for those who inhabit its natal settings. However, the teacher does not pretend that students can experience the same meaning as its creators, much less reside in their outlook. There remains a sacral quality to their original, artful creation; it was born of distinctive sufferings, joys, and yearnings. But this sense of reverence, which mirrors cosmopolitan reverence for the sheer fact of the world, does not convert creations into possessions that cannot be genuinely shared with others. The idea of a cosmopolitan education encourages a sense of hospitality. People can participate in and welcome other traditions into their lives. They can come to understand aspects of how people far and wide have responded to the world's address.

As we have seen, the process is neither simple nor automatic. Mehta (2000) illuminates why this is so in evoking an insight from Montaigne and the philosopher David Hume. They recognized, Mehta writes,

> that it is the hallmark of a truly reflective consciousness that it subverts the pride of reflective consciousness . . . Cosmopolitanism requires, properly speaking, more than simply the willingness or ability to adopt a reflective

standpoint that allows distance from one's own presuppositions. It may also require a prior ethic grounded in the supposition that in dealing with important matters like the meaning of life and the practices that express those meanings, the conclusions of reflection will be necessarily varied and indeterminate and that reflection will only heighten this sense, not transcend it. It may require a sensibility that renounces the confidence that one can easily possess that which is different.

(Mehta, 2000, pp. 627–628)

Cosmopolitan understanding differs from possession, just as education differs from socialization. The teacher in the example here presumes that students will need time and space to engage new traditions. They will need it because of the scholastic challenge involved, and because the process will bring into the open their own sense of tradition, shaped through socialization, and subject it to the light of genuine human variability.

Appiah (2005, pp. 252–272) rightly argues that philosophical agreement regarding fundamental values is not required as a ground for inter-communal or international political negotiation. It is enough at the start, he shows, that people comprehend particular concerns, circumstances, and options. However, in the project of cosmopolitan education it is vital to engage students with philosophical diversity such as that which resides in different musical traditions. Figuratively speaking, the teacher here is helping students understand not only what it means to study flamenco, but to imagine it as addressing them with questions about who they are and what they wish to become. The teacher is assisting students to come to grips with what it means to be a human being in a changing world, as well as how they themselves can help constitute their humanity. The teacher is encouraging students to perceive why all curriculum represents, in principle, their inheritance, to which in due course they can contribute even if it may be hard to isolate and assess their eventual imprint.

Moreover, they are all learning – teacher and students alike – more about what it means to be a critical rather than idolatrous custodian of inheritances of meaning, of purposiveness, and of responsiveness to the world (Hansen, 2001, pp. 114–156; and see Hogan, 1996). They are cultivating, at least in germ, a posture of what Arendt (1961) described as care for the world. That care begins with the local, in this case their classroom. In discerning the reality of how each of them responds to the curriculum, they move closer and closer apart. In realizing the depth and meaning in a tradition new to them, they move further and further together. At the same time, they experience the value and the wondrousness in acting as cosmopolitan creators. They learn, construct, and put forward cultural resources for themselves and others. They see the value in recognizing flamenco tradition as more than "just another nice sound" but as educational and as potentially edifying in its distinctive response to the experience of being human. This emerging, always dynamic sensibility can help position them to participate that much more actively and constructively in the affairs of life into which they enter.

Human beings cannot turn the tides of the sea, as Bryan Ferry and Roxy Music beautifully express in their song, "More Than This." But whether as children or as adults, they do not need to drift on the tides of chance. They can draw on their own latent aesthetic and intellectual capacity, and thereby turn their energies to constructive account. As Dewey (1985) posed the matter in a statement quoted previously, "Interest in learning from all the contacts of life is the essential moral interest" (p. 370). This interest is moral, in part, because it substantiates concern, responsibility, and creative guardianship of creativity itself at whatever level it occurs.

Exercises of the Self for the Teacher in the World

To prepare and practice for the orientation addressed here, teachers can absorb in their own ways the exercises characterized in Chapters 2 and 3. Those exercises constitute an ethic: a way of cultivating a person's aesthetic, moral, and reflective capacity and outlook. As such they contrast with modes of sacrificial self-abnegation sometimes triggered by stereotypical expectations of the "selfless" teacher (Higgins, 2003). The exercises bring the teacher *into* the conjunction "and" referred to throughout this book: reflective openness and reflective loyalty, the teacher and the world. Let me briefly rehearse several exercises in light of the present discussion.

We encountered one in a previous section: the identification of handbooks, or of a canon. These are meaningful works that help the teacher negotiate her or his way through the always complicated, conflicted, and redeeming realm of educating. The works may be philosophical texts, poems, histories, auto-biographies, novels, films, paintings, and more. They do not provide a blueprint or specific, blow-by-blow advice. They cannot do so, since each teacher's situation is unique and distinctive. But nor is it their office to do so. What they do provide is the voice of wisdom, courage, and imagination. In effect they say to the teacher: "Are you actually surprised that educating is difficult, and yet also wondrous? Are you really shocked that your school is rent by competing agendas and yet also positions you to mature? Are you really stunned to be witness to both the good and the bad in human nature? You, teacher, dwell at a crossroads of people, places, institutions, and more. There are no preset boundaries there that rule out the manifold expressions of human nature – remembering, too, that that very nature is ever-changing in ways nobody can mark or calculate, since we all are too close to it to see it. You will encounter every day, every hour, and perhaps every minute the problematic and the promising, the frustrating and the liberating, the depressing and the delightful."

While reminding teachers to engage reality rather than seek escape, handbooks can also comfort, soothe, and calm. They can reinvigorate and replenish. They become good company to keep, to recall a trope from the literary scholar Wayne Booth (1988). Booth illustrates how works of literature can become, in almost literal terms, friends and companions. They become a voice within, conversing with the person, serving as a kind of sympathetic observer and commentator. They help, as does any text or text-analogue that takes on the role of a handbook in the individual's life. I encourage teachers to identify their handbooks early and to hold them close, even as those works hold the teacher close, while also seeking new guides as well. Without knowing it, this practice can deepen one's care for the world itself. After all, it is human creativity in and for that world which has generated such inspiring works in the first place. Such caring, in turn, can ramify throughout the teacher's daily work, not so much overtly as in the subtle yet firm gestures of encouragement that mark any dedicated educator's craft.

If handbooks and a canon do not provide concrete advice, one's trusted peers can. Thus another exercise is focused companionship with colleagues, who may work in the same institutional setting or elsewhere. This exercise complements the spirit of induction programs and the now conventional, and sound, advice to teachers to collaborate, interact, share ideas, and learn to speak as a community. It does so by spotlighting the tone and the tenor of companionable talk. Rather than just addressing the latest problem or challenge, this talk can mirror what women made possible for themselves and others in the salons they began to generate some four hundred years ago. They created a space for thinking, for reflection, for criticism, and for imagination. They selected readings, topics, and broad questions to address. Teachers can do the same, creating thereby an intellectual sanctuary, a place apart, a place for them. Their talk in these sanctuaries – which may be in a colleague's home, in a café, in a public park – can inform the modes of practical, on-the-spot thinking they must practice in the classroom and office.

Their talk can turn philosophical in the sense of thinking out loud together about their respective philosophies of education. A philosophy of education can be understood as an embodiment of values, an ethical and moral compass, and a well-spring of practical ideas (Hansen, 2007, p. 7, *passim*). For example, a teacher may value dialogue with students, the give and take of interpretive questions revolving around subject matter. That value, in turns, provides a compass on how to conduct herself. It points inward, in the manner of ethics, guiding her to cultivate her arts of questioning, listening, and responding creatively, allied with deepening her knowledge of the subject matter at issue. It also points outward, in the manner of morals, guiding her to take note of events in the classroom that support richer discussion, and those events that may be distracting or undermining and to which she must therefore attend. And to value discussion is to develop a practical radar, a capacity to be on the lookout for any moment in the class where the teacher can pose a question, take students to the text or text-analogue, spark an exchange between individuals, and pick up on a quizzical look on a student's face. Teachers can learn endlessly from one another, in ways that at the same time provide real pleasure, as they think out loud about philosophies of education.

Another exercise, to practice with colleagues and with students, is the art of waiting – or, put another way, the art of silence. Confucius and Socrates, both founding figures in philosophy as the art of living, demonstrate an acute mindfulness of the virtues of silence. At many moments in their interaction with others they listen, they hold their tongue, they bide their time. Their silence becomes an active mode of non-action, just as patience as a pedagogical virtue denotes a highly active posture of attentiveness and alertness.

A related exercise is thinking carefully and systematically about particular events, persons, and issues in one's teaching. Here thinking denotes not just thinking *about* events but *thinking them*, which is to say describing them to oneself, rendering them in as full a color as possible to oneself, feeling them as delicately as one can. This thinking can be embodied in writing, whether in the familiar form of a journal or in other modes. However, it is not journaling for its own sake. I make this point heedful of teacher candidates with whom I worked as director of a teacher education program who one day complained to me they were being asked to write a journal in almost all their courses (!) – a sure sign of the fashionable trumping the reasonable. The writing exercises that mirror philosophy as the art of living would be more along the lines of *thinking teaching*. They would not necessarily be undertaken regularly like a conventional journal or diary. They would be more composed, like doing a painting or mastering how to play a particular piece of music.

Recall Marcus Aurelius' astute, thoughtful descriptions of what he learned from influential people across his life, including family members, teachers, politicians, and others. Those miniature set pieces that open his book seemed to influence his subsequent thinking in generative ways. Consider as another example "descriptive review," developed over the years by Patricia Carini and colleagues (see, for example, Himley and Carini, 2000). The term encompasses the practice of taking time to write about the doings of a particular student in order (a) to get to know that student better and thereby respond more efficaciously and helpfully, and (b) to see the classroom ethos itself in a fresh, more enriched way. The teacher can conduct this thinking over the whole year, shifting in her or his writing from one student (or class, as the case may be) to another. What Carini dubs the review portion has to do with sharing and discussing the descriptions, primarily with colleagues but also, in principle, parents and students. I would recommend teachers complement this fruitful exercise with fine-grained, essay-like miniatures where they focus closely on an aspect of their curriculum. In this way, they slowly but surely engage more fully with inheritances, in time bringing them from the mind to their very finger-tips for purposes of classroom work.

As difficult as it can be to find the time – or, better, to make the time – for these exercises of the self, it is hard to picture crafting a meaningful teaching life without a place for them. They fuel what Christopher Day and Quin Gu (2010), in an important study of teachers' lives, characterize as teachers' resilience in the face of challenge and difficulty. The exercises call for what the ancients called *otium*, which we translate today as "leisure" (cf. Ildefonso, 2010). But otium meant something other than free time, spare time, after work time, being entertained, and other connotations of the contemporary notion of leisure. Otium was not merely a reaction to work, a way to get away from work, a way to recuperate and relax. Leisure meant moving *toward something*: namely, toward inhabiting the world more fully. It often implied the creative use of solitude, not to be confused with being solitary. The idea was to balance the phases of one's life – something that many people today often have a hard time doing, given the way modern life prioritizes work and its corollary, entertainment, and makes everything else a tributary to them. Moreover, in the absence of otium and of the other exercises reviewed here, teaching can itself become a relentless, devouring beast, rather than the wondrous (i.e., joyful and painful, frustrating and fulfilling) human experience it can be when one brings to it a balanced orientation.

This talk of exercises of the self may well sound quaint if not strange to contemporary ears (to echo a trope from Nietzsche). It is one thing to refer to the endless self-help materials available on the internet and at bookstores every-where. It is quite another to imagine *working* on the self in the spirit of *rendering* oneself capable of dwelling in and for the world. However, as we have seen, to revitalize ancient practices of the self is not backward-looking. Quite the contrary. In figurative terms these practices come from the future, as an offering. They position people to look beyond the always seductive aspects of the present zeitgeist and to ask the questions with which this chapter began. What *are* you doing here? How are you dwelling? How are you relating to self, other, and world? These are questions human beings have asked since time immemorial, questions they have either sought to respond to in their own terms, or have let others do so for them. Today's technological rush, wherein everybody becomes endlessly hooked up in endless ways, is one such answer. Is it the teacher's, too? The student's own answer, too? Perhaps so, but it is one thing to swallow the answer unreflectively, and quite another to arrive at this response through one's own creative thought and conduct. Let a thousand technological and other wonders bloom. But let teachers and students do their own gardening as well, drawing upon technology as well as other resources as appropriate.

The exercises re-imagined here constitute a method. They constitute a self-pedagogy, an ongoing process of *forming* oneself into the person and teacher one can become. They make possible a continuous re-greening and re-flowering of the mind, heart, and imagination – all so essential, given the managerial pressures that bombard many teachers today (Day and Gu, 2010). Through such exercises, the teacher teaches herself or himself in an ongoing way, coming further and further into the role, and further and further into the world. In turn, teachers can infuse the exercises, in reconfigured form, into their curriculum, their teaching, their advising, and their mentoring in the school, university, or other setting.

Teaching, Curriculum, and the Cosmopolitan Prism

In this chapter, I have sought to elucidate aspects of educational cosmo-politanism as a distinctive outlook on curriculum and its realization through teaching and learning. Curriculum as cosmopolitan inheritance highlights the quest for meaning that can be understood as informing, in a natal sense, what is called subject matter. Curriculum as cosmopolitan inheritance is an educational idea that presupposes socialization but is not identical with it. This curriculum can fuel a cosmopolitan orientation that embodies respect for the reality of self, other, and world. This orientation propels persons to communicate with others and with other traditions and inheritances. It disposes people not only to be open to new values and ideas but to consider them, on the one hand, as responses to the world and, on the other hand, as addresses to them from the world.

This orientation can accompany, in a reflective spirit, students' growth in knowledge, information, and skills. Put another way, it is not a substitute for the curriculum but a re-imagining of its larger significance. Its virtue is that it can be enacted in any subject at any level of the system. That feature mirrors the virtues of cosmopolitanism touched on in the Preface: its suppleness as an attentive, open-ended philosophy of life, its longevity across history as a generative response to change, and its hopefulness rooted, in part, in awareness of the inextinguishable human quest for meaning.

The Direct and the Indirect

The orientation can complement more explicit efforts at a cosmopolitan-minded education. Such initiatives have barely begun, although those that have provide a glimpse of the possibilities. Walter Parker (2007) conceives "a critical, post-national, cosmopolitan school curriculum." This curriculum would aim to deepen students' sensibilities as what Parker calls "world citizens." It would aspire to cultivate a growing sense of stewardship for the world rather than solely for one's local setting. Parker acknowledges the values in traditional international and global curricula, which typically aim to enlarge students' knowledge of the world, to promote democratic thinking, and to strengthen tolerance of differences that are expressed non-violently. In fact he offers a reconstructed international curriculum, in what he dubs "Comparative Studies," that he argues would advance such aims.

However, he juxtaposes this proposal with a curriculum called "World Studies," with world standing for cosmos, i.e. for all those countless realms of human interaction and need not reducible to the expression of national characteristics or interests. This curriculum would focus on case studies of globalization, on earth studies (based upon the Earth Charter[8]), and above all on developing perspectives from the point of view of a world citizen. These elements instantiate Nussbaum's (1997a) perspective that to "cultivate humanity" around the globe requires, in her view, self-examination, learning to see oneself as a world citizen, and what she calls narrative imagination: the ability to think intelligently about other people's situations and to learn to respond well to them. Like Nussbaum (1997a, 2002) and other critics, Parker argues that the United States – with its still formidable power – needs not just an international or global curriculum but one centered explicitly upon cosmopolitan values.

Hiro Saito (2010) adopts a different though parallel tack. His brief for what he calls "Cosmopolitan-National Education" pivots around the education of emotion, and in this sense echoes both Confucian and Stoic philosophical motifs.[9] Saito draws upon an array of detailed examples from several school sites in Japan to illuminate how teachers can help students extend their emotional and cognitive affiliations to people elsewhere in the world. He does not conceive the cosmopolitan as a rival with the national. In his view, each perspective informs the other. He criticizes universalistic notions of cosmopolitanism – what Kok-Chor Tan (2004, p. 24) calls "extreme cosmopolitanism" – that oblige people to transcend their local rootedness in the name of world solidarity. Saito counters this view with a more grounded cosmopolitanism, such as that illuminated above in Chapter 4, in which people learn to move across rather than rise above local borders and boundaries. As with Parker's proposal, Saito highlights the power of dialogue in a cosmopolitan education. He emphasizes how it can generate expanded emotional affiliations which can, in turn, become a basis for intellectual, moral, and ultimately political commitments to transnational justice.

Leonard Waks (2008) takes up a policy orientation. He articulates mechanisms for expanding communication between individuals, schools, and communities as a way to deepen an ethos of shared cosmopolitan-minded responsibility. "A cosmopolitan citizenship education project," he writes,

> aims to soften oppositional identities and provide access to settings for cosmopolitan exchange. People form and strengthen cosmopolitan attitudes, interests and loyalties by engaging in such exchanges. Existing cosmopolitan settings, where people from different groups habitually and positively cooperate, whether in formal academic or "real world" settings, thus play a singularly important role in this process. The project as a result aims primarily to (a) enlarge the cosmopolitan potential of academic settings and (b) establish access routes between them and the city.
>
> (Waks, 2008, p. 213)

Waks discusses the promise in diversifying schools, in opening the doors of schools to adults who can bring to bear the resources of cosmopolitan networks, in allowing for much greater exchange and movement between local schools so they can establish cosmopolitan-minded relations, and more.

While there are many reasons to foreground the familiar concept "global (or world) citizen," this book has taken a different tack. I have rendered the original Greek term, *kosmopolites,* as inhabitant rather than as citizen of the world. One of the term's roots, *polis,* means not a state or nation but a community of human beings aspiring to dwell together. Dwelling implies inhabiting.

To me the educational priority in places of learning is coming into the world: becoming an inhabitant, becoming at home, cultivating roots in, and consciousness of, the stream of human meaning-making across space and time. This orientation fuels the core value of reflective openness to the new and reflective loyalty to the known. Without the orientation, the requirements of citizenship – even something we might dub cosmopolitan citizenship – may remain hard to meet or even to conceive. They may become brittle and formalistic. They may override or put in the shadows the deep modes of caring and participating painted in these pages. They may, paradoxically, render education into a mere means to an end, which is the very antithesis of learning to inhabit the world. If

I fail to cultivate this mode of dwelling in space and time, how can I be expected to take on the mentalities and habits of a so-called global citizen? How can I be expected to truly learn how to listen, to reflect, to take seriously the claims and needs of others? I will hear them only partially, see them only fitfully, and be motivated only intermittently. While there is no essential or preordained rivalry between the concepts, it seems to me that learning to inhabit the world in the manner portrayed in this book is a precondition for learning to be a responsible, and responsive, citizen of it.

In a spirit I take to be one of inhabitation, Glynda Hull and colleagues (2010) describe the creative uses of an online international social network that was juxtaposed with offline local programs intended to cultivate cosmopolitan-minded dispositions and capacities. The study focuses on a group of teenage girls in India, all living in poverty and who work each day to support their families, but who also have access to an organized educational program several times a week. Among other activities, the girls interacted and exchanged digital arts-based artifacts with youth from Norway, South Africa, and the United States. Hull and colleagues interpret the data to show how the girls reconstructed their sense of self and world. They deepened in their thoughtful receptivity to ideas from beyond the local and also enhanced their sense of personal agency and creativity. Through their "hospitable readings" of others' creations, and through their spontaneous communications, the girls enacted meaningful moments of intercultural exchange. The authors characterize the exchanges as "everyday cosmopolitanism" (p. 349), a term of art they develop from Corpus Ong (2009). Hull and colleagues illuminate, in fine-grained detail, the educational substance and meaning of this everyday mode of being.

The argument in this book conjures a curriculum reaching from childhood through university. Along with other more familiar fare, the curriculum would feature ongoing study of local inheritances and traditions which may reach back far into the past. At the same time, it would feature – again, over the space of years – an in-depth study of at least one other civilization, examining its arts, economic structures, politics, educational practices, religious institutions, and the like over the course of history. Teachers would slowly but surely encourage students studying in both streams to come to grips with the philosophical underpinnings of the respective cultures, how they embody responses to the quest for meaning and as such pose questions to students about how they are leading their own lives. The aim would not be coverage, or information or knowledge alone, valuable as they are. Nor would the aim be to replicate the teaching of national histories, whose privileging in school curricula distorts human experience in the world given how recently the nation-state itself came into being. The purposes would be (1) to come to grips with lives in various places across space and time, and (2) to experience fully, and then to render into an object of inquiry in its own right, reflective openness to the new juxtaposed with reflective loyalty to the known.

As a mirror to this idea, Anne-Marie Drouin-Hans (2006) argues that just as North African immigrant youth in France should study Montaigne and Montesquieu, so French youth with centuries-old roots in the land should study

Ibn Khaldun and other important Arab scholarly and literary works. All can benefit from a long-term, serious immersion in these twin universes of art, religion, philosophy, architecture, and so forth. Saranindranath Tagore (2003, pp. 87–91) sketches how an introductory course on philosophy (for roughly 16–20 year olds) can become genuinely comparative and cosmopolitan in its educational reach. It overcomes the "cafeteria" problem in some multicultural education programs by constantly generating intersection points, or crossroads, where inheritances meet or can be introduced to one another. Tagore refers to his approach as cultivating a "deep" rather than "shallow" cosmopolitanism (p. 89). In the terms of this book, it would be more than *in*formative but also *trans*formative in students' outlooks.

Another guide for curriculum-making is to select objects formed in cosmopolitan circumstances. For example, musicologists surmise that flamenco was born in late medieval Andalusia, the southern region of Spain that for centuries had been co-inhabited by Muslims, Christians, Jews, and various mixtures thereof. They were hardly conflict-free centuries in that region, and yet in many moments and places a genuine cosmopolitan-minded ethos obtained in the midst of cultural difference. The fundamentalist turn the Spanish court took, with its final assault on Moorish Spain in the late 1400s, erased this ethos. Flamenco seems to embody much of this history. In its singing that wells up from someplace beyond the heart, and in its earthy dancing that mesmerizes, flamenco transfigures the suffering of people shattered by discrimination. At the same time, it expresses the inextinguishable quest for meaning, for joy, and for dwelling fully in the here and now. There are countless forms of art, science, music, architecture, poetry, mathematics, physical education, and more, that teachers can draw upon from across the field of cosmopolitan-minded human endeavor.

In the spirit of exercises for the teacher, there are also numerous classroom-based activities that can activate reflective openness to new ideas, values, and people, juxtaposed with reflective loyalty to the known. A primary school teacher in a course I taught explained that, across her curriculum, she works with students to understand the relation between windows and mirrors: to see their work in arithmetic, reading, writing, art, and so forth as opening windows to the world while also raising mirrors for them to gaze in and thereby learn how their respective minds work. Another teacher routinely brings in portraits of various people associated with academic topics, as a way for students to imagine the fundamentally human origins and trajectories of subject matter. Other teachers I know make use of the familiar question Where do you come from? to help students see themselves as participants in multiple, often inter-cultural "spaces" in the world: family, friendships, various activities and interests, not to mention town, city, region, nation, continent. The teachers also transform that question into queries such as Where do you think they [other individuals and communities] think they are from? What would it take for us to try to understand how they address the question of roots, origins, and affiliations? As discussed in Chapter 3, to appreciate the plurality of home opens a door to appreciating the plurality of the human. Such questions can be delicate and sensitive, depending on students' circumstances, so as ever would need to be incorporated with a judicious touch.

Every subject holds out opportunities comparable to the music example sketched previously. Countless contemporary artifacts – a poem, scientific explanation, song, argument, painting, novel, geometric proof – can become an occasion for moving far into the past to study what has made that artifact possible in the first place. It can trigger thought about what might make it possible for the artifact to have continued life in the future. This method shines a light on another mode of being at home in the world: namely, through a vivid, organic relation with the human past, which in this kind of exercise no longer is merely past but becomes vitally present. The exercise can help students imagine why, and how, many works from the past speak to us from the future: their possibilities, like our own, are still ahead of us.

The ever-changing menu of cosmopolitan-minded educational work in the school seems endless. Many of these undertakings cost no more than Confucius' and Socrates' practice of raising questions with the young people who often surrounded them. Such work evokes or calls out a state of mind, and invites its enactment in activity with others and with the inheritances of the world. A cosmopolitan orientation encourages teachers and students alike to move from listening *to* others to listening *with* them. To be sure, it can be invaluable to learn to listen *to* other people; such learning constitutes the road to tolerance. But as important as this accomplishment is, cosmopolitanism as education encourages listening *with* others: an imaginative, aesthetic exercise of trying to see the world as they do, to try to grasp the underlying values, beliefs, and aspirations that inform their ways of looking and knowing. All persons live in the same world, and all develop modes of perception. But persons see that same world differently depending on their upbringing, experience, and concerns. To listen *with* others is to try to discern *their* response to being in the same world. This orientation pushes beyond tolerance – a posture in which I can listen to others but without being affected by the experience – into a realm of formative learning, in which who and what I am comes into play. I open myself to being influenced by my encounters.

Some of the concrete ideas suggested in these pages are idealistic. But ideals, even if unattainable, can provide light: they can suggest a sense of direction and the changes consistent with that direction. It bears underscoring that, as always with educational work, each step would require care, tact, and patience. The sorts of formal programs the studies above illustrate can complement the organic approach featured elsewhere in this book. This complementarity links the direct and the indirect, the explicit and the implicit, the formal and the ongoing, that have always constituted educational practice. What is stated programmatically, at discrete moments in teaching, often has a less enduring impact than all the everyday statements and doings in the work that are typically taken for granted (cf. Dewey, 1977). Just as cosmopolitanism on the ground does not await top-down initiatives to spring to life, so a cosmopolitan-minded education does not wait upon them either. In the example of the music classroom sketched above, the teacher never formally used the term cosmopolitan, though the experience that unfolded was saturated with meanings that term expresses.

Teachers as a Cosmopolitan Community

Cosmopolitanism points toward a way of living, not in the sense of grasping final truths that one can trumpet to others, but rather in respecting truth so much – that is, respecting the reality of world, other, and self so much – that one appreciates what it means to dwell educationally. We have seen enactments of these ideas – or, better, their very sources – in the tradition of philosophy as the art of living and in what research has illuminated about cosmopolitanism on the ground. This interweaving of philosophical and field-based anthropology fuels the idea of cultivating through education arts of speaking, listening, and inquiring.

These arts have long been at play, in concrete and distinctive ways, across the different subjects taught in school. A cosmopolitan prism illuminates additional significance embedded in them. Put another way, it reveals their dual character. On the one hand, these skills enable the student to learn to solve problems and to build a knowledge base. On the other hand, they open a door to participating in the world's very transformation – something which occurs with every creative act on the part of a community or individual. In other words, these skills are not merely for observing the world or for getting along in it, indispensable as such abilities always are, but for participating *in* it. Students can learn that in parsing a sentence, solving an equation, conducting an experiment, training for a sport – or composing music – that what is gained are not merely technical skills but an expanding orientation toward the world. This process can move them to participate in the world, to inhabit the world, as creatively as their time, resources, and strength allow.

In many if not most schools at all levels of the system, there are teachers and administrators who can exemplify for students how to do this. These men and women may operate under the proverbial radar screen, focused as they are day-by-day and moment-by-moment on their students' well-being. In my life I have met many educators from quite different communities, cultures, nations, regions, and the like, who are able to talk meaningfully with one another about educational matters. When they meet they build common ground, sometimes with startling swiftness and with fluency. This common ground does not spring from agreement per se on issues of curriculum, instruction, assessment, and the like. Rather it derives from their ability to generate language for expressing the importance of such issues, for articulating the significance of the very endeavor that goes by the name of education. To adapt a turn of phrase from Hans-Georg Gadamer (1984), one could describe this phenomenon as the natural propensity toward philosophy by some (obviously not all) who educate. Their efforts sustain a continuous, worldwide conversation undertaken in numerous registers about what it means to be a teacher, what makes teaching more than merely socializing others, and many related questions.

This conversation constitutes more than a sum of its national, cultural, and individual parts. It is not difficult to imagine instances in which, if a teacher did not explicitly identify herself or himself as, say, Chinese or Nigerian, or Catholic or Muslim, or as a math or art teacher, an outsider to the dialogue might be hard-pressed to determine the person's "origins." This familiar occurrence does not reflect a universalized homogeneity. On the contrary, it signals the ability of some educators to bring to bear an intimate grasp, literally at their finger-tips, of their local domains fused with an equally intimate, thoughtful receptivity to new outlooks and ideas. In their shared aspiration to get at the meaning of education, and to perform the work well, these educators stand between the universal and the particular, between the global and the neighborhood. They stand between the naïve and the cynical, between the local and the parochial. They stand in a cosmopolitan space.

Teacher educators can help candidates appreciate that approaching this space takes time, experience, and thought. They can help candidates plant the seeds of their emerging philosophies of education, knowing that it takes years to bring vision and practice together in a reciprocally informing, dynamic manner. That fact mirrors the claim in Chapter 1, that education in all its many forms cannot be rushed or forced. It can instead be nurtured, nourished, and supported through times of both frustration and fulfillment.

Educational work the world over has often been uncanny in its trajectories. Extensive testimony and research demonstrates that there are teachers everywhere who resist being molded into functionaries or hired hands (Day and Gu, 2010). They do not cast off the charge of socialization which is a critical aspect of their work. However, they also enact the longstanding fact that education means voyaging into the new, the unscripted, the unexpected, the unplanned, and the unpredictable – and not just for the individuals in question but for the world itself. That is, every person and every classroom or school community who undergo this process – in which they respond creatively to being in the world – have contributed thereby to the human richness of the cosmos. Their effort may be microscopic in comparison with the whole, and it may also have a family resemblance to others' gestures. But every genuinely educational experience embodies dimensions that are unique and irreducible.

Teachers constitute an already existing cosmopolitan community. Many have an abiding disposition to share ideas, methods, and philosophies across any number of cultural markers. The most serious-minded and playful of them seem to draw pleasure, insight, and edification from this trans-communal and trans-personal exchange. In so doing, they can trace their roots to pioneering educational influences such as Confucius and Socrates – who still teach through their words and legacies. Teachers are among those in our time who play an irreplaceable role in cultivating reflective openness to the new and reflective loyalty to the known.

Epilogue
Cosmos, Demos, and the Teacher

In his novel *Narcissus and Goldmund*, first published in 1930, Herman Hesse portrays two modes of life. The soulful, artistically compelled Goldmund embodies the spirit of the nomad, the wanderer, the adventurer. His life is marked by intensity – in joy and in sorrow, in love and in hate – and by almost nonstop epiphany as he encounters remarkable people and creates beautiful art works. He leads a life of endless risk, danger, and promise, calling to mind Henry Fielding's challenge to Fate: "Tomorrow, do thy worst, for today I have lived." In contrast, Narcissus dwells in a cloister – literally, a cloistered world. He teaches and governs within that world. He contemplates being and time. He finds depth in study and in what is given daily through its ordinary hours. Intensity and epiphany, risk and danger, are not hallmarks of his days. But his vocation has its own creative dimensions and it yields him satisfactions that Goldmund could never imagine. Hesse's achievement is to render convincingly the values in each mode of life. He does so, in part, by artfully making it easy for the reader to come to love both figures, their many imperfections notwithstanding.

Goldmund and Narcissus' different pathways illuminate the tensions between home and road, the local and the universal, and the familiar and the strange. Their ways of moving in the world reveal the constraints and losses, as well as the opportunities, which accompany any life trajectory. At the same time, their heartfelt, lifelong friendship mirrors how those apparent antinomies – old and new, near and far, the one and the many – can in metaphorical terms be companions. They do not necessarily cancel each other out. Seen through a cosmopolitan prism, they become richer and more robust through their mutual, ineradicable presence. Goldmund and Narcissus move closer and closer apart, as they see more clearly the reality of their differences and the consequences for life that flow from them. They move further and further together as they learn, if not in so many words, to acknowledge, understand, and appreciate those very differences.

A cosmopolitan orientation lacks the purity, the constancy, and the poetic heroism in the nomadic and monastic ways of life, respectively, that Goldmund and Narcissus embody. As we have seen, however, it has its own inhabitable appeal, holding out images of life as educative, meaningful, and transactive. To recall Chan Kwok-bun's (2005, p. 13) trope, such a life conjures the possibility of roots and routes – of place and places, of the known and the new, of memory and anticipation. In educational terms, it gives rise to the possibility of broadening people's horizons, which as documented here does not necessitate physical movement per se but rather aesthetic, ethical, moral, and intellectual movement, however modest each step may be. The orientation propels persons to express, *to create*, a generous response to the world.

Are human beings fundamentally inclined toward such creativity? Are they most fulfilled when they dwell in a permeable world, when they accept and indeed cultivate porosity rather than close it off? While there is considerable evidence for believing so, the portrait remains incomplete. History and current events demonstrate that it is equally natural to human beings to turn the portrait on its head – to become shrilly tribal, violent, and death-dealing.

It is true that power-grasping persons have throughout history proclaimed themselves the guardians of the faith, be it ethnic, political, religious, or whatever, and have wreaked terrible destruction by inciting people to fear, hate, and kill the ever-present "enemy." By ever-present I mean the human capacity to create foes in their very midst where before there were only neighbors, associates, even comrades and friends. Consider a remark from the 1990s made by the new mayor of a war-ravaged town in Bosnia whose longstanding Muslim residents had recently been expelled, and whose places of worship had all been destroyed. In an interview with a foreign journalist, the mayor declared: "There were never any mosques in Zvornik" (quoted in Bevan, 2006, p. 7). The mind recoils at this kind of demagogic "leadership." Its persistent emergence the world over is perhaps one origin among others of the concept evil. The novelist Erich Maria Remarque conjures a dream that has doubtless occurred many times to people over the centuries. In his well-known war novel, *All Quiet on the Western Front*, several infantrymen at rest behind the lines – who have just survived yet another terrible battle dictated by the powers that be – muse that all the world's ills could be cured if so-called "leaders" were stripped down to their underwear and thrown into a pen to fight it out, while the rest of the world went on with its affairs.

But demagogues do not spring *de novo* out of the cosmos. They are creatures of culture, as are all human beings. They absorb and are formed in particular ways by the zeitgeist in which they and others dwell. There is a chord in people they are able to strike, sometimes all too easily. The fact that most persons, most of the time, do not act as they do offers perennial hope for educational and political work. Nonetheless, the human capacity for openness to the new does not always trump the equally visible capacity to reject the unknown and the different. The scene is further complicated because of evolutionary aspects of human biology, which according to many scientists cannot be arrested and which influence though do not determine both capacities. The beloved bird, the dove, comes to mind. A universal symbol of peace, doves will sometimes attack one another if they are not kept in separate cages.

The historical record reveals that cosmopolitan capacities and accomplishments, manifest since virtually the dawn of culture, have been fragile and susceptible to rupture by tribalistic and nationalistic impulses. In addition, as mentioned previously, cosmopolitan-minded people have often been singled out for persecution in various parts of the world. They have been cast as scapegoats for societal ills and otherwise treated as foreign to an alleged human norm. Finally, while we have seen that cosmopolitanism on the ground does not depend upon wealth, power, and privilege, a sympathetic critic could point out that today's elites might be quite willing to conclude: Fine then, let them be cosmopolitan and poor, and let us be parochial and rich.

For these sobering reasons, the educational focus in this book walks hand-in-hand with a democratic political commitment with its fundamental value of universal justice. While all humans are vulnerable, they are not vulnerable in the same way or at the same time (Fischer, 2007, p. 161). Moreover, not all social conditions today support people in dwelling meaningfully in the space of paradoxical transitions that cosmopolitanism evokes: of leaving *and* remaining home, of engaging the strange *and* the familiar, of witnessing *and* participating. As Shirley Pendlebury (2009) observes, "the ordinary and the everyday are not everywhere the same" (p. 21). Thus an important aspect of the current literature and energy that surrounds cosmopolitanism has to do with its focus on institution-building to support the sort of orientation illustrated in this book. The literature appears attuned to Dewey's cautionary remark about the otherwise vibrant cosmopolitan thinking of Kant and his eighteenth-century contemporaries:

> One of the fundamental problems of education in and for a democratic society is set by the conflict of a nationalistic and a wider social aim. The earlier cosmopolitan and "humanitarian" conception suffered both from vagueness and from lack of definite organs of execution and agencies of administration. In Europe, in the Continental states particularly, the new idea of the importance of education for [universal] human welfare and progress was captured by national interests and harnessed to do a work whose social aim was definitely narrow and exclusive. The social aim of education and its national aim were identified, and the result was a marked obscuring of the meaning of a social aim.
>
> (Dewey, 1985, p. 103)

For Dewey, a social aim is always a trans-personal and trans-community aim, whether the community be family, neighborhood, city, region, nation, or any other category. He argues repeatedly for making educational provision available to all people in its fullest, most inter-personal and inter-communal form.

I touched on the issue of institution-building in Chapter 1 in characterizing political cosmopolitanism, and have returned to it periodically. Numerous scholars and activists today have argued that the idea of the cosmopolitan necessitates the ongoing construction of constitutional arrangements, international agreements, open-door exchanges, formal structures of hospitality, and more, to support persons suffering under unjust constraints. Some writers emphasize the economic aspect, conceiving reconstructed institutions worldwide that, ideally, would position all persons to fashion creative and humane lives. For example, the capabilities approach to socioeconomic development referred to previously complements a bottom-up rather than top-down strategy, while calling at the same time for formal international agreements and structures of support. Scholars and activists alike are holding up a mirror to the wealthiest nations today, urging a reconstructed moral consciousness which would also link up with a new consciousness regarding the shared, and threatened, physical environment in which all life dwells. These and related undertakings are invaluable and they will become ever more so as the world becomes more crowded.

At the same time, in my view a focus on institution-building constitutes, figuratively speaking, the last not the first word – though all the words and associated actions are needed to improve the world's prospect. To me, the first word must be given to people who in their everyday lives create space for their impulse toward openness and hold in check the temptation to shut doors. They may be working-class, professional, young or old; they may be cab-drivers, artists, or executives; they may be teachers and students. They are everywhere in our midst, and perhaps inside our own skins if we let them breathe. Cosmopolitan interaction, so often spontaneous in origin and contagious in practice, does not require pre-established institutions to make it possible. It has historically accompanied, or preceded, every known form of governmental organization: from empires to kingdoms, from city states to liberal democracies. In all parts of the globe some people have responded with curiosity, respect and interest to new ideas and cultural forms, even if they have also found them a source of uncertainty, concern, and fear. They have genuinely learned from such contacts in ways examined throughout this book.

This propensity gives rise to democracy. It does not depend first upon the establishment of democratic institutions. This fact suggests that forming such institutions, if they are themselves to be just and efficacious, depends upon recognizing the active resources in life on the ground. I take this perspective to be a fundamental lesson of Dewey's still timely *Democracy and Education*, first published in 1916 in the midst of a world war. In the book, Dewey does not address democracy until after he has characterized his conception of education. The latter pivots around notions of communication, everyday interaction, and what it means to realize one's gifts. Put another way, for Dewey education constitutes the continued reconstruction of experience, by which he means a process of continually learning from experience and using the results of that learning to shape subsequent experience. Education involves developing dynamic habits, or what I have called in this book arts and practices of listening, speaking, attending, contemplating, and acting. Perhaps the most fundamental art of all, in cosmopolitan perspective, is the habit of keeping habit itself responsive, dynamic, and expansive. That ability positions the person to develop her or his bent as fully as circumstances permit while also interacting richly and responsively with other people.

In Chapter 7 of his book, Dewey poses the question What kind of society would best support the mode of education touched on above? What set of institutions, what relational order between people, will most likely support every human being in fulfilling his or her unique potential? Dewey finds the answer in democracy. But democracy does not *provide* the answer. The idea of democracy does not dictate or orchestrate what kind of education people need and deserve. For Dewey democracy denotes more than a system of laws, principles, regulations, and institutions, indispensable as they are, given the realities of injustice and the need for organs of collective action. Democracy's root is the demos, the people: all people, not just a select few. Democracy comes alive, first and foremost, in concrete, constructive interaction between people. Democracy happens when people exchange thoughts freely around a meal, when they share views in the market place or in the public park, when they comment on shared concerns and solutions on email or over the phone, and in countless other venues. All such exchanges contribute, in principle, to an ethos that encourages more of the same. Democratic laws, guidelines, and other institutional arrangements – including in education – should be conceived, at least in part, as expressive of, and supportive of, the human desire for genuine communication, for innocent and fresh interaction, and for crafting lives of meaning and purpose.

From the very emergence of the idea of education, as contrasted with social-ization, thinkers have struggled with the question: Which comes first, the kind of society people would like which can then give rise to the right mode of education? Or does one start with the right mode of education on the premise that people educated this way will form the right kind of society? From a cosmopolitan perspective, this chicken-and-egg question does not require an either/or response. Institutions are necessary for securing human goods. But education, especially in a rapidly changing and shrinking world like ours, is necessary for continually reflecting upon and in some cases reconstructing such goods. Educational work is not a mere tool of particular interests however estimable the latter may be. In the name of democracy itself understood as conduct, teachers and students merit some space *on their own terms* to move closer and closer apart as they create ways to communicate, and further and further together as they engage in a serious way human inheritances embodied in the curriculum.

In the cosmopolitan, nobody knows what each interaction of the new and the old will look like nor what it will generate. The willingness to learn, to cultivate reflective openness and reflective loyalty, can carry people through this perma-nent uncertainty. People can come to see that a feeling for paradox can promote balance in human affairs. In likeness, in the adventure of education nobody knows the destination, though academic subjects with their facts, frameworks, and ways of thinking provide indispensable resources. In metaphorical terms these subjects constitute handbooks, in the spirit of Epictetus' effort, which can accompany people as they move in the world. Education is not mere absorption, not merely following along in other people's footsteps. While socialization positions persons to get underway in the first place, education propels them forward as individuals and as social beings.

Political reform and institution-building do not create cosmopolitanism on the ground but they can support and release it for fuller and wider expression.

Experienced teachers show a way here because they know they cannot "make" education happen – and they know they do not have to. Their students are quite alive and on the move, even if sometimes habituated to think of the classroom as strangely outside the world. Good teachers tap into the ever-rushing life within students and provide occasion after occasion for them to experience why curriculum is itself a vivid, ever-changing response to life. It is itself emblematic of the quest for meaning and it can teach people how to focus the mind, expand the spirit, and discover how best to deploy their individual bent. Teacher narratives, research studies, and other sources attest to how challenging it is to walk the delicate line between, on the one hand, ignoring students' latent powers and forcing material upon them and, on the other hand, ignoring curriculum and indulging idiosyncratic, fashionable caprice. In likeness, it takes artfulness on the part of those who would nominate themselves change-agents and institution-builders not to force material on people while also not ignoring the genuine service that meaningful support can provide them. Through a cosmopolitan prism, the watchword seems to become: be wary of the top-down, but be equally wary of self-abnegation. Not forcing things on others can morph into holding back invaluable knowledge and experience. The teacher and the cosmopolitan reformer, each in her or his own way, must be the most open and the most loyal of all.

Notes

1 A Perspective on Teaching and Education for Our Time

1 See, for example, the first volume in John Baldacchino's (2010) projected trilogy on the Mediterranean, and Predrag Matvejevic's (1999) cultural portrait of the region.

2 To be sure, "Western" influence in the form of colonial and imperial ventures has been relentless, today taking the form of what some call neoliberalism (which I touch on later in the chapter). As we will see, cosmopolitanism as an educational outlook contrasts markedly with invasive, ethnocentric, or other one-sided orientations toward the world.

3 Sankar Muthu (2003) responds in depth to concerns about the moral contradictions perceived in some Enlightenment thinkers, for example with regards to class, race and gender. Along with Carter (2001), Schlereth (1977), and others, Muthu illuminates productive alternatives to either a totalizing endorsement or rejection of Enlightenment thought, especially with regards to its cosmopolitan strands which provide telling grounds for a critique of bigotry and intolerance. Muthu provides an especially wide-ranging, generative assessment of Kant's highly creative position. Kant's writing on cosmopolitanism and morality is many-sided, nuanced, and ever underway. In my view his thought is distorted if described as "universalistic," given the homogenizing if not ethnocentric overtones that term connotes. For a related treatment of Kant's outlook, as well as application of his thought to contemporary (and often controversial) human rights theory and practice, see Bynum (2007).

4 Recent studies include:

Conceptual: Appiah's (2005, 2006) pioneering work on the moral and political dimensions of cosmopolitanism through a reconstructed liberal lens; Benhabib's (2006) influential political focus on issues in cosmopolitanism and democracy, which can be productively paired with the set of studies on political cosmopolitanism edited by Brock and Brighouse (2005); Carter's (2001) wide-ranging study of moral and political questions; Cheah and Robbins' (1998) important edited set of inter-disciplinary studies; Corpus Ong's (2009) recent work in media studies; Derrida's (2001) oft-cited perspective on the limits and possibilities of cosmopolitan hospitality; Hannerz's (1990) widely noted cultural perspective; Heater's (1996) initiative in reanimating the political promise in cosmopolitan thinking; Hill's (2000, 2009) critique of identity politics through a cosmopolitan lens; Lu's (2000) careful account of cosmopolitan-minded thinking as contrasted with stereotypical versions of the concept; Nussbaum's (1997a, 1997b, 2002) influential, universalist outlook; Scheffler's (2001) trenchant interpretation of political and cultural aspects of cosmopolitanism; and S. Tagore's (2003, 2008) clarifying work on cosmopolitanism, including through studies of the poetry and essays of his famous relation, Rabindranath Tagore.

Historical research: See Holton (2002) on an international conference held in 1911 that addressed race and cultural diversity in the world; Jacobs (2006) on early modern expressions of cosmopolitan-minded practices; Jasanoff's (2005a, 2005b) accounts of cosmopolitan-mindedness in, respectively, Ottoman Alexandria and India when under English imperial rule; Majluf (1997) on a celebrated nineteenth-century art exhibit in Paris in which critics took to task cosmopolitan-minded artists for not being "authentically national"; Muthu's (2003) aforementioned study of Kant's and others' cosmopolitan outlooks; Reydam-Schils' (2005) examination of Stoic practices in the Roman world; Richardson's (2008) ethnographic and historical study of cosmopolitanism and other themes in Odessa, Russia; Rosenfeld's (2002) and Schlereth's (1977) studies of the history of the cosmopolitan idea in eighteenth-century Europe.

Literary studies: Under the heading of "cosmopolitan modernism," Walkowitz (2006) examines cosmopolitan motifs in novels of Joseph Conrad, James Joyce, and Virginia Woolf; under the heading of "modernist cosmopolitanism," she interprets work by Kazuo Ishiguro, Salman Rushdie, and W. G. Sebald. For general discussion of these themes, see Huyssen (2007). Berman (2001) elucidates cosmopolitan perspectives in works by Henry James, Marcel Proust, Virginia Woolf, and Gertrude Stein. Stanton (2006) does the same for fiction by Kazuo Ishiguro, Michael Ondaatje, Jamaica Kincaid, and J. M. Coetzee. Fojas (2005) and Loss (2005), among others, have recently examined cosmopolitan patterns in numerous Latin American authors. Kirkbright (2000) has edited a set of studies of cosmopolitanism in German and Austrian writers, among them Heinrich Heine, Marie Herzfeld, and Johann Wolfgang von Goethe. Also see Choo (2011) and Jollimore and Barrios (2006) for direct connections with education.

Field-Based studies: I will provide details about a range of recent studies in Chapter 4.

Educational work: See Costa (2005) on questions of education and cultural hybridity through a cosmopolitan lens; Gregoriou (2004) on relations between cosmopolitanism, hospitality, and education; McDonough (1997) on the crossroads of justice and education when considering oppressed communities; Papastephanou (2002, 2005) on questions of politics, human relations and education in globalized conditions; Pinar (2009) on exemplars of "worldliness" understood through a cosmopolitan framework; Popkewitz (2008) for a critique of schooling which collapses cosmopolitanism and neoliberalism into a rationalist, universalistic ideology; Rizvi (2005, 2009) on why cosmopolitanism, as a frame for understanding today's cultural relations, can inform practices in international education; Todd (2009) on questions of ethics, justice, and education in conflicted domains of contemporary society; and Waks (2008) on cosmopolitan-minded educational policy, school relations, and theory. Edited sets of analyses include McDonough and Feinberg (2003), which focuses on a variety of questions concerning justice, culture, and educational provision in contemporary societies, and Lingard et al. (2008) though only a few entries in that book attend to cosmopolitanism per se. Two educational journals have also featured special issues on the topic: *Studies in Philosophy of Education* (Strand, 2010) and *Educational Philosophy and Theory* (Roth and Burbules, 2011).

5 Beck (2004), Donald (2007), Hansen (2010b), and McDonough (1997) discuss distinctions between cosmopolitan and humanist, liberal, and multicultural outlooks. The literature touched on in this chapter also sheds light on differences between cosmopolitanism and the recently coined term "glocalism." That descriptive term addresses how global processes have infiltrated local spaces, and how persons adapt strategically to this influence. There is nothing inherently cosmopolitan – in its aesthetic, educational, ethical, or moral senses – about glocalism as typically construed. Unlike cosmopolitanism, which is a descriptive *and* normative concept, glocalism cannot form the ground of a philosophy of education. Another familiar term is

"internationalism," which historically has referred to workers' movements which band together, across national borders, to resist what they see as oppressive capitalist practices. Its origins reach back to the First International, or International Workingmen's Association, established in Europe in 1864. Still another current term is Eleanor Roosevelt's idea of "worldmindedness." This concept mirrors one aspect of cosmopolitanism: reflective openness to the world. But as I have argued, cosmopolitanism constitutes an educational orientation toward the meaning and necessity of the local as much as of the world writ large.

6 For recent applications of the capabilities approach to education see, for example, Terzi (2008) and Walker (2006).

7 Another form emerging today could be called *geographic cosmopolitanism*. It denotes environments, settings, and milieus in which people enact trans-cultural, trans-rational, and trans-traditional habits of thought and conduct. Geographic cosmopolitanism is not coterminous with administrative boundaries. In this outlook, the five boroughs of New York City do not constitute "a cosmopolitan city." Rather they embody numerous permeable sites and porous scenes of interaction that are surrounded by or in the midst of localized practices (cf. Earle and Cvetkovich, 1995, p. 157 and *passim*).

   Scholars and activists have also begun articulating what has been dubbed *environmental cosmopolitanism* (cf. Heater, 2002, pp. 122–129). This outlook takes seriously notions of the cosmos as comprising all beings, rather than just persons, all of whom merit moral concern and political support. In this perspective cosmos connotes what William James called a "pluriverse" of "entities" (Latour, 2004a, p. 454) that includes birds, rocks, human beings and their creations, the sky above, wind, trees, insects, rivers, and all the rest. In this light a cosmopolitan ethic, as contrasted with a humanist ethic as sometimes conceived, implies an attitude of responsibility toward the totality of nature – as if, to deploy a trope from the songwriter Nick Drake (2000), each of us "could have been one of these things first." It would require a full-blown analysis to do justice to this outlook, in which one could draw on an array of writers who illuminate relations between cosmopolitanism and the environment (see, for example, Harrison, 1992; Latour, 2004b; Schwartz, 2009; Sebald, 2006; and Tresch, 2007).

   A cosmopolitan orientation does not presuppose a particular philosophy of nature any more than it presupposes a fixed conception of human nature. But cosmopolitanism can ally itself organically to a depth vision of the environment in which life dwells. The opposite of environmentalism, in cosmopolitan perspective, is not anthropocentrism but misanthropy.

8 For Arendt, education ushers the young into the universe of human makings so that they can, in turn, be equipped to (re)make the world as adults. Education and the future of the world are compromised, in her view, if adults selectively narrow the curriculum so that it coheres with their current politics and values, rather than providing the young the fullness of human creativity as expressed in traditions of art, science, letters, and the like. For discussion see, for example, Gordon (2001) and Higgins (2010).

9 See, for example, Sebald's powerful inquiry into moral remembrance in his book, *The Emigrants*.

10 The international school of thought and practice represented by the organizational title "Philosophy for Children" (P4C) has documented the keen sensibility children often have for truth, justice, and passionate dispassion, even if they may not use such terms (cf. Sharp, 1983; Donne, 2005).

11 Some general claims about cosmopolitanism seem to precede what research has documented. For example, Sheldon Pollock and colleagues (2000) contend that "cosmopolitanism is not some known entity existing in the world, with a clear genealogy from the Stoics to Immanuel Kant, that simply awaits more detailed description at the hands of scholarship" (p. 577). However, as we will see, cosmopolitanism *is* in the world – rather than merely in somebody's theory – and it does have a

discernible ancestry. Scott Malcomson (1998), after some arbitrary and attenuated remarks about the Stoics and Kant, concludes that they "are not of great use" (p. 238) in thinking about cosmopolitan practices. In this book I show, in part by drawing on recent research, how untrue that viewpoint is. Kant's and the Stoics' ideas and conduct have a wondrous contemporary pertinence including for teachers everywhere.

12 I have sketched some of this literature in a study of the poetics of teaching (Hansen, 2004).

2 Becoming a Teacher in and of the World

1 The French language provides a felicitous way of expressing the point. "Stoïque" refers to a person who withdraws from life and suffers its wounds in silence. "Stoïcien" refers to a person who embodies the public, agentive aspect of Stoicism at issue in this chapter.

2 Platonist ideologies should not be confused with Plato himself, just as Confucianist doctrines should not be confused with Confucius' actual thought. Neither figure's outlook is reducible to a single "ism" (including cosmopolitanism). Writers in the tradition under discussion here emphasize that, for the student of the art of living, it is important to return to the primary texts themselves rather than to rely upon the layers of sometimes dogmatic commentary that have settled upon them over time.

3 Zweig was himself a widely read, cosmopolitan-minded novelist, short story writer, cultural commentator, and more. His *The World of Yesterday* (1964) paints a telling portrait of the vitality yet also fragility of cultural creativity, in this case in his native Europe before the rise of Nazism and fascism.

4 I am grateful to Jeff Frank for this quote.

5 Diogenes Laertius, who lived sometime in the second–third century CE, is an important source of knowledge about Diogenes and other Greek thinkers. I use the conventional "D.L.6.passage number" system in order to refer to those passages in Laertius' Book 6 of his *Lives of Eminent Philosophers* where he describes Diogenes' practice.

6 In a previous work (Hansen, 2001, pp. 178–187), I wrote how Hillesum shows teachers the meaning of tenacious humility, which is a disposition that fuses a strong commitment to educating with an equally strong commitment to the values of open-mindedness and a spirit of inquiry. Susan Gubar (2006) writes elegantly of Hillesum's affecting prose.

7 Marcus and Dewey hold different views of the cosmos. For the ancient writer, cosmos constitutes a unity of all things patterned, in part, after mathematical presumptions of order, symmetry, and connection. For Dewey, whose attitude toward the issue is naturalistic, cosmos is a name, among other suitable ones, for the ever-changing surroundings in which living beings try to make their way. In following the tradition of philosophy as the art of living, from Socrates through today's figures, one encounters different pictures of the cosmos. As mentioned previously, I share Hadot's view (1995, p. 212) that it is not necessary to privilege a particular picture in order to cultivate in a meaningful way the exercises of the self touched on here. I am struck by the passionate concern for arts of self-improvement and for humane modes of dwelling that mark the tradition across time and space.

3 On the Human Condition and its Educational Challenge

1 For discussion of current debates about "whither the human cosmos," see Beck (2006), Dallmayr (2003), Habermas (1998), McCarthy (1999), Morin and Kern (1999), Papastephanou (2005), and Savage et al. (2005).

2 Emerson knew Montaigne's essay "On Repenting" (1991) with its memorable opening bars on the plasticity of self, humanity, and world:

> Others form Man; I give an account of Man and sketch a picture of a particular one of them who is very badly formed and whom I would truly make very different from

what he is if I had to fashion him afresh. But it is done now. The brush-strokes of my portrait do not go awry even though they do change and vary. The world is but a perennial see-saw. Everything in it – the land, the mountains of the Caucasus, the pyramids of Egypt – all waver with a common motion and their own. Constancy itself is nothing but a more languid rocking to and fro.

(Montaigne, 1991, p. 907)

3 A point of logic: If an event has happened, one can say it will remain permanently true that that event happened. Thus the cosmos can be taken to feature a form of permanence, namely all that is past and therefore untouchable. A core principle in philosophy as the art of living is that all the knowledge in the world cannot prevent future change, although it can be of service in influencing the direction that change takes. All that people know cannot necessarily predict, much less guarantee, the contours of what is to come, including in the very next moment. Those contours are, as such, permanently impermanent. A related point is that the past and *the inter-pretation of the past* are not synonyms. What's done is indeed done, but its *meaning* is not, and humans are creatures who live by meaning.

4 It is hard to conceive what permanent cultural preservation could mean as compared with preservation-within-and-through-change. There may have been a time in human history when this condition did not hold. For example, the famous cave paintings of Cro-Magnon people in modern-day France and Spain were undertaken over the course of 25,000 years. During this time the techniques and subjects barely changed. One investigator of the cave art (discussed in Thurman, 2008) argues that for these conventions to have endured intact for (in effect) four times as long as recorded history implies that the culture must have been "deeply satisfying" to its members – and, as Thurman adds, "stable to a degree it is hard for modern humans to imagine." One could conjecture that the longevity of this remarkable tradition reflects the fact that the artists encountered no other models. Once cultural interaction does begin in earnest, with the close of the Ice Age, artistic forms begin to proliferate, a process that has continued unabated through the present.

5 On the basis of his decades-long consideration of what it means to be human, Montaigne concludes:

I leave it to the graduates – and I do not know if even they will manage to bring it off in a matter so confused, intricate and fortuitous – to arrange this infinite variety of features into groups, pin down our inconsistencies and impose some order. I find it hard to link our actions one to another, but I also find it hard to give each one of them, separately, its proper designation from some dominant quality; they are so ambiguous, with colours interpenetrating each other in various lights.

(Montaigne, 1991, p. 1222, III.13)

6 For a sociological perspective on Feinberg's point, see Hiro Saito's (2010) application of Bruno Latour's "Actor-Network Theory" in a study of students' cosmopolitan-minded outlooks.

7 Judith Shklar (1984) comments insightfully on Montaigne's outlook. For a related discussion of education and questions of cruelty in society, see Neil Burtonwood's (2006) study of the educational ramifications of Isaiah Berlin's political philosophy. Leonard Waks (2009) comments on Burtonwood's study in an overview of themes in cosmopolitanism and education.

8 This claim does not imply that the homeless – in a physical or spiritual sense – are *ipso facto* excluded from the platform of concern expressed in these chapters. Quite the contrary. I hope the analysis sheds further light on the plight of being rendered homeless by revealing another layer of deprivation it can inflict on people, namely taking away the creative cultural space marked by openness and loyalty. This point does not mean homeless people, in the physical or spiritual sense, cannot be creative. As

discussed in the previous chapter, cosmopolitanism is not a "totalizing" concept much less a new "church," as David Held rightfully cautions. However, it does insist on the very real cost to a person or community of being stripped of any sense of rootedness, whether in a geographic sense or in the sense of being rooted in – which means *participating in* and *shaping* – a calling, an art, a religious practice, a human relation, in short that which constitutes an enduring source of meaning and hope. (For an evocative treatment of the need for roots, see Simone Weil's (2002) classic text.)

Kevin McDonough (1997) shows that for people in oppressed circumstances, a multicultural rather than cosmopolitan-minded education may be the priority, in order to revitalize a sense of local tradition that may have been sundered or fractured by the powers that be. This revitalization, in turn, supports people in entering the crossroads of reflective openness and reflective loyalty (for further discussion see Hansen, 2010b, pp. 158–159). My thanks to Shilpi Sinha (personal communication, November 1, 2008) for calling attention to difficult situations in which alternatives to a cosmopolitan approach may be most appropriate.

Another version of homelessness has cropped up in conversations I have had with teachers in recent years. They have been uncertain of what to make of some students' apparent indifference to, or obliviousness of, any sense of home, tradition, or roots. They report that some students, from across the socioeconomic spectrum, not only do not seem to care about anything that might go under the heading of tradition or roots, but are perplexed by the very notion that somebody would care. The teachers suggest that talk of home, in the register of this chapter, would befuddle these students. The teachers do not imply students are callous, jaded or cynical (with a small "c" since Diogenes, a founding figure of the philosophical school known as Cynicism, held values to which he was strongly attached). Rather they attest to a flatness or casualness of outlook, a sense that one thing is as significant, or as insignificant, as anything else. The discussion in Chapter 5 will address this apparent absence of commitment or engagement, the latter being constitutive of a sense of home in the world however conceived. In that orientation it does matter – and people are aware that it matters – what one thinks, believes, and does.

4 Cultural Crossroads and Creativity

1 "The word *rihla*," writes Predrag Matvejevic (1999), "refers both to a journey and to its description. Such descriptions constitute a genre that flourished more than any [in Battuta's era] and served scholarship – geography and cartography – as well as literature. It was capacious enough to include almanacs, calendars, grammars, zodiacs, horoscopes, the occasional map, and all sorts of accounts connected with peregrinations through the Mediterranean and beyond" (p. 111).

2 To my knowledge, Ibn Battuta's and Ibn Khaldun's work was unavailable in Latin or Greek translation in Montaigne's era – even while it was Arab scholarship that had helped make Aristotle and various commentators on his work available to Europe. This cosmopolitan gesture, of a culture receiving back one of its own inheritances from another, can be discerned time and again in the human record. Consider, for example, the role non-African writers played in documenting and publicizing African history, a process that helped inform the anti-colonial impulses that eventually led to the end of European empire.

3 The eighteenth century also featured an explosion of books in the genre of imaginary voyages, sometimes dubbed "robinsonades" after Daniel Defoe's *Robinson Crusoe* (published 1719). Philip Babcock Gove (1941) annotates over 200 examples, published in numerous languages from English to Japanese, and ranging from Jonathan Swift's *Gulliver's Travels* (1726), to Voltaire's *Candide* (1759), to many anonymous works.

Incidentally, the Arab tradition of *rilah*, or travel-writing – of which Ibn Battuta's oeuvre is exemplary – precedes all this by several centuries. Again, as far as I am aware these writings were unavailable in translation into Greek, Latin, or other European languages, although not necessarily unknown to Europeans, given the trans-cultural interaction endemic in the Mediterranean.

4   Mary Midgley (1991) and Michele Moody-Adams (1997) provide persuasive accounts of why criticism of other cultures is not only necessary, given an interconnected world, but morally legitimate. They show how such criticism can move beyond uncritical, ethnocentric judgmentalism and become a basis for creative, productive modes of communication.

The hermeneutic principle underlying this chapter (and book) is that what we call bias, or prejudice, is a necessary ground for any interpretive act. Otherwise such an act cannot get underway and persons remain mute and unblinking before the world. These prejudices emerge through the course of socialization and life experience. Through coming to grips with them, a process triggered by the encounter with the new, persons can gain reflective distance and begin to grasp difference as well as similarity. Prejudice becomes a pre-condition for interpretive movement. Prejudice, which is another word for "pre-judgment," provides the point of departure for coming into a diverse world. It makes possible *arriving*, in ever-dynamic ways, at a broader, richer platform for judgment. From this point of view, humans should be grateful for the prejudices that put them into the world in the first place, without which they would remain in limbo; and they can be equally grateful that such a beginning is not an ending. (My thanks to M. Mei-lin Ng for valuable criticism on this point.)

5   In contrast, it makes sense to refer to cosmopolitanism *in* Buddhist thought and practice, or in Polynesian ideas and culture, or in European practices and concepts.

6   For discussion of values in cosmopolitan perspective, see Hansen et al. (2009).

7   For another generative treatment of "cosmopolitan nationalism," see Louise Blakeney Williams' (2007) comparative study of Rabindranath Tagore's and W. B. Yeats' cosmopolitan outlooks. A parallel study to Edmunds and Turner's effort is Emma Tarlo's (2007) interview-based inquiry into the cosmopolitan-minded practice of three successful and well-known Muslim women whose work is centered in London.

8   Also see Peter Nyers' (2003) complementary account of legal initiatives from below that support the needs of refugees, asylum seekers, and undocumented immigrants. Bonnie Honig (2006) and Gilbert Leung (2009) provide spirited critiques of privileging institutionalized categories of world citizenship and of rights over alternative, bottom-up, and horizontal cosmopolitan experience in everyday life. Honig dramatizes her concern when she writes that formal institutions, if unduly privileged on the landscape of human endeavor, can become "our principal addressees, our guardians, ventriloquizers, impersonators, shapers and censors of our voice, our desires, our aspirations, our solidarities" (2006, p. 120). For Kurasawa, "the socially self-constituting character" of on-the-ground cosmopolitanism "is the font of its robustness and vibrancy" (2004, p. 252).

9   The philosopher Friedrich Nietzsche sheds light on this ideal by distinguishing between what he calls two kinds of equality: "The thirst for equality can express itself either as a desire to draw everyone down to oneself (through diminishing them, spying on them, tripping them up) or to raise oneself and everyone else up (through recognizing their virtues, helping them, rejoicing in their success)" (1996, p. 136). By success Nietzsche does not have in mind conventional markers such as wealth or prestige. Rather, to recall a trope from Emerson, he has in mind success in the sometimes demanding educational process of drawing a new circle – that is, becoming a person with a broader, richer, deepened sense of life's possibilities and limits. Another person's success, in this light, should provoke not envy but rather trigger the desire to make a comparable move.

5 Curriculum and Teaching in and for the World

1 In Hansen et al. (2009), my co-authors and I describe cosmopolitan arts, or methods, of hope, of memory, and of dialogue.

2 Andrew Abbott sheds light on this point:

> Is education years in schools? Testable knowledge of particular areas? Ability to quickly master new material? Grasp of "classic" texts? Experience of the world? These may indicate education, but they are not the thing itself. When we say "after she left school she began her real education," we show our properly deep ambivalence about the nature of education itself. This ambivalence defines education interstitially, emergently, not as years in school, or experience, or whatever, but rather as their intersection or as something beyond them to which each points.
>
> (Abbott, 1988, p. 318)

3 Darryl De Marzio (2007a, pp. 23–27, *passim*) builds on ideas from Richard Rorty to discuss how the study of philosophical texts can be understood as a mode of "canon-formation" – a process as germane to teachers, De Marzio argues, as it is to philosophers or anyone else.

4 Camilla Fojas (2005) provides, through the lens of cosmopolitanism, an insightful, fair-minded, and comprehensive study of *Ariel*. Among other accomplishments, she spotlights the limitations in Carlos Fuentes' rich and often haughty introduction that accompanies Margaret Sayers Peden's translation. Fuentes takes *Ariel* to task for, among other things, what he sees as its neglect of Latin American sources and its lack of critique of Latin American culture writ large.

5 Terence's turn of phrase also recalls the importance of humor, touched on in Chapter 4 (p. 71), in any inhabitable way of life including the cosmopolitan. The phrase in fact appears in the voice of Chremes, a busybody and rather shaky character. He has been peeking into his neighbor's courtyard and, when called on it by the neighbor, replies with Terence's now-famous words! The Roman writer and orator Cicero (106–43 BCE) was apparently the first commentator to transform the witticism into a cosmopolitan motif (Nussbaum, 1997b, p. 33). In my view, this dual framing of Terence's splendid words is marvelous. It shows why a sense of humor can denote not frivolity but a mature and richly serious outlook on the human condition (Tozer, 1907). The filmmaker Krzysztof Kieslowski evidently shares this outlook. The cosmopolitan prism mentioned in the first paragraph of Chapter 1, through which the character played by Irene Jacob looks out on the world, is in fact made of plastic and can be bounced like a ball – as she does later in the film.

6 Thus it might be unseemly and potentially dangerous to create a category called "Cosmopolitan Teachers" as contrasted with teachers who bring a cosmopolitan orientation to bear in their work. The unseemliness resides in the presupposition that any teacher, at any level – like any author, in any genre – can fully grasp the idea and consequences of cosmopolitanism. The danger is something I witnessed years ago in a job where I worked with many groups of educators. In one group I encountered a small sub-set of Special Education teachers whose obnoxious, arrogant attitude toward their peers made me realize that they had transformed their title – Special Education teachers – into an existential assumption that they themselves were special, and therefore were entitled to carte blanche in their conduct. In the view of everyone else in the room they specialized in rudeness. Happily they were the exception among numerous other, typically quite dedicated Special Education teachers with whom I worked.

7 I base the example on what I have witnessed in a variety of classrooms over the years. I have chosen music, in part, because of its timeless universality in human culture. The specific example, of flamenco, was introduced to me as a boy when my parents took me to behold the great dancer Maria Benitez, and her great singers and guitarists. I have

never recovered from that experience, a condition for which I am ever grateful. I hope the example illustrates how a cosmopolitan dimension can in principle accompany teaching any subject, and I invite readers to substitute any curricular object they have in mind.

8 For discussion of the Earth Charter in cosmopolitan perspective, see Macgregor (2004).

9 However, like some social scientists writing on cosmopolitanism, Saito seems to associate philosophy (mistakenly) with universalizing theory alone and to be unaware of its modes of practical embodiment as presented in this book. To be sure, some philosophical writing on cosmopolitanism is highly abstract, far above the oxygen necessary for everyday life on the ground. But some takes its point of departure precisely from close attention to that life. These remarks recall one way to distinguish between philosophy as theory, in which the answers to a question (e.g., What is knowledge?) need not affect the person's life in any overt manner, and philosophy as the art of living, in which the answers to a question (e.g., How shall I conduct my life?) ramify directly into one's outlook and action. For millennia, teachers have benefited from both modes of philosophy.

References

Abbas, A. (2000). Cosmopolitan de-scriptions. *Public Culture* 12 (3), 769–86.

Abbott, A. (1988). *The System of Professions* (Chicago: University of Chicago Press).

Achebe, C. (1958). *Things Fall Apart* (London: Heinemann).

Aciman, A. (1994). *Out of Egypt: A Memoir* (New York: Picador).

Aloni, N. (2002). *Enhancing Humanity: The Philosophical Foundations of Humanistic Education* (Dordrecht: Kluwer).

Ambrosio, J. (2008). Writing the self: Ethical self-formation and the undefined work of freedom. *Educational Theory*, 58 (3), 251–267.

Appiah, K. A. (2005). *The Ethics of Identity* (Princeton: Princeton University Press).

Appiah, K. A. (2006). *Cosmopolitanism: Ethics in a World of Strangers* (New York: W. W. Norton).

Arendt, H. (1961). The crisis in education. In H. Arendt, *Between the Past and Future*, pp. 173–196 (New York: Penguin).

Bader, V. (1999). For love of country. *Political Theory*, 27 (3), 379–397.

Bailin, S. (2006). An inquiry into inquiry: (How) can we learn from other times and places? In D. Vokey (Ed.), *Philosophy of Education 2006*, pp. 1–12 (Urbana, IL: Philosophy of Education Society).

Baldacchino, J. (2010). *Makings of the Sea: Journey, Doubt, and Nostalgia* (Gorgias Press).

Barnett, A., Held, D. and Henderson, C. (Eds.) (2005). *Debating Globalization* (Cambridge: Polity Press).

Beck, U. (2002). The cosmopolitan perspective: Sociology of the second age of modernity. In S. Vertovec and R. Cohen (Eds.), *Conceiving Cosmopolitanism: Theory, Context, and Practice* (Oxford: Oxford University Press).

Beck, U. (2004). The truth of others: A cosmopolitan approach. *Common Knowledge*, 10 (3), 430–449.

Beck, U. (2006). *The Cosmopolitan Vision*, trans. C. Cronin (Cambridge: Polity).

Benhabib, S. (2006). *Another Cosmopolitanism* (Oxford: Oxford University Press).

Berman, J. (2001). *Modernist Fiction, Cosmopolitanism, and the Politics of Community* (Cambridge: Cambridge University Press).

Bevan, R. (2006). *The Destruction of Memory: Architecture at War* (Chicago: University of Chicago Press).

Bhattacharya, S. (1997). *The Mahatma and the Poet: Letters and Debates Between Gandhi and Tagore, 1915–1941* (New Delhi: National Book Trust).

Bloom, A. (1968). Notes. In *The Republic of Plato*, trans. A. Bloom, pp. 439–472 (New York: Basic Books).

Bok, S. (2006). "No one to receive it"? Simone Weil's unforeseen legacy. *Common Knowledge* 12 (no. 2), 252–260.

Booth, W. C. (1988). *The Company We Keep: An Ethics of Fiction* (Berkeley: University of California Press).

Bose, S. and Manjapra, K. (Eds.) (2010). *Cosmopolitan Thought Zones: South Asia and the Global Circulation of Ideas* (Basingstoke, UK: Palgrave Macmillan).

Bouriau, C. (2007). *Qu'est-ce que l'Humanisme? (What is Humanism?)* (Paris: J. Vrin).

Branham, R. B. and Goulet-Cazé, M.-O. (Eds.) (1996). *The Cynics: The Cynic Movement in Antiquity and its Legacy* (Berkeley: University of California Press).

Brann, E. T. H. (1979). *Paradoxes of Education in a Republic* (Chicago: University of Chicago Press).

Brock, G. and Brighouse, H. (Eds.) (2005). *The Political Philosophy of Cosmopolitanism* (Cambridge: Cambridge University Press).

Brown, E. (2000). Socrates the cosmopolitan. *Stanford Agora: An Online Journal of Legal Perspectives* 1, 74–87.

Brown, E. (2006). Hellenistic cosmopolitanism. In M. L. Gill and P. Pellegrin (Eds.), *A Companion to Ancient Philosophy*, pp. 549–558 (Oxford: Blackwell).

Brown, P. (1971). *The World of Late Antiquity* (London: Thames & Hudson).

Bruckner, P. (2000). *Le Vertige de Babel: Cosmopolitisme ou Mondialisme (The Vertigo of Babel: Cosmopolitanism or Globalism)* (Paris: Arléa).

Burtonwood, N. (1995). Beyond local cultures: Towards a cosmopolitan art education. *International Journal of Art and Design* 14 (2), 205–212.

Burtonwood, N. (2006). *Cultural Diversity, Liberal Pluralism and Schools: Isaiah Berlin and Education* (London: Routledge).

Bussis, A. M., Chittenden, E. A. and Amarel, M. (1976). *Beyond Surface Curriculum: An Interview Study of Teachers' Understandings* (Boulder, CO: Westview Press).

Bynum, G. L. (2007). Human Rights Education and Kant's Critical Humanism. Unpublished doctoral dissertation, Columbia University, New York.

Calhoun, C. (2007). *Nations Matter: Culture, History, and the Cosmopolitan Dream* (London: Routledge).

Calvino, I. (1993). *Six Memos for the Next Millennium* (New York: Vintage International).

Carter, A. (2001). *The Political Theory of Global Citizenship* (London: Routledge).

Cheah, P. and Robbins, B. (Eds.) (1998). *Cosmopolitics: Thinking and Feeling Beyond the Nation* (Minneapolis: University of Minnesota Press).

Choo, S. (2011). On literature's use(ful/less)ness: Reconceptualizing the literature curriculum in an age of globalization. *Journal of Curriculum Studies* 43 (1), 47–67.

Clark, K. (1969). *Civilisation* (film series) (London: British Broadcasting Corporation).

Confucius (1993). *The Analects*, trans. R. Dawson (Oxford: Oxford University Press).

Connolly, W. E. (2000). Speed, concentric circles, and cosmopolitanism. *Political Theory* 28 (5), 596–618.

Copleston, F. (1985). *A History of Philosophy*, vol. 1 (Garden City, NY: Doubleday).

Corpus Ong, J. (2009). The cosmopolitan continuum: Locating cosmopolitanism in media and cultural studies. *Media, Culture and Society* 31 (3), 449–466.

Costa, M. V. (2005). Cultural cosmopolitanism and civic education. In K. Howe (Ed.), *Philosophy of Education 2005*, pp. 250–258 (Urbana, IL: Philosophy of Education Society).

Cremin, L. A. (1970). *American Education: The Colonial Experience 1607–1783* (New York: Harper & Row).

Dallmayr, F. (2003). Cosmopolitanism: Moral and political. *Political Theory* 31 (3), 421–442.

Dawson, R. (1993). Note on the translation of key terms. In Confucius, *The Analects*, pp. xvi–xxvii (Oxford: Oxford University Press).

Day, C. and Gu, Q. (2010). *The New Lives of Teachers* (London: Routledge).

DeMartino, G. F. (2000). *Global Economy, Global Justice: Theoretical Objections and Policy Alternatives to Neoliberalism* (London: Routledge).

De Marzio, D. M. (2007a). The Teacher as Ethical Subject: A Foucauldian Analysis of Plato's *Alcibiades I* and Montaigne's "On Educating Children." Unpublished doctoral dissertation, Columbia University, New York City.

De Marzio, D. M. (2007b). The care of the self: *Alcibiades I*, Socratic teaching and ethics education. *The Journal of Education* 187 (3), 103–127.

Derrida, J. (2001). *On Cosmopolitanism and Forgiveness*, trans. M. Dooley and M. Hughes, ed. S. Critchley and R. Kearney (London: Routledge).

DeSisto, L. A. (2007). Education and the Human Condition: Reconceptualizing the Activities of Teaching and Learning. Unpublished doctoral dissertation, Columbia University, New York City.

Dewey, J. (1977). Moral principles in education. In *John Dewey: The Middle Works 1899–1924: Vol. 4, Essays on Pragmatism and Truth 1907–1909*, ed. J. A. Boydston, pp. 265–291 (Carbondale: Southern Illinois University Press). Original work published 1909.

Dewey, J. (1985). *John Dewey: The Middle Works 1899–1924: Vol. 9, Democracy and Education 1916*, ed. J. A. Boydston (Carbondale: Southern Illinois University Press). Original work published in 1916.

Dewey, J. (1988). *John Dewey: The Later Works 1925–1953: Vol. 1, Experience and Nature*, ed. J. A. Boydston (Carbondale: Southern Illinois University Press). Original work published 1925.

Dewey, J. (1989). *John Dewey: The Later Works 1925–1953: Vol. 7, Ethics*, ed. J. A. Boydston (Carbondale: Southern Illinois University Press). Original work published 1932.

Dewey, J. (1991). Knowing and the known. In *John Dewey, The Later Works 1925–1953: Vol. 16, Essays, Typescripts and Knowing and the Known*, ed. J. A. Boydston, pp. 1–279 (Carbondale: Southern Illinois University Press). Original work published 1948.

Dillon, J. T. (2004). *Musonius Rufus and Education in the Good Life: A Model of Teaching and Living Virtue* (Dallas: University Press of America).

Diogenes Laertius (2005). *Lives of Eminent Philosophers*, vol. 2, trans. R. D. Hicks (Cambridge, MA: Harvard University Press). Original work published third century CE.

Domanski, J. (1996). *La Philosophie, Théorie ou Manière de Vivre? Les Controverses de l'Antiquité à la Renaissance* (*Philosophy as Theory or as a Way of Life? The Controversies from Antiquity through the Renaissance*) (Paris: Éditions de Cerf).

Donald, J. (2007). Internationalisation, diversity and the humanities curriculum: Cosmopolitanism and multiculturalism revisited. *Journal of Philosophy of Education* 41 (3), 289–308.

Donne, J. (2005). To begin in wonder: Children and philosophy. *Thinking: the Journal of Philosophy for Children* 14 (2), 9–17.

Drake, N. (2000). One of these things first. *Bryter Layter*, Universal-Island Records (New York: Island Def Jam Music Group). Original work published 1970.

Drouin-Hans, A.-M. (2004). *Éducation et Utopies* (*Education and Utopias*) (Paris: J. Vrin).

Drouin-Hans, A.-M. (2006). Identité (Identity). *Le Télémaque* 29, 17–26.

Du Bois, W. E. B. (1987). *W. E. B. Du Bois: Writings* (New York: Library of America).

Duneier, M. (1992). *Slim's Table: Race, Respectability, and Masculinity in America* (Chicago: University of Chicago Press).

Dunn, R. E. (2005). *The Adventures of Ibn Battuta: A Muslim Traveler of the 14th Century* (Berkeley: University of California Press).

Earle, T. C. and Cvetkovich, G. T. (1995). *Social Trust: Toward a Cosmopolitan Society* (Westport, CT: Praeger).

Edmunds, J. and Turner, B. S. (2001). The re-invention of a national identity? Women and "cosmopolitan" Englishness. *Ethnicities* 1 (1), 83–108.

Elon, A. (2002). *The Pity of it All: A Portrait of the German-Jewish Epoch 1743–1933* (New York: Picador).

Emerson, R. W. (1983). *Emerson: Essays and Lectures* (New York: Library of America).

Englund, H. (2004). Cosmopolitanism and the devil in Malawi. *Ethnos* 69 (3), 293–316.

Epictetus (1983). *Handbook of Epictetus*, trans. N. White (Indianapolis: Hackett).

Erskine, T. (2000). Embedded cosmopolitanism and the case of war. *Global Society* 14 (4), 569–590.

Feinberg, W. (2003). Reflection and rationality. *Philosophy of Education 2003*, pp. 76–78 (Urbana: University of Illinois Press).

Fischer, M. (2007). A pragmatist cosmopolitan moment: Reconfiguring Nussbaum's cosmopolitan concentric circles. *Journal of Speculative Philosophy* 21 (3), 151–165.

Flory, S. (1987). *The Archaic Smile of Herodotus* (Detroit: Wayne State University Press).

Fojas, C. (2005). *Cosmopolitanism in the Americas* (W. Lafayette, IN: Purdue University Press).

Forman-Barzilai, F. (2005). Sympathy in space(s): Adam Smith on proximity. *Political Theory* 33 (2), 189–217.

Foucault, M. (1988). *Madness and Civilization: A History of Insanity in the Age of Reason*, trans. R. Howard (New York: Vintage Books). Original work published 1961.

Foucault, M. (1994). The ethic of care for the self as a practice of freedom. In J. Bernauer and D. Rasmussen (Eds.), *The Final Foucault*, pp.1–20 (Cambridge, MA: MIT Press).

Foucault, M. (2005). *The Hermeneutics of the Subject*, ed. F. Gros, trans. G. Burchell (New York: Picador).

Frost, R. (2007). *The Notebooks of Robert Frost*, ed. R. Faggen (Cambridge, MA: Harvard University Press).

Fuller, T. (1989). Introduction. In M. Oakeshott, *The Voice of Liberal Learning: Michael Oakeshott on Education*, pp. 1–16 (New Haven, CT: Yale University Press).

Gadamer, H.-G. (1984). On the natural inclination of human beings toward philosophy. In *Reason in the Age of Science*, trans. F. G. Lawrence, pp. 139–150 (Cambridge, MA: MIT Press).

Gallas, K. (2003). *Imagination and Literacy: A Teacher's Search for the Heart of Learning* (New York: Teachers College Press).

Gallie, W. B. (1956). Essentially contested concepts. *Proceedings of the Aristotelian Society*, 56, 167–198.

Gaudelli, W. (2003). *World Class: Teaching and Learning in Global Times* (Mahwah, NJ: Lawrence Erlbaum).

Geertz, C. (1983). *Local Knowledge* (New York: Basic Books).

Gilroy, P. (2004). *After Empire: Melancholia or Convivial Culture* (London: Routledge).

Giri, A. K. (2006). Cosmopolitanism and beyond: Toward a multiverse of transformations. *Development and Change* 37 (6), 1277–1292.

Goldsmith, O. (1762). *The Citizen of the World* (London: Dent).

Gordon, M. (Ed.) (2001). *Hannah Arendt and Education: Renewing our Common World* (Boulder, CO: Westview Press).

Gournay, M. le Jars de. (1998). *Preface to the* Essays *of Michel de Montaigne by his Adoptive Daughter*, trans. R. Hillman and C. Quesnel (Tempe, AZ: Medieval and Renaissance Texts and Studies). Original work published 1595.

Gournay, M. le Jars de. (2002). *Apology for the Woman Writing and Other Works*, ed. and trans. R. Hillman and C. Quesnel (Chicago: University of Chicago Press).

Gove, P. B. (1941). *The Imaginary Voyage in Prose Fiction* (New York: Columbia University Press).

Graffigny, F. de (2002) *Lettres d'une Péruvienne* (*Letters of a Woman from Peru*) ed. J. Mallinson (Oxford: Voltaire Foundation). Original work published 1747.

Green, P. (2008). The great marathon man. *New York Review of Books* 55 (no. 8, May 15).

Gregoriou, Z. (2004). Resisting the pedagogical domestication of cosmopolitanism: From Nussbaum's concentric circles of humanity to Derrida's *aporetic* ethics of hospitality. In K. Alston (Ed.), *Philosophy of Education 2003*, pp. 257–266 (Urbana, IL: Philosophy of Education Society).

Gubar, S. (2006). Falling for Etty Hillesum. *Common Knowledge*, 12 (2), 279–301.

Habermas, J. (1998). Learning by disaster? A diagnostic look back on the short 20th century. *Constellations* 5 (3), 307–320.

Hadot, P. (1995). *Philosophy as a Way of Life*, ed. A. I. Davidson, trans. M. Chase (Oxford: Blackwell).

Halbwachs, M. (1992). *On Collective Memory* (Chicago: University of Chicago Press).

Halevy, D. (1948). *Essai sur l'Accélération de l'Histoire* (*An Essay on the Acceleration of History*) (Paris: Îles d'or).

Hall, M. L. (1997). Montaigne's uses of classical learning. *Journal of Education*, 179, 61–75.

Hannerz, U. (1990). Cosmopolitans and locals in world culture. *Theory, Culture and Society*, 7, 237–251.

Hansen, D. T. (1992). The emergence of a shared morality in a classroom. *Curriculum Inquiry* 22, 345–361.

Hansen, D. T. (1995). *The Call to Teach* (New York: Teachers College Press).

Hansen, D. T. (2001). *Exploring the Moral Heart of Teaching: Toward a Teacher's Creed* (New York: Teachers College Press).

Hansen, D. T. (2002). Well-formed, not well-filled: Montaigne and the paths of personhood. *Educational Theory* 52, 127–154.

Hansen, D. T. (2004). A poetics of teaching. *Educational Theory* 54, 119–142.

Hansen, D. T. (Ed.) (2007). *Ethical Visions of Education: Philosophies in Practice* (New York: Teachers College Press).

Hansen, D. T. (2008). Curriculum and the idea of a cosmopolitan inheritance. *Journal of Curriculum Studies* 40, 289–312.

Hansen, D. T. (2009). Walking with Diogenes: Cosmopolitan accents in philosophy and education. In D. Kerdeman (Ed.), *Philosophy of Education 2009*, pp. 1–13 (Urbana, IL: Philosophy of Education Society).

Hansen, D. T. (2010a). Cosmopolitanism and education: A view from the ground. *Teachers College Record* 112, 1–30. Published online 2008, http://www.tcrecord.org ID Number: 15411.

Hansen, D. T. (2010b). Chasing butterflies without a net: Interpreting cosmopolitanism. *Studies in Philosophy and Education* 29, 151–166.

Hansen, D. T. and Laverty, M. J. (2010). Teaching and pedagogy. In C. McCarthy et al. (Eds.), *Handbook of Philosophy of Education*, pp. 223–235 (London: Sage).

Hansen, D. T., Burdick–Shepherd, S., Cammarano, C. and Obelleiro, G. (2009). Education, values, and valuing in cosmopolitan perspective. *Curriculum Inquiry* 39, 587–612.

Harrison, R. P. (1992). *Forests: The Shadow of Civilization* (Chicago: University of Chicago Press).

Hartog, F. (1988). *The Mirror of Herodotus: The Representation of the Other in the Writing of History*, trans. J. Lloyd (Berkeley: University of California Press). Original work published in 1980.

Harvey, D. (2000). Cosmopolitanism and the banality of geographic evils. *Public Culture* 12 (2), 529–564.

Heater, D. (1996). *World Citizenship and Government: Cosmopolitan Ideas in the History of Western Political Thought* (New York: St. Martin's Press).

Heater, D. (2002). *World Citizenship: Cosmopolitan Thinking and its Opponents* (London: Continuum).

Heilman, S. C. and Cohen, S. M. (1989). *Cosmopolitans and Parochials: Modern Orthodox Jews in America* (Chicago: University of Chicago Press).

Held, D. (1995). *Democracy and the Global Order: From the Modern State to Cosmopolitan Governance* (Stanford, CA: Stanford University Press).

Held, D. (2005). Principles of cosmopolitan order. In G. Brock and H. Brighouse (Eds.), *The Political Philosophy of Cosmopolitanism*, pp. 10–27 (Cambridge: Cambridge University Press).

Hesse, H. (1968). *Narcissus and Goldmund* (New York: Farrar, Straus & Giroux). Original work published 1930.

Hiebert, D. (2002). Cosmopolitanism at the local level: The development of transnational neighborhoods. In S. Vertovec and R. Cohen (Eds.), *Conceiving Cosmopolitanism: Theory, Context, and Practice*, pp. 209–223 (Oxford: Oxford University Press).

Higgins, C. R. (2003). Teaching and the good life: A critique of the ascetic ideal in education. *Educational Theory* 53 (2), 131–154.

Higgins, C. R. (Ed.) (2010). Special issue on Education, Crisis, and the Human Condition: Arendt after 50 years. *Teachers College Record* 112 (2), 375–385. http://www.tcrecord.org ID Number: 15750, (accessed: 1/7/2011).

Hill, J. (2000). *Becoming a Cosmopolitan: What it Means to be a Human Being in the New Millennium* (Lanham, MD: Rowman & Littlefield).

Hill, J. (2009). *Beyond Blood Identities: Posthumanity in the Twenty-First Century* (Lanham, MD: Lexington Books).

Himley, M. and Carini, P. (Eds.) (2000). *From Another Angle: Children's Strengths and School Standards* (New York: Teachers College Press).

Hirsch, E. D. (1987). *Cultural Literacy: What Every American Needs to Know* (Boston: Houghton Mifflin).

Hogan, P. (1996). *The Custody and Courtship of Experience: Western Education in Philosophical Perspective* (Blackrock, Ireland: Columba Press).

Hollinger, D. A. (1995). *Postethnic America: Beyond multiculturalism* (New York: Basic Books).

Hollinger, D. A. (2002). Not universalists, not pluralists: The new cosmopolitans find their own way. In S. Vertovec and R. Cohen (Eds.), *Conceiving Cosmopolitanism: Theory, Context, and Practice*, pp. 227–239 (Oxford: Oxford University Press).

Holton, R. J. (2002). Cosmopolitanism or cosmopolitanisms? The Universal Races Congress of 1911. *Global Networks* 2 (2), 153–170.

Honig, B. (2006). Another cosmopolitanism? Law and politics in the new Europe. In

S. Benhabib, *Another Cosmopolitanism*, ed. R. Post, pp. 102–127 (Oxford: Oxford University Press).

Huizinga, J. (1952). *Erasmus of Rotterdam*, trans. F. Hopman (London: Phaidon). Original work published 1924.

Hull, G. A., Stornaiuolo, A. and Sahni, U. (2010). Cultural citizenship and cosmopolitan practice: Global youth communicate online. *English Education*, 42 (4), 331–67.

Huyssen, A. (2007). Geographies of modernism in a globalizing world. *New German Critique*, 34 (1), 189–207.

Ildefonso, G. (2010). The place of leisure in education. Unpublished manuscript, Teachers College, Columbia University.

Issawi, C. (1987). An Arab Philosophy of History: Selections from the Prolegomena of Ibn Khaldun of Tunis (1332–1406) (Princeton, NJ: Darwin Press).

Jackson, P. W. (1968). *Life in Classrooms* (New York: Holt, Rinehart & Winston).

Jackson, P. W., Boostrom, R. E. and Hansen, D. T. (1993). *The Moral Life of Schools* (San Francisco: Jossey–Bass).

Jacobs, M. (2006). *Strangers Nowhere in the World: The Rise of Cosmopolitanism in Early Modern Europe* (Philadelphia: University of Pennsylvania Press).

Jasanoff, M. (2005a). Cosmopolitan: A tale of identity from Ottoman Alexandria. *Common Knowledge* 11 (3), 393–409.

Jasanoff, M. (2005b). *Edge of Empire: Lives, Culture, and Conquest in the East 1750–1850* (New York: Vintage Books).

Jaspers, K. (1990). *Socrates, Buddha, Confucius, Jesus*, trans. R. Manheim, ed. H. Arendt (San Diego: Harcourt Brace). Original work published in 1957.

Jollimore, T. and Barrios, S. (2006). Creating cosmopolitans: The case for literature. *Studies in Philosophy and Education* 25 (5), 363–383.

Kant, I. (1963a). Idea for a universal history from a cosmopolitan point of view. In *On History*, ed. L. W. Beck, trans. L. W. Beck, R. E. Anchor and E. L. Fackenheim, pp. 11–26 (New York: Macmillan). Original work published 1784.

Kant, I. (1963b). Perpetual peace. In *On History*, ed. L. W. Beck, trans. L. W. Beck, R. E. Anchor and E. L. Fackenheim, pp. 85–135 (New York: Macmillan). Original work published 1795.

Kant, I. (1990). *Foundations of the Metaphysics of Morals*, second edition, trans. L. W. Beck (Englewood Cliffs, NJ: Prentice Hall). Original work published 1785.

Kant, I. (1993). *Critique of Practical Reason*, ed. and trans. L. W. Beck (Upper Saddle River, NJ: Prentice Hall). Original work published 1788.

Kirkbright, S. (2000). *Cosmopolitans in the Modern World: Studies on a Theme in German and Austrian Literary Culture* (Munich: Iudicium).

Kleingeld, P. (1999). Six varieties of cosmopolitanism in late eighteenth-century Germany. *Journal of the History of Ideas*, 60 (3), 505–524.

Kleingeld, P. and Brown, E. (2006). Cosmopolitanism. *Stanford Encyclopedia of Philosophy* (http://plato.stanford.edu/entries/cosmopolitanism/.).

Konrad, G. (2007). *A Guest in My Own Country: A Hungarian Life*, trans. J. Tucker, ed. M. H. Heim (New York: Other Press).

Kraye, J. (1996). *The Cambridge Companion to Renaissance Humanism* (New York: Cambridge University Press).

Kristeva, J. (1993). *Nations without Nationalism*, trans. L. S. Roudiez (New York: Columbia University Press).

Kurasawa, F. (2004). A cosmopolitanism from below. *European Journal of Sociology*, 145 (2), 233–55.

Kwok-bun, C. (2005). *Chinese Identities, Ethnicity and Cosmopolitanism* (London: Routledge).

Lamont, M. and Aksartova, S. (2002). Ordinary cosmopolitanism: Strategies for bridging racial boundaries among working-class men. *Theory, Culture and Society* 19 (4), 1–25.

Latour, B. (2004a). Whose cosmos, which cosmopolitics? *Common Knowledge* 10 (3), 450–462.

Latour, B. (2004b). *Politics of Nature: How to Bring the Sciences into Democracy*, trans. C. Porter (Cambridge, MA: Harvard University Press).

Laverty, M. J. (2010). Learning our concepts. *Journal of Philosophy of Education* 43 (S1), 27–40.

Leung, G. (2009). A critical history of cosmopolitanism. *Law, Culture and the Humanities* 5, 370–390.

Levenson, J. R. (1971). *Revolution and Cosmopolitanism: The Western Stages and the Chinese Stages* (Berkeley: University of California Press).

Lingard, B., Nixon, J. and Ranson, S. (Eds.) (2008). *Transforming Learning in Schools and Communities: The Remaking of Education for a Cosmopolitan Society* (London: Continuum International).

Locher, C. (1976). Primary and secondary themes in Montaigne's 'Des Cannibales'. *French Forum*, 1, 119–126.

Locke, A. (1989). Cultural relativism and ideological peace. In L. Harris (Ed.), *The Philosophy of Alain Locke: Harlem Renaissance and Beyond*, pp. 69–78 (Philadelphia: Temple University Press). Original work published 1944.

Long, A. A. (1996). *Stoic Studies* (Cambridge: Cambridge University Press).

Long, A. A. (2006). *From Epicurus to Epictetus* (Oxford: Oxford University Press).

Loss, J. (2005). *Cosmopolitanisms and Latin America: Against the Destiny of Place* (New York: Palgrave Macmillan).

Lovlie, L., Mortensen, K. P., and Nordenbo, S. E. (Eds.) (2003). *Educating Humanity: Bildung in Postmodernity* (Oxford: Blackwell Publishing).

Lu, C. (2000). The one and many faces of cosmopolitanism. *The Journal of Political Philosophy*, 8 (2), 244–253.

Macgregor, S. (2004). Reading the Earth Charter: Cosmopolitan environmental citizenship or light green politics as usual? *Ethics, Place and Environment*, 7 (1–2), 85–96.

Mackintosh-Smith, T. (2002). *The Travels of Ibn Battutah* (London: Picador).

Majluf, N. (1997). "Ce n'est pas le Pérou," or, the failure of authenticity: Marginal cosmopolitans at the Paris Universal Exhibition of 1855. *Critical Inquiry* 23 (4), 868–893.

Malcomson, S. L. (1998). The varieties of cosmopolitan experience. In P. Cheah and B. Robbins (Eds.), *Cosmopolitics: Thinking and Feeling Beyond the Nation*, pp. 233–245 (Minneapolis: University of Minnesota Press).

Marcus, Aurelius (2003). *Meditations*, trans. G. Hays (New York: Modern Library).

Masschelein, J. and Simons, M. (2002). An adequate education in a globalized world? A note on immunization against being–together. *Journal of Philosophy of Education* 36 (4), 589–608.

Matvejevic, P. (1999). *Mediterranean: A Cultural Landscape*, trans. M. H. Heim (Berkeley: University of California Press).

McCarthy, T. (1999). On reconciling cosmopolitan unity and national diversity. *Public Culture* 11 (1), 175–208.

McCarty, L. P. (2009). Failing to cosmopolitanize Diogenes in Montreal: A peripatetic excursion. In D. Kerdeman (Ed.), *Philosophy of Education 2009*, pp. 14–17. Urbana, IL: Philosophy of Education Society.

McDonough, K. (1997). Cultural recognition, cosmopolitanism and multicultural education. In S. Laird (Ed.), *Philosophy of Education 1997*, pp. 127–135 (Urbana, IL: Philosophy of Education Society).

McDonough, K. and Feinberg, W. (Eds.) (2003). *Citizenship and Education in Liberal-Democratic Societies: Teaching for Cosmopolitan Values and Collective Identities* (Oxford: Oxford University Press).

Mehta, P. B. (2000). Cosmopolitanism and the circle of reason. *Political Theory* 28 (5), 619–639.

Mei-lin Ng, M. (2006). Valuation, evaluation, and value education – On acquiring the ability to value: A philosophical perspective. In R. H. M. Cheng, J. C. K. Lee and L. N. K. Lo (Eds.), *Values Education for Citizens in the New Century*, pp. 49–66 (Sha Tin, Hong Kong: Chinese University Press).

Merleau-Ponty, M. (1964). Eye and mind. In Merleau-Ponty, *The Primacy of Perception*, pp. 159–190 (Evanston, IL: Northwestern University Press).

Midgley, M. (1991). *Can't We Make Moral Judgments?* (New York: St. Martin's Press).

Mijolla, E. de (1994). *Autobiographical Quests: Augustine, Montaigne, Rousseau, and Wordsworth* (Charlottesville: University of Virginia Press).

Mintz, A. (2008). The Pains of Learning. Unpublished doctoral dissertation, Columbia University, New York City.

Mitchell, K. and Parker, W. C. (2008). I pledge allegiance to . . . Flexible citizenship and shifting scales of belong. *Teachers College Press*, 110 (4).

Montaigne, M. de (1991). *The Essays of Michel de Montaigne*, trans. M. A. Screech (London, Penguin).

Montesquieu. (1991). *Pensées* (Thoughts), ed. L. Desgraves (Paris: Robert Laffont). Original edition first appeared 1758.

Montesquieu. (2004). *Persian Letters*, trans. C. Betts (London: Penguin). Original work published 1721.

Moody-Adams, M. (1997). *Fieldwork in Familiar Places: Morality, Culture, and Philosophy* (Cambridge, MA: Harvard University Press).

Morin, E. and Kern, A. B. (1999). *Homeland Earth: A Manifesto for the New Millennium* (Cresskill, NJ: Hampton Press).

Murdoch, I. (1970). *The Sovereignty of Good* (London: Routledge & Kegan Paul).

Muthu, S. (2003). *Enlightenment against Empire* (Princeton, NJ: Princeton University Press).

Nancy, J.-L. (1996). The Deleuzian fold of thought. In P. Patton (Ed.), *Deleuze: A Critical Reader*, pp. 107–113 (Oxford: Blackwell).

Nehamas, A. (1998). *The Art of Living: Socratic Reflections from Plato to Foucault* (Berkeley: University of California Press).

Nietzsche, F. W. (1996). *Human, All Too Human*, trans. R. J. Hollingdale (Cambridge and New York: Cambridge University Press). Original work published 1878.

Norton, G. (1904). *Studies in Montaigne* (New York: Macmillan).

Nussbaum, M. C. (1994). *The Therapy of Desire: Theory and Practice in Hellenistic Ethics* (Princeton, NJ: Princeton University Press).

Nussbaum, M. C. (1997a). *Cultivating Humanity: A Classical Defense of Reform in Liberal Education* (Cambridge, MA: Harvard University Press).

Nussbaum, M. C. (1997b). Kant and cosmopolitanism. In J. Bohman and M. Lutz-

Bachman (Eds.), *Perpetual Peace: Essays on Kant's Cosmopolitan Ideal*, pp. 25–57 (Cambridge, MA: MIT Press).

Nussbaum, M. C. (2000). *Women and Human Development: The Capabilities Approach* (Cambridge: Cambridge University Press).

Nussbaum, M. C. (2002). *For Love of Country?*, ed. J. Cohen (Boston: Beacon Press).

Nwankwo, I. K. (2005). *Black Cosmopolitanism: Racial Consciousness and Transnational Identity in the Nineteenth-Century Americas* (Philadelphia: University of Pennsylvania Press).

Nyers, P. (2003). Abject cosmopolitanism: The politics of protection in the anti-deportation movement. *Third World Quarterly* 24 (6), 1069–1093.

Oakeshott, M. (1989). *The Voice of Liberal Learning: Michael Oakeshott on Education*, ed. T. Fuller (New Haven, CT: Yale University Press).

O'Connell, K. M. (2007). Art, nature, and education: Rabindranath Tagore's holistic approach to learning. In D. T. Hansen (Ed.), *Ethical Visions of Education: Philosophies in Practice* pp. 126–140 (New York: Teachers College Press).

Osler, A. and Starkey, H. (2003). Learning for cosmopolitan citizenship: Theoretical debates and young people's experiences. *Educational Review* 55 (3), 243–254.

Papastephanou, M. (2002). Arrows not yet fired: Cultivating cosmopolitanism through education. *Journal of Philosophy of Education* 36 (1), 69–86.

Papastephanou, M. (2005). Globalisation, globalism and cosmopolitanism as an educational ideal. *Educational Philosophy and Theory* 37 (4), 533–551.

Papastergiadis, N. (2007). Glimpses of cosmopolitanism in the hospitality of art. *European Journal of Social Theory* 10 (1), 139–152.

Parker, W. C. (2007). Imagining a cosmopolitan curriculum. Unpublished paper, University of Washington at Seattle.

Pendlebury, S. (2009). Accommodating cosmopolitanism. In D. Kerdeman (Ed.), *Philosophy of Education 2009*, pp. 18–22. Urbana, IL: Philosophy of Education Society.

Piel, G. (1972). *The Acceleration of History* (New York: Knopf).

Pinar, W. F. (2009). *The Worldliness of a Cosmopolitan Education: Passionate Lives in Public Service* (New York: Routledge).

Plato (1992). *Republic*, trans. G. M. A. Grube and C. D. C. Reeve (Indianapolis: Hackett).

Pollock, S. Bhabha, H. K., Breckenridge, C. A. and Chakrabarty, D. (2000). Cosmopolitanisms. *Public Culture* 12 (no. 3), 577–590.

Popkewitz, T. (2008). *Cosmopolitanism and the Age of School Reform* (New York: Routledge).

Reydams-Schils, G. (2005). *The Roman Stoics: Self, Responsibility, and Affection* (Chicago: University of Chicago Press).

Richardson, T. (2008). *Kaleidoscopic Odessa: History and Place in Contemporary Ukraine* (Toronto: University of Toronto Press).

Rizvi, F. (2005). Identity, culture and cosmopolitan futures. *Higher Education Policy*, 18 (4), 331–339.

Rizvi, F. (2009). Toward cosmopolitan learning. *Discourse: Studies in the Cultural Politics of Education*, 30 (3), 253–268.

Robbins, B. (1999). *Feeling Global: Internationalism in Distress*. New York: New York University Press.

Rodó, J. E. (1988). *Ariel*, trans. M. S. Peden (Austin: University of Texas Press). Original work published 1900.

Rosenblatt, L. M. (1978). *The Reader, the Text, the Poem: The Transactional Theory of the Literary Work* (Carbondale: Southern Illinois University Press).

Rosenfeld, S. (2002). Citizens of nowhere in particular: Cosmopolitanism, writing, and political engagement in eighteenth-century Europe. *National Identities* 4 (1), 25–43.

Roth, K. and Burbules, N. C. (Eds) (2011). Special issue: Philosophical perspectives on cosmopolitanism and education, *Educational Philosophy and Theory*, 43 (3), 205–316.

Saito, H. (2010). Actor-network theory of cosmopolitan education. *Journal of Curriculum Studies*, 42 (3), 333–351.

Sallis, J. (2006). *Topographies* (Bloomington: Indiana University Press).

Salomon, N. (1979). Cosmopolitanism and internationalism in the history of ideas in Latin America. *Cultures* 6 (1), 83–108.

Savage, M., Bagnall, G. and Longhurst, B. (2005). *Globalization and Belonging* (London: Sage).

Scarry, E. (1998). The difficulty of imagining other persons. In E. Weiner (Ed.), *The Handbook of Interethnic Coexistence*, pp. 40–62 (New York: Continuum).

Scheffler, S. (1996). Review of *For Love of Country*. *Times Literary Supplement* December 27, 8–9.

Scheffler, S. (2001). Conceptions of cosmopolitanism. In Scheffler, *Boundaries and Allegiances: Problems of Justice and Responsibility in Liberal Thought*, pp. 111–130 (Oxford: Oxford University Press).

Scheuerman, W. E. (2004). *Liberal Democracy and the Social Acceleration of Time* (Baltimore, MD: Johns Hopkins University Press).

Schlereth, T. J. (1977) *The Cosmopolitan Ideal in Enlightenment Thought: Its Form and Function in the Ideas of Franklin, Hume, and Voltaire, 1694–1790* (Notre Dame, IN: University of Notre Dame Press).

Schofield, M. (1991). *The Stoic Idea of the City* (Cambridge: Cambridge University Press).

Schwartz, E. (2009). *At Home in the World: Human Nature, Ecological Thought, and Education after Darwin* (Albany: State University of New York Press).

Sebald, W. G. (2006). *Campo Santo*, trans. A. Bell (New York: Modern Library).

Sellars, J. (2003). *The Art of Living: The Stoics on the Nature and Function of Philosophy* (Aldershot, UK: Ashgate).

Sen, A. (1999). *Development as Freedom* (New York: Knopf).

Sen, A. (2006). *Identity and Violence: The Illusion of Destiny* (New York: W. W. Norton).

Sharp, A. M. (1983). Children's intellectual liberation. *Educational Theory* 31 (2), 197–214.

Shayegan, D. (1992). *Sous les Ciels du Monde* (*Under the Skies of the World*) (Paris: Éditions du Félin).

Shklar, J. N. (1984). *Ordinary Vices* (Cambridge, MA: Belknap Press of Harvard University Press).

Shusterman, R. (1997). *Practicing Philosophy: Pragmatism and the Philosophical Life* (New York: Routledge).

Siebers, T. (1993). The ethics of anti-ethnocentrism. *Michigan Quarterly Review* 32 (1), 41–70.

Skrbis, Z., Kendall, G. and Woodward, I. (2004). Locating cosmopolitanism: Between humanist ideal and grounded social category. *Theory, Culture and Society* 21 (6), 115–136.

Smith, H. J. (1926). *Oliver Goldsmith's* The Citizen of the World (New Haven, CT: Yale University Press).

Smith-Ponthieu, J. F. (1971). Oliver Goldsmith as Social Critic in *A Citizen of the World* (Unpublished doctoral dissertation, Texas Tech University).

Snyder, J., Bolin, F. and Zumwalt, K. (1992). Curriculum implementation. In P. W. Jackson (Ed.), *The Handbook of Research on Curriculum*, pp. 402–435 (New York: Macmillan).

Sontag, S. (2001). Remarks on literature. Panel featuring W. G. Sebald and Susan Sontag, chaired by André Aciman, held at the 92nd Street Young Men's Christian Association, New York City, October 15.

Stanton, K. (2006). *Cosmopolitan Fictions: Ethics, Politics, and Global Change in the Works of Kazuo Ishiguro, Michael Ondaatje, Jamaica Kincaid, and J. M. Coetzee* (New York: Routledge).

Starmer, N. (2009). Growth in connection. Unpublished manuscript, Klingenstein Center, Teachers College, Columbia University, New York City.

Strand, T. (Ed.) (2010). Special issue on cosmopolitanism in the making, *Studies in Philosophy and Education*, 29 (2), 103–242.

Szerszynski, B. and Urry, J. (2002). Cultures of cosmopolitanism. *The Sociological Review* 40, 461–481.

Tagore, R. (1966). From *My Life*. In A. Chakravarty (Ed.), *A Tagore Reader*, pp. 80–89 (Boston: Beacon Press). Original work published 1928.

Tagore, R. (1997). *Gitanjali* (New York: Scribner). Original work published 1913.

Tagore, S. (2003). Tagore, education, cosmopolitanism. In S. F. Alatas, L. T. Ghee, and K. Kuroda (Eds.), *Asian Interfaith Dialogue*. Washington, DC: World Bank.

Tagore, S. (2008). Tagore's conception of cosmopolitanism: A reconstruction. *University of Toronto Quarterly*, 77 (4), 1070–1084.

Tan, K.-C. (2004). *Justice Without Borders: Cosmopolitanism, Nationalism, Patriotism* (Cambridge: Cambridge University Press).

Tarlo, E. (2007). Islamic cosmopolitanism: The sartorial biographies of three Muslim women in London. *Fashion Theory*, 11 (2/3), 143–172.

Terence (1988). *The Self-Tormentor*, trans. A. J. Brothers (London: Aris & Phillips).

Terzi, L. (2008). *Justice and Equality in Education: A Capability Perspective on Disability and Special Educational Needs* (New York: Continuum).

Thurman, J. (2008). First impressions: What does the world's oldest art tell us? *The New Yorker*, June 23.

Todd, S. (2009). *Toward an Imperfect Education: Facing Humanity, Rethinking Cosmopolitanism* (Boulder, CO: Paradigm).

Toulmin, S. (1990). *Cosmopolis: The Hidden Agenda of Modernity* (Chicago: University of Chicago Press).

Tozer, B. (1907). Cosmopolitanism and humour. *The Monthly Review* 27 (79), 129–136.

Tresch, J. (2007). Technological world-pictures: Cosmic things and cosmograms. *Isis*, 98, 84–99.

Tuan, Y-F. (1996). *Cosmos and Hearth: A Cosmopolite's Viewpoint* (Minneapolis: University of Minnesota Press).

Varenne, H. (2007). Difficult collective deliberations: Anthropological notes toward a theory of education. *Teachers College Record*, 109, 1559–1588.

Venturi, F. (1972). *Italy and the Enlightenment: Studies in a Cosmopolitan Century*, ed. S. Woolf, trans. S. Corsi (New York: New York University Press).

Waks, L. J. (2008). Cosmopolitanism and citizenship education. In M. A. Peters, A. Britton and H. Blee (Eds.), *Global Citizenship Education: Philosophy, Theory and Pedagogy*, pp. 203–220 (Rotterdam: Sense Publishers).

Waks, L. J. (2009). Reason and culture in cosmopolitan education. *Educational Theory*, 59 (5), 589–604.

Waldron, J. (2000). What is cosmopolitan? *The Journal of Political Philosophy*, 8 (2), 227–243.

Waldron, J. (2003). Teaching cosmopolitan right. In K. McDonough and W. Feinberg (Eds.), *Education and Citizenship in Liberal-Democratic Societies: Teaching for Cosmopolitan Values and Collective Identities*, pp. 23–55 (Oxford: Oxford University Press).

Waldron, J. (2006). Cosmopolitan norms. In S. Benhabib, *Another Cosmopolitanism*, ed. R. Post, pp. 83–101 (Oxford: Oxford University Press).

Walker, M. (2006). *Higher Education Pedagogies: A Capabilities Approach* (Maidenhead, UK: Open University Press).

Walkowitz, R. L. (2006). *Cosmopolitan Style: Modernism Beyond the Nation* (New York: Columbia University Press).

Wardle, H. (2000). *An Ethnography of Cosmopolitanism in Kingston, Jamaica* (Lampeter, UK: Edwin Mellen).

Weil, S. (2002). *The Need for Roots: Prelude to a Declaration of Duties Toward Mankind*, trans. A. Wills (London: Routledge). Original work published 1949.

Weiming, T. (1985). *Confucian Thought: Selfhood as Creative Transformation* (Albany: State University of New York Press).

Weiming, T. (1998). Epilogue: Human rights as a Confucian moral discourse. In De Bary, W. T. and Weiming, T. (Eds.), *Confucianism and Human Rights*, pp. 297–307 (New York: Columbia University Press).

Werbner, P. (1999). Global pathways: Working-class cosmopolitans and the creation of transnational ethnic worlds. *Social Anthropology* 7 (1), 17–35.

White, B. W. (2002). Congolese rumba and other cosmopolitanisms. *Cahiers d'Études Africaines*, 168, 663–686.

Williams, L. B. (2007). Overcoming the 'contagion of mimicry': The cosmopolitan nationalism and modernist history of Rabindranath Tagore and W.B. Yeats. *American Historical Review* 112 (1), 69–100.

Wineburg, S., Mosborg, S., Porat, D. and Duncan, A. (2007). Common belief and the cultural curriculum: An intergenerational study of historical consciousness. *American Educational Research Journal*, 44 (1), 40–76.

Woolf, V. (1984). Montaigne, in V. Woolf, *The Common Reader: First Series*, pp. 58–68 (New York: Harcourt Brace & Company). Original work published 1925.

Yourcenar, M. (1990). *Memoirs of Hadrian*, trans. G. Frick (New York: Noonday Press). Original work published 1951.

Zubaida, S. (2002). Middle Eastern experiences of cosmopolitanism. In S. Vertovec and R. Cohen (Eds.), *Conceiving Cosmopolitanism: Theory, Context, and Practice*, pp. 32–41 (Oxford: Oxford University Press).

Zweig, S. (1956). *Erasmus of Rotterdam* (New York: Viking Press). Original work published in 1934.

Zweig, S. (1964). *The World of Yesterday* (Lincoln: University of Nebraska Press). Original work published in 1943.

Name Index

Abbas, A. 47, 63
Abbott, A. 132
Achebe, C. 13, 68
Aciman, A. 57–8, 64
Addams, J. 102
Aksartova, S. 81–2, 102
d'Alembert, J. R. 38
Aloni, N. 12
Ambrosio, J. 36
Antisthenes 7
Appiah, K. A. 9, 11, 34, 49, 74, 81, 107, 125
Arendt, H. 12, 102, 107, 127
Aristotle 77, 130

Bader, V. 34, 81
Bailin, S. 11
Baldacchino, J. 125
Balzac, H. de 74
Barnett, A. 10
Beck, U. 10, 64, 75, 83, 126, 128
Benhabib, S. 125
Benitez, M. 132
Berlin, I. 129
Berman, J. 126
Bevan, R. 120
Bhattacharya, S. 6, 18
Bloom, A. 25
Bobbio, N. 85
Bok, S. 103
Booth, W. C. 108–9
Bose, S. 6
Bouriau, C. 68
Branham, R. B. 7, 38
Brann, E. T. H. 9
Brighouse, H. 125
Brock, G. 125
Brown, E. 6, 7, 10, 11, 24, 73
Brown, P. 36

Bruckner, P. 63, 75
Burbules, N. C. 126
Burtonwood, N. 98, 129
Bussis, A. M. 94
Bynum, G. L. 125

Calhoun, C. 10
Calvino, I. 4
Carini, P. 110
Carroll, L. 74
Carson, A. 35
Carter, A. 8, 125
Castoriades, C. 62–3, 64
Cephalus (*The Republic*), 25
Cheah, P. 75, 83, 125
Choo, S. 126
Cicero 7, 41, 132
Clark, K. 31
Cohen, S. M. 65
Confucius 6, 7, 21–4, 32, 33, 45, 55, 59, 102, 104, 109, 116, 118, 128
Connolly, W. E. 57
Copleston, F. 38
Corpus Ong, J. 114, 125
Costa, M. V. 74, 126
Cremin, L. A. 90
Cvetkovich, G. T. 8, 127

Dallmayr, F. 128
Dawson, R. 22
Day, C. x, 110, 111, 118
DeMartino, G. F. 10
De Marzio, D. M. 36, 132
Derrida, J. 125
Descartes, R. 59, 68
DeSisto, L. A. 96, 98
Dewey, J. 27, 30, 32, 40, 44, 49–51, 59, 84, 100, 102, 106, 108, 116, 121–3, 128

Subject Index

CPSIA information can be obtained
at www.ICGtesting.com
Printed in the USA
FFOW02n0153160116
20454FF